CLINICAL MANAGEMENT OF BEREAVEMENT

CLINICAL MANAGEMENT OF BEREAVEMENT
A Handbook for Healthcare Professionals

George M. Burnell, M.D.
Kaiser Permanente Medical Center
Honolulu, Hawaii

Adrienne L. Burnell, R.N., Ph.D.
University of Hawaii
Honolulu, Hawaii

 **HUMAN SCIENCES PRESS, INC.**

Copyright © 1989 by Human Sciences Press, Inc.
A Subsidiary of Plenum Publishing Corporation
233 Spring Street, New York, N.Y. 10013

Printed in the United States of America

Library of Congress Cataloging in Publication Data

Burnell, George M.
   Clinical management of bereavement : a handbook for healthcare professionals /
George M. Burnell, Adrienne L. Burnell.
      p.   cm.
   Bibliography: p.
   ISBN 0-89885-424-5
   1. Bereavement—Psychological aspects.   2. Death—Psychological aspects.
3. Consolation.   I. Burnell, Adrienne L.   II. Title.
[DNLM: 1. Grief.   BF 575.G7 B963c]
RC455.4.L67B87 1989   616.85′2—dc19   87-35613
DNLM/DLC for Library of Congress   CIP

This book is dedicated to our parents and our children.
And in memory of Eric.

CONTENTS

ACKNOWLEDGMENTS

This book could not have been written without the help of many people who contributed in a variety of ways. We wish to thank those who have generously given their time for the lengthy interviews which have provided much of the material for this book. Among them, special thanks go to Professor Mitsuo Aoki, Lennie McMorine, R.N., M.S., Dr. Martin Leftik, Dr. Karl Pregitzer, Dr. Albert Mariani, Dr. John Mueh, Dr. Norman Levey, Ruth Stewart, R.N., Elaine Miller, R.N., Carol Chang, R.N., Sandy Cruz, R.N., Olivia Castro, R.N., Judy Boomer, R.N., Frances Fowler, R.N., Jean Grippin, R.N., M.S., Dr. Ruta Summers, Dr. George Manning, Dr. Jacob Gerritsen, Dr. Gardner Bemis, Dr. Yi Ching, Dr. Paul Glen, Dr. Alfred Scottolini, Dr. Robert Wilkinson, Professor Shelley Horton, Patricia Tolleson, and William Sleeman.

We are also grateful to the many families we have interviewed and gotten to know at the chapters of the Compassionate Friends in Los Gatos and Palo Alto, California. Their insights and frank communications have been incorporated into many pages of this book. Similarly, we are indebted to the few hundred grieving patients and families we have seen in consultation and therapy over the last 20 years. Many pages in this book are filled with the knowledge and awareness they gave us in the course of learning about their grief.

We especially want to thank Dr. William Cody, Chief of Psychiatry,

Kaiser Medical Center, Honolulu, for his warm support and steady encouragement, Dr. Alex Roth and Dr. James Bennett for their insights and wisdom, Professor Ann Clark for suggestions and feedback, and Dr. Michael Bridge (Life Foundation) for updated information on AIDS.

Finally, we want to acknowledge the diligent assistance from Jodie Fukuda, medical librarian at the Kaiser Hospital in Honolulu, and give special thanks to Dr. Ellen Colburn-Rohn for her invaluable editorial contributions. Last but not least, we wish to thank the staff of Human Sciences Press and Norma Fox, Executive Editor, for giving us her support, advice, and guidance throughout the course of this project.

INTRODUCTION

The purpose of this book is *to give physicians, nurses, and social workers in the hospital setting some guidelines in the management of bereavement reactions following the death of an immediate family member.* Although we know that in the hospital the exposure to bereavement is a frequent occurrence, relatively little attention and training are given to that topic in current medical, nursing, and social work curriculae. This book aims to answer that need.

Although bereavement seems to be a universal phenomenon with predictable patterns and outcomes, its manifestations and course often vary from person to person. Special circumstances can set off different pattens of intensity and duration of grief, and these should be recognized.

Research of the 1970s and 1980s has shown that various grief reactions can lead to or exacerbate physical and mental health problems. It is becoming clear that clinicians and health professionals may play a crucial role in preventing complications of the grief experience. Therefore we shall discuss the basic patterns of acute and chronic grief in order to provide a basis for the understanding of interventions.

Too often we have heard from surviving families that medical and nursing staff feel helpless and awkward, at times even responding inappropriately in the aftermath of a patient's death. There are many reasons for this, including a lack of knowledge about the grief process, some discomfort about the death situation itself, insufficient training in dealing with troubled families, a deliberate attempt to remain distanced from the process, and some unresolved personal attitudes and feelings about death and dying.

There is also the matter of myths about bereavement. Patients, their families, and health professionals have all been exposed to beliefs and expressions that can prove to be counterproductive to the grief process. We will attempt to dispel the most common myths with each succeeding chapter by providing information from research and other sources, plus guidelines for managing some of the problems inadvertently caused or perpetuated by mistaken notions.

It is indeed a paradox that the health professions, although dedicated to the prevention and alleviation of pain and suffering until the patient has died, can often see no further obligation or need to help the survivors who themselves are in acute pain. One explanation is that the contract was made with the patient, leading to the usual thinking that "everything possible was done"; thus nothing more seems necessary. The family of the patient is not technically part of the doctor-patient contract, and family members do not possess the status of "patienthood." Therefore there is little or no sense of responsibility toward the family or friends of the deceased (Krant, 1975).

Yet, each year approximately 8 million Americans experience the loss of an immediate family member, 800,000 widows and widowers experience the pain of grief, and another 800,000 parents mourn the loss of a child below the age of 25. A significant proportion of these mourners will be at risk for changes in their physical and mental status. Studies have shown that many bereaved individuals will experience new illnesses or an exacerbation of existing or chronic physical and mental health problems. In some cases the bereavement experience is so stressful that it leads to the increase of self-destructive behaviors, such as smoking, drinking, and drug abuse. In other cases it can even result in the premature death of the closest survivor. This is why educators in medical, nursing, and social work schools are becoming more aware of the toll of bereavement and the need to provide more knowledge and training for clinicians, who will be dealing with the realities of dying, the fears of terminal patients, and the bereavement experience of families.

Up to now, information dealing with death, dying, and its aftermath has been given predominantly to hospice personnel. However, after interviews with hundreds of families in acute grief, we have become aware of the need for both knowledge and skills for professional staff in the various services of the hospital and clinic practice as they deal with dying patients and their families. This book attempts to fill the gap in the literature.

Through our survey we have drawn material from a variety of sources in an attempt to present information that is balanced and useful. Besides reviewing the pertinent literature, we have interviewed clinicians, chiefs of services, and nursing supervisors of various units in two different hospitals. We have also analyzed and reviewed data and clinical notes of approximately 300 cases of bereavement and grief counseling seen by us from 1972 to 1987. Much of the feedback from those cases has been incorporated in the guidelines suggested throughout the book.

We have purposely avoided the reporting of detailed clinical histories except for a few vignettes, because it was our feeling that students and clinicians learn best from their own case histories rather than from those they read about in books. The material is so arranged that each chapter can be read as a separate source.

Chapter 2, "Definitions and Theories of Bereavement," provides a good foundation for the following chapters. Chapters 1 through 6 review the basic knowledge of normal and abnormal grief patterns, the signs and symptoms of grief, bereavement following specific losses, and anticipated versus unanticipated grief. Chapter 7 examines the roles of physicians, nurses, and social workers in the aftermath of the death situation. Chapter 8 discusses the particular circumstances of bereavement in specialized hospital services such as the ICU, the CCU, Oncology Unit, pediatric and geriatric services, OBGYN, and surgical and general medical services. It also deals with the management of bereaved patients seen in the clinic setting and the controversial issue of medicating these patients.

Chapter 9 analyzes the ethical, legal, and special personal problems of health professionals in their confronting death and bereavement issues. Chapter 10 gives concrete guidelines and suggestions for dealing with survivors while dispelling common myths about bereavement. Chapter 11 provides material for training and support programs in the hospital setting, plus some sources of information for course material and nursing care planning and education. Chapter 12 gives the rationale and basis for referring bereaved individuals to mental health professionals and self-support groups. Additional references and source materials are provided in the appendixes. They deal with concepts of death in children, nursing procedures for handling still-births, and an example of a nursing care plan. A categorized reading list is included for any health professional who is asked about material that may help the bereaved survivor to understand or cope with the death of a loved one.

Because the technology of today's medical practice is becoming increasingly more complex and impersonal, the interaction with the families involves discussions of many alternatives, complicated machines, difficult decisions, numerous specialized procedures, and increased responsibilities. It is much more delicate and fraught with risks and problems than in times when the practice of medicine was based essentially on a supportive relationship between the doctor, the patient, and the family. In the increasing complexity of the modern world of medicine, some of the old-fashioned common-sense ideas about the supportive roles in family relationships have been lost.

This book is an attempt to lay down some basic foundations for preventions and intervention in the area of bereavement. It tries to correct practices based on long-standing myths and to provide guidelines backed by updated research and clinical findings. It is our hope that the suggestions and recommendations made throughout the book will help those who want to relieve the pain in people whose plight begins with the loss of a significant person.

Chapter 1

THE STRESS OF BEREAVEMENT

In contrast to previous decades, most people today die in hospitals or in institutions. And it is there that the trauma of bereavement is experienced and that grief reactions are witnessed. Doctors, nurses, social workers, and members of the clergy are expected to coordinate the complex process of dying, death, and bereavement, providing a buffer between participants and their feelings. As a result, death and bereavement have become a source of major stress for both families and health care professionals (Vachon, 1987).

The stress can be experienced along a continuum which starts when the patient and family learn about a terminal diagnosis or about an imminent death. It continues with the experience of dying, and it ends with the reactions following death. The ordeal is extremely acute for the family. The experience of watching someone die, plus the feeling of loss that follows the death, especially, of a spouse or a child, have been reported as among the most intense and stressful experiences an individual can endure in a lifetime (Elliott & Eisdorfer, 1982; Holmes & Rahe, 1967).

The reactions that follow bereavement encompass a wide range of symptoms that are usually predictable and usually include crying, sighing, sadness, anxiety, agitation, sleeplessness, and loss of appetite. These symptoms are considered part of a syndrome of normal grief which was best described by Lindemann (1944), a psychiatrist who studied the reactions of 101 bereaved persons who were seen following the disastrous fire of the Coconut Grove night club in Boston. Some of the bereaved followed a predictable course, while others went on to develop pathological outcomes of grief because the reaction was inhibited, delayed, or prolonged. His study was a milestone in aiding our understanding of bereavement, because he not only gave an accurate description of the syndrome, but he also provided some account of the atypical forms of grief.

Lindemann proposed some practical guidelines for those who are in a position to help the bereaved. He noted that sometimes individuals are so distressed by the bereavement reaction that they seek help from health professionals, especially for relief from symptoms of insomnia, restlessness, agitation, and anxiety. Even though these people exhibited symptoms severe enough to require tranquilizers, sedatives, or emotional support, they were seen as suffering from a normal condition.

Some raised the question of whether grief should be considered a disease (Engel, 1961) or simply a basic human response to a significant loss in life. Others saw the reactions as a form of separation anxiety in adult life, affected by the nature of the prototypical attachment formed during bonding between mother and child and the child's reactions to losses in later life (Bowlby & Parkes, 1970).

The question of whether grief is a disease or a normal psychological reaction to a major life event is still receiving attention in the literature (Osterweis, 1984). And many other questions are still the subject of intensive study.

Why do some individuals fare better than others in coping with the stress of bereavement? Why do some people become ill, while others go on with their lives after a period of readjustment?

What can health professionals do to ease the process of dying and grieving? What can they do to alleviate the pain and stress of bereavement? Is it really part of their responsibility, or does their responsibility end with the death of the patient? Do their interventions have an impact on the bereaved and their subsequent behaviors? To what extent is the management of bereavement influenced by the attitudes of doctors and nurses?

Whether we like it or not, people turn to physicians, nurses, and social workers for emotional support and for answers to their questions. Families expect help during the dying process as well as during bereavement. In this regard Fulton and Langton (1964) have commented that ". . . the nurse is often the person who is confronted with the task of making the act of dying as smooth a process as possible.

Yet, the nurse's role in meeting the needs of the dying and his relatives is seldom clearly defined" (p. 110).

There is some evidence today from various studies that our own attitudes toward death and dying have considerable influence on our ways of dealing with survivors (Aries, 1974). We live in a death-denying society. Therefore we do not have any well-established roles and learned behaviors to help us cope or help us help others cope with the reality of death (Feifel, 1971). Our society tells us, "Laugh and the world laughs with you, weep and you weep alone."

Many of us feel that it is morbid to talk about death and grief. In fact, many of us have built an elaborate set of defenses to avoid being hurt by death (Kavanaugh, 1974). We even have expressions to avoid the mention of the words "death" or "dying," referring instead to "passing on" or "passing away." For some, there is the belief that the dead person goes on to a better place and happiness, thereby relieving the survivors of the need to worry. For others, death is akin to sleep. Some funeral establishments even provide "slumber rooms," and families are told and expected not to be sad, but to go on with their lives as if the dead person were only asleep. Yet death is not simply a biological event. It is also a psychosocial reality which calls for major social and psychological readjustments (Sudnow, 1967).

Among health professionals, the awareness of death and bereavement is much more acute because of the unavoidable exposure in the hospital setting. Yet despite this exposure, studies have shown that physicians and nurses have a high degree of anxiety when dealing with death and bereavement issues (Feifel, 1965; Poppoff, 1975; Schultz & Alderman, 1978).

Various explanations have been offered for this unusually high sensitivity to the death situation. It has been suggested that physicians, in treating dying patients, are reminded of their sense of failure and loss of mastery and control over the situation (White, 1977). Many physicians choose to avoid specialties that are more heavily involved with dying patients. Some prefer to deal with patients in an intensive care unit, where patients recover or die quickly, rather than in an oncology unit where the care is prolonged, often palliative, and requires closer and more intense involvement with patients and their families. On the other hand, nurses seem to choose to work with the dying and the bereaved as a way to overcome their own fears of death (Poppoff, 1975). But it is certain that the phenomenon of bereavement in the hospital setting is stressful for both the families and caregivers (Vachon, 1987).

Our attitudes toward the bereaved are influenced by the society we live in. Western society tends to set certain standards which encourage us to fit bereaved people into one pigeonhole. We tend to see all the bereaved as belonging to one category of sufferers. We often fail to take into account such factors as the circumstances of the death, the personality of the griever, and the nature of the relationship with the deceased (Davis, 1984). Fortunately, one of the lessons we have learned from the bereavement research of the second half of the twentieth century is that although patterns of grieving are generally predictable, the grief reaction has unique manifestations from one individual to another. It is therefore most important to allow survivors to grieve in their own way rather than to force them into a stereotypical pattern (Kubler-Ross, 1981).

Bereavement is considered a stressor with biological, psychological, and social consequences for families. For a detailed review of the literature, two excellent books are recommended: Therese Rando's *Grief, Dying and Death* (1984) and *Bereavement: Reactions, Consequences and Care* written by a panel of American scientists and edited by M. Osterweis, F. Solomon, and M. Green (1984). Both books contain extensive reviews of published studies and both have extensive lists of references.

BEREAVEMENT AS A PHYSICAL STRESSOR

Research has shown that bereavement can result in adverse consequences to people's lives, especially if they have predispositions to certain types of illnesses (Elliott & Eisdorfer, 1982). Many studies have shown that bereavement can:

lead to physical illness;

aggravate existing medical conditions;

generate new physical symptoms and complaints;

increase utilization of medical services.

There is no doubt today that bereavement is a major factor in increasing the risk for mortality and morbidity (Parkes, 1986). The question that remains to be answered is under what circumstances and to what extent does bereavement impact upon the health of grieving persons.

Studies have adopted various designs, all with a variety of methodological problems. Generally speaking, it is difficult to study bereavement because of the multiplicity of demographic, cultural, psychological, and physical factors involved.

Basically, there have been three major approaches to studying mortality and morbidity:

1. Epidemiologic studies which survey the incidence of bereavement in general or of special populations. Most studies agree that bereavement occurs at a rate of 5 to 10 percent in the general population (Osterweis et al., 1984).

2. Retrospective studies, which tend to be less precise because they depend on past records and conclusions based on extrapolations of old rates of bereavement.

3. Prospective studies of whole populations or of bereaved samples compared with controlled groups or case control studies, in which individuals with a particular condition (ulcerative colitis, depression, diabetes, etc.) believed to be associated with bereavement are compared to an appropriate control group.

With these various designs and criteria for defining bereavement, plus differing sample sizes, it is understandable that conflicting results are often reported. Furthermore, the duration of the bereavement follow-up period, plus the fact that individuals sometimes remarry, both constitute significant variables that can alter the reporting of results. In this book we shall report only the findings that seem to be in agreement in most studies. We shall avoid areas that remain controversial and inconclusive.

Most of the research has been done on individuals who have lost a spouse (Parkes, 1972). A few studies have been done on individuals who have lost a child. Virtually none have been made of other losses, such as of parents, children, siblings, or lovers.

Let us now review the salient findings on physical health outcomes in terms of mortality and morbidity.

Mortality

From all retrospective and prospective studies it is clear that bereavement increases the survivor's risk for dying. After a review of nine major studies, Osterweis and her colleagues (1984) concluded that widowed men, up to age seventy-five, have an increased risk for death, especially if they remain unmarried. The risk is greater in the first year following bereavement, but the mortality rate can remain elevated for as long as 6 years (Kraus & Lilienfeld, 1959; Parkes et al., 1969) Widows, on the other hand, for reasons which remain unclear, show an increased mortality only in the second year (Cox & Ford, 1964; Krauss & Lilienfeld, 1959; Gerber et al., 1975).

As for the cause of death, there are also some interesting differences between men and women after bereavement. Among widows, there is a higher percentage of deaths from cirrhosis of the liver, whereas bereaved men, proportionately, tend to die more from infectious diseases, accidents, cardiovascular diseases, and suicides (Helsing & Szklo, 1981; Helsing et al., 1982). It is interesting to note that remarriage has a definite impact on the mortality rate. In one study, where half of the men who had remarried before age fifty-five were compared to those who had not remarried, the mortality rate of those who remained single was significantly higher (Helsing et al., 1982).

The majority of studies of mortality deal with the loss of a spouse. Very little has been reported on the mortality following other types of losses. One study did note a significant increase in deaths of bereaved parents (34.3 percent) compared to nonbereaved parents (6.9 percent) (Levau, 1982), but these results were somewhat difficult to interpret because they were derived from a reanalysis of a previous study (Rees & Lutkins, 1967). Nevertheless, the loss of a child does indeed carry a high mortality risk for bereaved parents (Clayton, 1982).

Morbidity

The extent to which bereavement acts as a stressor on the physical health of individuals is still a matter of controversy despite a vast number of studies in the psychosomatic literature. Many studies have reported that bereavement can predispose to, aggravate, or precipitate various types of medical illnesses.

Klerman and Izen (1977) have summarized the literature, which has implicated bereavement in various medical conditions, including acute, closed angle glaucoma, cancer, cardiovascular diseases, Cushing's disease, disseminated lupus erythematosus, pernicious anemia, pneumonia, rheumatoid arthritis, hyperthyroidism, tuberculosis and ulcerative colitis. Yet, the evidence for linking bereavement to these conditions remains weak, and the question of whether bereavement acts as a specific stressor or a nonspecific one remains unclear (Parkes, 1970). Furthermore, it is difficult to reach definite conclusions as to the role of bereavement per se in the subsequent course of illness because one is never sure about the extent and impact of predisposing factors. Clinicians and researchers both agree that other variables, such as genetic factors, differences in physiologic responsiveness, and psychological vulnerability all play a role.

To appease the purists, the literature refers to bereavement as an *antecedent;* that is, an event that precedes the onset of the disease, with greater regularity than would be expected in the general population. These studies are careful not to mention a direct cause/effect relationship, but they do imply a strong association between the two conditions of bereavement and a specific illness. For example, hyperthyroidism in adults (Kleinschmidt et al., 1965) and asthma in adults (Levintan, 1985) and in children (Morillo & Gardner, 1979) seem to be exacerbated after a traumatic event, such as a loss from divorce, separation, or death. The same has been postulated for children (Leaverton et al., 1980) as well as adults (Grant et al., 1974; Treuting, 1962) who develop diabetes. However, in these reports, bereavement is not singled out as a specific stressor, but rather as one of life's stressful events.

Similarly, various types of cancer have been associated with bereavement. Retrospective studies so far tend to generalize the type of loss, attempting to identify whether the loss was actual or perceived. Along these lines, Schmale and Iker (1966) observed an association between bereavement and cancer of the cervix, while Greene in a series of studies (Greene, 1954; 1965; Greene et al., 1956), found a high incidence of leukemia and lymphoma in individuals who suffered a recent loss. Unfortunately, these studies all present methodological difficulties due to lack of matched controls, small sample size, and generalization of the type of loss (actual or perceived), and therefore cannot be considered conclusive. Nevertheless, there is a renewed interest among researchers today in exploring the relationship between immunologic mechanisms, bereavement, and cancer (Osterweis et al., 1984).

Others have implicated bereavement in the occurrence of cardiac arrests or arrhythmias (Engel, 1971; Parkes & Weiss, 1983). But the most frequently implicated conditions following bereavement are myocardial infarction, congestive failure, and essential hypertension (Wiener et al., 1975). This, of course, is of importance to all physicians who follow their patients for such conditions, for if they are known to be grieving, the patients may need to be carefully medicated and given additional support (see Management Guidelines, in Chapter 3).

In most such cases, it is well recognized that the stress of bereavement seems to exacerbate the disease rather than to cause it. As earlier noted, some studies have reported significant increases in cirrhosis of the liver in women, and infectious diseases, accidents, and suicide in men (Helsing et al., 1982). Many of these conditions tend to occur as a result of self-damaging behaviors following bereavement (Jacobs & Ostfeld, 1977). People who grieve often tend to neglect themselves. They increase their smoking, drinking, and drug intake, all of which leads to a deterioration in health or an exacerbation of an existing condition. Poor health habits then can account for an increased incidence of alcoholism, suicide, and cardiac deaths. However, recent studies have not confirmed these findings in a group of widows in the San Diego area (Zisook & Shuchter, 1986; Zisook et al., 1987).

The utilization of services has been another focus of studies. Researchers have taken the number of hospitalizations or the frequency of office visits as an index of morbidity. Without debating the virtues or limitations of such an approach, the link between bereavement and an increase in the use of medical services remains inconclusive so far, because the findings show that use appears to vary significantly according to the type of health care system utilized (Parkes, 1970; Wiener et al., 1975). Bereaved individuals in a prepaid system of care are likely to make more visits than those utilizing a fee-for-service system. This observation suggests that the fee in the fee-for-service system might serve as an inhibiting factor for bereaved individuals. This hypothesis also needs further study.

BEREAVEMENT AS A PSYCHOLOGICAL STRESSOR

To what extent are bereaved individuals susceptible to mental illness? What are the factors that predispose these individuals to psychological problems and deterioration in their social functioning?

Among the factors studied so far are age and sex, prior psychological and social adjustment, prior health status and health habits, personality variables, sociocultural factors, socioeconomic status, relationship with the deceased, the nature of the death, alcohol and drug use, smoking, perceived social support, suicidal ideation, and guilt. We shall report only the salient and most important findings. Again, for a detailed review, the reader is referred to the book by Osterweis and her colleagues (1984).

Psychiatric complications do tend to occur in the first year of bereavement (Parkes & Brown, 1972), consisting mostly of increased alcohol and drug consumption, depressive disorders, and suicides. Clinically diagnosable depressions have been found in 10 to 20 percent of widows and widowers (Parkes & Brown, 1972; Clayton, 1982). Many of the depressed patients in these studies were observed to be high users of drugs, alcohol, and tobacco; therefore it can be speculated that such health-damaging behaviors also played a significant part in the subsequent course of depression. This has been particularly true for young widows and widowers. Also, widowed persons were found to make more use of prescribed medications, such as sleeping pills (Clayton, 1974), tranquilizers (Maddison & Viola, 1968) and various mixtures of sedatives, analgesics, and antidepressants (Thompson et al., 1984).

The most serious psychiatric complication of bereavement of course is commits suicide. The risk for suicide is relatively high for older widowers (MacMahon & Pugh, 1965) and for single men who have lost their mothers (Bunch et al., 1971). Researchers have speculated that a number of factors may be operating here. Pre-existing conditions, such as alcoholism and depression, obviously play a role and predispose bereaved individuals. But other factors, such as the nature of the death of the spouse, may be important as well, especially if the spouse died by suicide (Stroebe et al., 1981–1982). It is therefore important for health professionals to have a high index of alertness when the above factors are observed in survivors during their visits to the clinic.

Other forms of psychopathology occur when manifestations of grief take on extreme variations, which are usually referred to as "atypical or pathological grief." These variations are considered to be extreme when the grief is either inhibited, delayed, or prolonged. These extreme reactions are frequently diagnosed as reactive depressions. They occur at a frequency of 13 to 20 percent of widows and widowers during the first year of bereavement (Clayton & Darvish, 1979; Parkes & Weiss, 1983).

BEREAVEMENT AS A SOCIAL STRESSOR

Bereaved individuals often feel isolated, alienated, and lonely. They also feel rejected, misunderstood, and, when all alone, they feel that they have no one to turn to or to talk to. It is this perceived lack of social support that is one of the most significant predictors of poor outcome among the bereaved (Clayton, 1975; Vachon et al., 1982).

In addition to this perceived lack of social support, widows frequently experience additional stress because of financial difficulties or lack of experience in money matters. Other social stressors can complicate the picture if they occur concurrently with the bereavement, such as family conflicts, loss of job, retirement, illness, or even other deaths. All of these stresses can significantly aggravate the course of bereavement and cause further social deterioration (Parkes, 1975; Raphael & Maddison, 1976; Stroebe & Stroebe, 1983).

Sociological studies of bereavement have shown that there can be a serious impact on the widow's social status, social roles, and social adjustment. Loneliness which ensues as a result of social isolation following the loss of a spouse can be a most serious problem, especially for widows (Glick, Weiss, & Parkes, 1974). The impairment of social functioning in these widows can last months or even years. Following the loss of their spouses, many individuals undergo significant changes in their statuses and experience serious role and identity conflicts (Berardo, 1970; Lopata, 1973).

There are significant differences in the social adjustment of men and women. For women, the loss of a husband means the loss of income, the loss of a sexual partner, and possibly a loss of social status (Glick et al., 1974). For men, the loss of a wife means the loss of emotional support and social relationships outside the home. Glick, Weiss, and Parkes (1974) reported differences in how each sex perceived the loss of social roles. Men described the loss of their spouses in terms of feelings of dismemberment, whereas women spoke of the loss of their husbands in terms of feelings of abandonment. As for parents who have lost a child, they are at high risk for separation and divorce (Kaplan et al., 1976).

At any rate, whether we are talking about bereavement as a physical, a social, or a psychological stressor, the question of specificity remains unanswered. Nevertheless, there seems to be no doubt that bereavement remains a powerful event in the lives of most individuals. Anything that can be done to attenuate the blow is considered therapeutic and preventive.

None of the studies mentioned have prescribed regimens or recommendations for intervention programs to modify the course of bereavement and its complications. However, it is the general consensus that a knowledge of the stresses, the factors that play a role, and the populations that are at greater risk all help raise the awareness and sensitivity of health professionals in their dealings with bereaved individuals.

During a terminal illness or after a death, the stress of bereavement begins. It is at this point that the health care team can provide the emotional buffer for the intense distress that follows the death. Many of these bereaved individuals will be seen as patients in the office in the months that follow the loss. It is important to identify the individuals at higher risk, to check on their coping process, and on their social support system.

The health care team now has a moral and professional responsibility to provide the support needed by bereaved families. With the growing sophistication of patients as consumers of health services, families evaluate the attention they receive at the time of death and thereafter as an indicator of the quality of medical care. But providing effective support requires a medical team which feels secure in its approach to families. Each member must keep personal anxiety tolerable and manageable in order to be mutually supportive. Only then can they provide the professional support expected of them.

The dying and bereavement situation is stressful not only to families but also to the hospital and clinic staff. But stress is reduced as a feeling of security increases when we acquire knowledge about the dying and bereavement process, as well as about our own attitudes and feelings regarding death, dying, and bereavement. In the chapters ahead we shall attempt to dispel common myths about bereavement and to provide some guidelines for intervention based on current knowledge and clinical experience.

Chapter 2

DEFINITIONS AND THEORIES OF
BEREAVEMENT

In this chapter we shall (a) define the most common terms used in the area of grief, loss, and bereavement; (b) review the current conceptual models for bereavement theory; and (c) discuss the psychosocial factors influencing the bereavement process.

DEFINITIONS

For several decades the subject of grief and bereavement has been of special interest to many disciplines, including medicine, nursing, psychology, social work, theology, law, literature, philosophy, and anthropology. From this multifarious literature have emerged many terms which at times have been used interchangeably or ambiguously within varying contexts. For example, the meanings of grieving and mourning are frequently confused because the terms are used interchangeably. Both imply a sense of suffering caused by sorrow, sadness, and mental pain due to a loss through death. In both there is a deep sense of loss. Yet grieving tends to be a stronger word which implies deep mental suffering, usually endured alone. On the other hand, mourning usually refers to the outward and social expression of the sadness resulting from the loss. In his classic paper, *Mourning and Melancholia,* Freud did use the term *mourning* as denoting the normal process of suffering the loss of a love object. He ascribed the term to the psychological processes involved in this suffering (Freud, 1917).

To avoid confusion for the reader, we shall define the most common terms and expressions as they are used throughout this book and in the current medical and psychiatric literature. Our aim is to provide a common and consistent language to be used among clinicians, teachers, and students in conferences, workshops, in-service training programs, and research projects. Such consistent language should also help health professionals communicate and share their experiences within an interdisciplinary framework.

The term *bereavement* comes from the Old English *beroafian*, which means "to rob," "to plunder," or "to dispossess." The meaning is derived from the idea that death robs us of a loved one. The connotation of violence still remains in the current use of the term "bereft," but usually when referring to a possession (Funk, 1978). Today, the term "bereavement" refers to a separation or loss through death. More specifically, this event is marked by a given point in time.

Bereavement reactions consist of the physiologic, psychologic, or behavioral responses to bereavement. These responses vary in intensity, duration, and frequency from one individual to another. They do not refer to a physiological reaction or imply that they occur as a universal phenomenon (Osterweis et al., 1984).

The *bereavement process* refers to the bereavement reactions that occur *over time*. This process can last from weeks to several years.

As mentioned above, the word *mourning* is an ambiguous term, because sometimes it is used interchangeably with "grief." The most useful definition has been provided by James R. Averill (1968), a psychologist, who regards it as the "conventional behavior established by traditions, customs and mores of a given society." Thus, mourning dictates the behavior of the individual following a loss through death. But it should be noted that this socially prescribed behavior may or may not coincide with the feelings of the bereaved. *Mourning*, as we shall use it in this book, will refer to the social expression of grief, namely, mourning rituals and associated behaviors, for example, wearing black.

Various cultures and religions provide the bereaved with rules of conduct before the burial or cremation, and with what should be done and observed on holidays and anniversaries (Rosenblatt et al., 1977). For example, in Orthodox Judaism, after the initial period of grief, families are expected to go to the temple twice a day for 11 months, then four times a year thereafter (Lamm, 1969). In the Irish culture, the wake is a time for everyone to share in the grief through viewing of the body, lamenting, and paying tribute through eulogies. In India, mourning lasts 13 days, and the family is not expected to show sadness because this demonstration of feeling is believed to impede the deceased soul from proceeding to the next "level of attainment" toward Nirvana (salvation and union with God).

Grief is an intense feeling or emotional suffering caused by a loss through death. The term was derived from the Latin *gravis* which means "heavy." Later the word evolved through the French to convey that the "spirits were heavy with sorrow."

The *grief process* refers to the change of feeling states *over time*. The reactions to grief are physiological (like crying and sighing) and psychological (sadness, anger, guilt) rather than cultural, as in mourning. The grief process may coincide with mourning, particularly if the feelings are supported by social customs such as funeral rites. Mourning can take place with little or no expression of grief, but the rituals then help the bereaved save face when true feelings cannot be expressed without incurring serious criticism.

The expression *grief work* comes from the German *Trauerarbeit* which means mourning. The term was coined by Lindemann (1944), who explained that the process of experiencing grief required a tremendous amount of both physical and emotional energy. He felt that this expenditure of energy was necessary for the process of "working through" the loss by the individual. When the grief work proceeds without complication, the griever is able to reach the point of resolution and reinvestment in living.

In order to accomplish this work, the bereaved must complete four tasks which have been described by Worden (1982), a researcher in the area of dying and grieving. To accomplish these tasks the griever must:

(a)   accept the reality of the loss,

(b)   accept the grieving as painful,

(c)   adjust to the changed environment without the help or companionship of the deceased, and

(d)   be able to withdraw much of the energy invested in the deceased and reinvest it in new relationships.

The various aspects of grief work will be discussed in greater detail in Chapter 3, "Signs and Symptoms of Bereavement."

Finally, when the tasks of grief work do not proceed in a healthy manner, the result is *pathological grief*. Reactions in this case tend to be extreme and lead to prolonged distress and poor psychological and social functioning. The grief process then tends to be delayed, inhibited, prolonged, or even absent (see Chapter 4).

THEORIES OF BEREAVEMENT

When a family experiences the sharp and intense pain of bereavement, the reactions that follow encompass a wide and confusing range. The spectrum includes, at first, a state of numbness and shock, later followed by anger, protest, guilt, and despair. Episodes of confusion are not uncommon, along with social withdrawal to varying degrees. In the initial period, the presentation of symptoms is such that it is difficult to distinguish the reaction from clinical depression. What eventually makes it possible to differentiate between these two conditions is the difference in the intensity and duration of the symptoms. Clinicians, researchers, and theorists have attempted to understand the underlying psychological mechanisms that would explain the genesis of these reactions. Although no one theory has been totally satisfactory, most theories have contributed valuable concepts toward the understanding of this universal phenomenon. Our feeling has been that health professionals should know the basic elements of the major theoretical models in order to understand their roles and their interventions in dealing with family grief.

The following is a summary of the major theoretical models presented for the understanding of bereavement. The material is adapted from the report of the Institute of Medicine.

Psychoanalytic Theory

Freud theorized in his 1917 paper, *Mourning and Melancholia*, that the more strongly he identifies with the deceased, the more the bereaved person has difficulty in "letting go" of the loved one. This is especially true if the bereaved person has had unresolved feelings of hate and resentment toward the deceased, or feelings of ambivalence. What Freud pointed out is that in normal grief, the person is able to deny the loss, then to increase the investment in the loss, later to become preoccupied with the deceased, and eventually to go on with readjusting to life and reinvesting in other relationships.

Contemporary Psychodynamic Theories

Clinicians working with bereaved patients have elaborated on psychoanalytic theory. On the basis of clinical observations, they have focused on various aspects of the bereavement process, some emphasizing intrapsychic mechanisms, others concentrating on interpersonal aspects and sociocultural factors, including cultural background, belief systems, values, health, and financial status. All of those clinicians found that two determinant factors play a major role. First, there is the personality of the griever with his own style of perceiving, interpreting, and coping with previous life situations (Vachon et al., 1982). This established style plays a significant part in the way the person adjusts to the loss of a loved one. The more flexible the person is, the more adaptable he or she is likely to be in adjusting to the crisis of bereavement. Second, the more psychopathology the griever has prior to the loss, the more difficulty this individual will have in coming to terms with the loss (Parkes & Weiss, 1983).

Further understanding of the bereavement process also comes from clinical studies and observations made on patients who were in psychotherapy for complicated grief reactions. Horowitz and his group (1980) have noted that individuals who have negative images of themselves in their unconscious do more poorly, because these images are "reactivated" by the loss. These distorted self-concepts complicate the bereavement process. Even normal individuals suffer from a lowering of self-esteem at the time of the loss, but this temporary shift is usually less intense and less disparate with the person's basic self-concept. The normal person can function without being overwhelmed by the bad thoughts about the self, without being overwhelmed by guilt feelings, and without feeling needful of the deceased. These views are also in agreement with cognitive theory (described below) in which a person's grief pattern is greatly influenced by the negative thought patterns generally used by the bereaved.

Most clinicians and researchers who focus on the interpersonal aspects agree that if the relationship with the deceased was ambivalent, the likelihood of developing a clinical depression is strong (Parkes & Weiss, 1983). Although it should be recognized that most relationships are tainted with some ambivalence or even hostility, these conflicts are usually mild in the normal bereaved when counterbalanced by affectionate ties. Other types of relationships can lead to complications in the grief process, such as those involving an excessively dependent personality. This is particularly true for wives who depended to a large extent on their husbands for taking responsibility for the management of finances, household duties, driving, and fixing things around the house. Their reaction tends mostly to be one of helplessness, fear, indecisiveness, and intense longing. And if the bereaved person depended on the deceased for socialization, the emotional support needed to generate spontaneity and enthusiasm is sorely missed (Lopata, 1973; Parkes & Weiss, 1983).

Attachment and Interpersonal Theories

These conceptual models emphasize the nature of the interpersonal relationship held with the deceased and the strength of the bond in the relationship. Bowlby, a psychoanalyst who had studied the nature of attachments made by human beings since childhood, concluded that the propensity toward such attachments is universal. What this means is that the stronger the bond with the deceased, the more difficult and the more painful the grief (Bowlby, 1970, 1973, 1980).

Interpersonal theory states that as the person is reacting, relationships will be greatly influenced by social withdrawal, anger, hostility, sadness, and explosive displays of tears and helplessness. At times, grievers may avoid relationships, while, at other times, they may desperately seek support. It is only after they have adopted a new identity, seen themselves in a different light, acted in different ways, that they can begin to make decisions and form new relationships (Parkes & Weiss, 1983).

Crisis Theory

In this model bereavement is regarded as a critical life event which disturbs the individual's emotional equilibrium (Caplan, 1963). It too emphasizes previous personality problems which make it difficult for the individual to function socially. But despite these problems, the reactions to the loss are regarded as an opportunity for growth and for change in a positive direction.

Cognitive Theory

Bereavement, according to these theories, sets off negative thoughts which, in predisposed individuals, accentuate the negative self-image (Beck et al., 1979). As mentioned above in the psychodynamic theories, the negative thinking in the individual becomes the central dominant force. This person tends to interpret the loss as a personal rejection, and the rejection is felt to be on the basis of personal shortcomings. Later, the individual sees the future only in pessimistic terms.

Behavioral Theory

The focus of this theory, as in cognitive theory, is on pathological grief (Mawson et al., 1981; Ramsay, 1979). Those bereaved who have a history of avoiding confrontations with stressful life events will tend to repeat the same pattern in the bereavement situation by avoiding the pain of grief. These people are said to be "stuck" in their grief. Another pattern of pathological behavior can develop if the bereaved person was receiving considerable approval from the deceased and now feels acutely deprived of such approval. This person may have a more difficult time of "letting go" of the approval and the loss.

At another extreme is the case where family and friends encourage the bereaved to continue living with grief. These encouragements may occur in subtle form within warm support and sympathy, but sometimes they serve to prolong the grieving in some people (Gauthier & Marshall, 1977).

Theories of Stages in the Grief Process

Several theoreticians have modeled the grief process according to the stages of the dying process described by Elisabeth Kubler-Ross (1969). Averill (1968) and Lindemann (1944) described three stages of grieving: shock, despair and recovery, while Colin Parkes (1970), a British psychiatrist, saw four stages: numbness, pining (searching behavior), depression and recovery. Since the 1960s there has been an academic debate over how many stages can be conceptualized in the grieving process. But it is clear now that there is much overlapping of stages. The reader should also keep in mind that these stages are not delineated by rigid boundaries and that it would be erroneous to assume that a person should move neatly from one stage to another in order to complete the grief process. The stage theory simply provides a rough guide to the understanding of the overall grief reaction, with a beginning, a middle, and an end, encompassing symptoms that wax and wane within the various stages (see Chapter 3).

The Reaction Theory

Therese Rando (1984), a clinical psychologist and researcher in the area of grief and loss, prefers to conceptualize the grief process in terms of reactions rather than stages. She warns against the tendency to "fit people" into defined stages and "push" them from one to another. Instead she distinguishes three broad categories of reactions: *avoidance*, in which there is shock, denial, and disbelief; *confrontation*, in which the grief is most intense and the reactions to the loss are most acutely felt; and *reestablishment*, whereby the grief declines and a reentry into the daily routine follows. Rando adds that these reactions are influenced by the individual characteristics of each person and by pertinent social and psychological factors. Even these reactions are not rigidly sequential, and the individual can move back and forth among them (Rando, 1984).

PSYCHOSOCIAL FACTORS AFFECTING THE GRIEF PROCESS

Acknowledging Rando's (1984) statement about the individual characteristics which influence the grief reaction, we shall briefly discuss the factors most important to the clinician.

1. The nature of the relationship to the deceased.

One can be closer to a grandparent than to a parent, and therefore grieve more acutely over the loss of that grandparent. The strength of the relationship will be the strong determinant in the intensity of the grieving. On the other hand, if there was much ambivalence and conflict in the relationship with the deceased, there will be complications in the grief process.

2. The individual's coping behaviors and mental health.

How the person copes with other crises in life is likely to influence the style of coping with grief as well. If a person is accustomed to running away from problems, there is a strong likelihood that this person will not accept the pain of grief, thus delaying the process and opportunity for recovery. Grievers will commonly:

1. avoid talking about the deceased;
2. plunge back into work or school;
3. indulge in drugs, alcohol, or food to help block out the reality;

4.   obsess about details of the death;

5.   make major decisions, such as to sell the home, move away, or become involved in a new relationship;

6.   turn to prayer as an outlet for feelings or relief of guilt;

7.   seek contact with others to relieve loneliness and despair.

When used with caution and in moderation, such coping behaviors are adaptive. When used excessively, they could lead to complications and pathological grief (Shuchter, 1984).

3. Basic beliefs and attitudes toward death.

Another factor that may affect the course of the grief process is the individual's basic beliefs and attitudes toward death. Both consciously and subconsciously, they affect feelings and dictate behaviors.

4. Level of intelligence and maturity.

The understanding and the meaning of the relationship with the deceased will be directly related to the griever's intelligence level and degree of maturity. Professionals must be prepared for wide variation in this area.

5. The individual's past history of losses.

Previous experiences with death and losses may influence the person positively or negatively. If previous grief experiences have shown that grief shall pass in due time, then the person may be more accepting of the new loss. On the other hand, a negative experience may further complicate the reaction to the new loss. Therefore, it is always useful to inquire from the griever whether other losses have occurred and how the grieving was experienced.

6. The individual's ethnic, cultural, and religious backgrounds.

As mentioned previously under the definition of mourning, ethnic, cultural, and religious factors can play a major role in the subsequent reactions to the loss. Therefore, these various backgrounds of the bereaved should always be noted by clinicians.

7. The "unfinished business" with the deceased.

This item refers to issues or conflicts that were never or only partially resolved with the deceased prior to the death. It is as if the death interfered with the closure or resolution of conflicts. This lack of completion leaves the griever with a sense of anxiety and a feeling of having missed the opportunity to tell the deceased that he or she was loved, appreciated, and needed.

8. The social support system.

How much support the griever perceives may greatly affect the subsequent course of bereavement (Vachon et al., 1982). Therefore it is important to inquire about the amount of support that the bereaved can realistically expect in the weeks ahead. If no support is available, follow-up and referral should be made. It has been shown that the support of health professionals is inversely proportional to that received by family or friends (Hart, 1971).

Summary of Major Theoretical Concepts of Bereavement

Theories of bereavement overlap in their conclusions and in their emphases. However, each model seems to complement the various pieces of the overall puzzle of the bereavement process. The ultimate model will have to take into account a multiplicity of factors, and the distinction between normal bereavement and pathological reactions to bereavement will need further study and analysis. Nevertheless, the following general conclusions can be drawn from the current state of knowledge:

1. Despite the existence of multiple theories of bereavement, each theory in its way contributes valuable elements to the overall understanding of the bereavement process.

2. Bereavement is universal and predictable. It has been observed since antiquity. Although it has some recognizable patterns in large groups of people, individual reactions are clearly dependent on sociocultural factors, preexisting personality traits, and the strength of the relationship with the deceased.

3. Grief has a purpose and a healing function. Despite the fact that pain appears to be intolerable to some individuals, there seems to be general agreement among clinicians that the bereavement process cannot proceed and reach completion without suffering. The process is viewed by most clinicians and researchers as having a healing and purposeful function because it enables the bereaved to progress to the stage of reinvesting in life and in new relationships.

4. Bereavement is unique to each individual. Bereavement reactions show considerable variation from one person to another. There are varying levels of intensity and duration, with different outcomes, even within the normal range of reactions. Signs and symptoms of grief encompass social withdrawal, physical discomfort, and feelings of distress that come and go throughout the bereavement process until

they finally subside. These symptoms and complaints fall within the norm and should be recognized as such.

5. There is a need for further research of the boundaries between normal and pathological bereavement. In the meantime, clinical observations remain our most important way to devise new forms of intervention. In later chapters, we shall provide concrete guidelines and suggestions based on clinical interviews and feedback from persons who have experienced various types of bereavement. Other interventions to be discussed have been derived from the various experiences reported by hospital and clinical staff members.

Chapter 3

SIGNS AND SYMPTOMS OF BEREAVEMENT

When a patient dies, the survivor experiences a tremendous emotional pain, as if something had been wrenched from his psychic life (Raphael, 1983). Bereavement experts have summarized the grief experience by saying that when your parent dies, you lose your past; when your spouse dies, you lose your present; and when your child dies, you lose your future. The grief process is the sequence of emotional reactions to the loss, following a predictable course which is both painful and healing.

Some clinicians conceptualize grief within a disease model, assuming that grief, like a fresh wound, must proceed according to the phases of healing and the reconstitution of damaged tissue (Engel, 1961). The disadvantage of this model is that it likens the grief process to a pathological condition, which it is not. The one thing that clinicians and researchers agree on, however, is that grief is a reaction, which must be allowed to take its course without being inhibited, delayed, or prolonged, if a favorable outcome is expected.

Experts who have observed the various stages of grief have identified certain signs and symptoms as characteristic of each phase. This conceptualization is useful for health professionals because it enables them to recognize whether a person is progressing as expected, or getting stuck in a particular phase of the grief process. The state of being arrested in a phase may lead the person into an unhealthy grief pattern with pathological consequences (see Chapter 4).

The disadvantage of the stage model is that it implies a linear progression of symptoms, which does not necessarily happen. Symptoms tend to wax and wane throughout the entire process, not always following an orderly succession. For example, although crying is predominant in the early phases of grief, it may subside and reappear in later phases. The same would be true for sighing, surges of sadness, anger, and despair. The grieving widow may be reminded of the deceased husband and of the past by a passing comment in casual conversation. "Remember how much fun George used to have with us?" Suddenly, even though it is years later, painful emotions are reactivated and tears flow spontaneously for seconds or minutes. The trigger could be any number of things, such as a piece of music or a song cherished by the loved one.

Experts have described three, four, or five phases of grief. A few have modeled the phases after the well-known Kubler-Ross stages of dying because of the similarity of symptom clusters and the psychological mechanisms. Not surprisingly, there are some parallels, since the dying person goes through what is believed to be a grieving process as well. In both the grieving or the dying process, there is much overlapping of symptoms from one phase to the next (see Figure 1). To clarify and simplify applicability for clinicians, we have adopted the following scheme proposed by Brown and Stoudemire (1983).

THE THREE PHASES OF GRIEF

Phase 1, described by the authors as the "shock" phase, begins immediately upon learning of the news of the death or the diagnosis of terminal illness. It usually lasts from 1 to 2 weeks and is dominated by a state of disbelief and emotional numbness. Somatic symptoms are not uncommon and include, besides crying and sobbing, feelings of tightness in the throat and chest, nausea, and a sensation of emptiness in the abdomen. Patients in the acute stage of grief appear confused, dazed, stunned, immobilized, and disorganized. They seem helpless, lost, and overwhelmed by the impact of the loss. This is more pronounced if the death was sudden or unexpected. The state of shock and numbness seems to serve the purpose of shielding the newly bereaved from the sudden and intense pain of the loss.

In the second phase, the bereaved person becomes obsessively

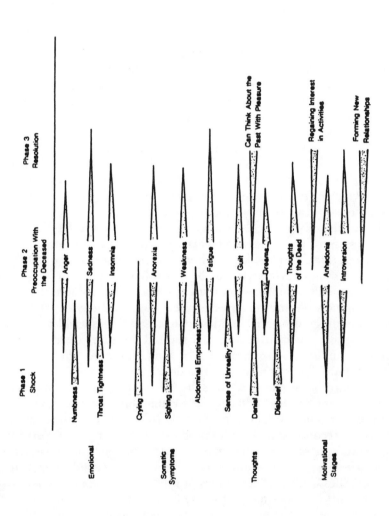

Figure 1 Phases of Uncomplicated Grief

preoccupied with thoughts of the deceased. The emotional numbness has subsided, and the acute awareness of the death begins to set in. The griever feels sad and new symptoms appear. They include insomnia, fatigue, anorexia, and *anhedonia*, the inability to experience any kind of pleasure. The predominant symptom in the second phase is a characteristic obsession with thoughts of the deceased, particularly memories of past actions and, seemingly, every aspect of the mutual relationship. Crying and episodes of sobbing tend to persist in most cases. Past conflicts, unresolved anger, resentment, and guilt are recalled and reexamined over and over again. There are repeated feelings that the deceased was neglected and that more could and should have been done. Vivid dreams of the deceased occur, including nightmares which are reported to be frightening. Sometimes there are hallucinatory episodes that consist of hearing the dead person's voice in the room, or mistaking strangers to look just like the deceased (Rees, 1975). Typically, the bereaved in this phase loses all desire to socialize, tending to withdraw from social obligations.

In the majority of cases, this second phase lasts from 1 to 6 months. Naturally, there is considerable variation in the duration of these phases, and this should be kept in mind by the clinician, who follows such a patient in the clinic. It may be confusing, at times, to see such a patient exhibiting similar symptoms years later, but recurrences are not uncommon on anniversaries of the death, birthdays of the deceased, weddings, or special holidays (Christmas, Memorial Day, New Year's Day), or special occasions that remind the survivor of the deceased. Upon listening to the report of such symptoms, the clinician should inquire about anniversary reactions.

The third phase, referred to as the "resolution" phase, is marked by the griever's gradual detachment of emotional energy from the deceased and reinvestment in new relationships. By this time, symptoms of the second phase have subsided for the most part, recurring only on occasion, but with lesser intensity and duration. They no longer immobilize the griever, who displays a general renewed interest in social activities, including new areas of interest and creative pursuits. Although this does not mean that the bereaved has recovered from the loss, it does reflect an adjustment. As Phyllis Silverman (1974), clinician and researcher aptly commented, "One doesn't get over it, but one gets used to it." Memories of the deceased are no longer viewed with sadness, but with a pleasant nostalgia and tenderness.

The above phases are characteristic of typical reactions seen in adults. Later, we shall describe the variations seen in adolescents and children.

The Four Categories of Adult Symptoms of Bereavement

When adults grieve, they exhibit a constellation of signs and symptoms which can be classified into four major categories:

(a) physical symptoms,

(b) mental symptoms,

(c) emotional symptoms, and

(d) behavioral manifestations.

As noted previously, these symptoms, responses, and manifestations do not occur in a progressive and linear fashion across the phases just described. There is some overlapping of symptoms between the various phases (see Figure 1).

Physical Symptoms

Lindemann (1944), a psychiatrist, observed the reactions of over 100 bereaved patients who survived the Coconut Grove fire of 1944. He described the following set of symptoms of acute grief: sensations of somatic distress, occurring in waves lasting from 20 minutes to an hour at a time, a feeling of tightness in the throat, choking with short- ness of breath, the need for sighing, an empty feeling in the abdomen, muscle weakness, and an intense subjective distress best described as "mental pain." Later, sobbing and crying were noted as occurring in waves over the following days. A feeling of numbness was observed, characterized by an absence of feelings or the expression of inappro- priate feelings. Additional symptoms, described by others, include sensitivity to noise, tightness in the chest, a sense of depersonalization (a feeling that nothing seems real), shortness of breath, lack of energy, muscular weakness, lack of coordination, and a dry mouth (Parkes & Brown, 1972; Worden, 1982).

Other complaints of physical discomfort might consist of pain or gastrointestinal disturbances. Frequently present are all of the vege- tative signs and symptoms of depression, such as insomnia, anorexia, weight loss, and lack of energy. Therefore, in acute or early phases it is difficult to distinguish normal grief from clinical depression.

In the elderly, in particular, it is important to consider the pos- sibility of bereavement reactions when similar complaints or symptoms are present, even though the patient may not mention a history of recent loss (Gallagher et al., 1983). In general, when such symptoms are present in the elderly, they are usually more pronounced and associated with marked irritability and negativistic thinking. Too often a misdiagnosis of major depression or dementia is made if a history of bereavement is not obtained. Sometimes the physical complaints may even take on a pattern similar to the one that was present in the deceased. For example, if the loved one died of a heart attack, the bereaved patient might later complain of tightness in the chest or pain in the heart (Zisook et al., 1982).

Studies of widows and widowers in England (Parkes & Weiss, 1983; Young et al., 1963) have shown that their mortality rate from heart disease increased in the 6-month period following bereavement. Other studies have reported that grieving individuals tend to develop numerous symptoms and illnesses in the first 6 months after the loss. For example, widows frequently complain of headaches, fainting spells, dizziness, skin rashes, indigestion, vomiting, and palpitations. Among some of the illnesses diagnosed were hyperthyroidism, diabetes, and hypertension.

Insomnia and poor appetite can lead to exhaustion, persistent fatigue, and poor nutrition. Not commonly, the beginning or increased use of alcohol, tobacco, or drugs brings on a deterioration of the health status. It is clear that the bereavement process takes a heavy toll on bodily functions and on the immune system, putting the individual at risk for major illness (Holmes & Rahe, 1967; Parkes & Weiss, 1983).

Mental Symptoms

Confusion and disbelief are characteristic of the shock phase, whereas preoccupation with thoughts about the deceased occur with the beginning of the second phase. The grieving patient may have experiences of seeing the dead person or of hearing the voice of the deceased, as if that person were very much alive (Rees, 1975). Most grievers will go through a detailed review of all the events that led to the death. Many will have a need to reexamine past actions and behaviors toward the deceased. While some people will retreat into silence, others will find comfort in sharing these recent experiences with people whom they trust, including their physicians.

It is important to recognize that these subjective experiences are within the normal range and do not call for a psychiatric referral at this stage. Most people will also experience an urge to solve the puzzle which led to the final stage of death, attempting to make some sense out of the course of illness. "When we saw him in the hospital last

weekend, he looked fine, and we all thought that he was getting better. . . ." "But then, the nurse did mention that he had had a bad day
yesterday." "I remember talking to him, and he seemed worried." "I
wonder if he knew that the end was coming."

The need to explain a chain of events is more or less present in
everyone (Kalish, 1985). Therefore, it is important for health professionals to be aware of this normal need and to assist the bereaved in
the hospital or during return visits to the clinic. The explanation given
by the physician is another link in the reconstruction of the events.
But it is not necessarily the last one. Sometimes the autopsy report
provides an additional rationale which can satisfy some individuals.
Others cannot be satisfied with the reality and find it necessary to
keep ruminating. This is especially true if the death was perceived as
senseless or unfair, such as the result of an accident, a disaster, a suicide, or murder. Although bits of news can occasionally relieve some
of the anguish, the bereaved typically spends time seeking some sort
of answer to gain some perspective or "to make some sense" of the
death, whether it be a case of divine intervention, punishment, or a
logical explanation of cause and effect. The search for meaning is, of
course, greatly determined by the cultural and religious background
of the survivor (Geertz, 1973; Rosenblatt et al., 1977).

There are also disturbances of cognitive functioning. Typical
manifestations include the inability to concentrate, which may cause
the person to be absent-minded, to get lost while driving, to misplace
money and other things, or to miss appointments. The bereaved may
also find it difficult to concentrate on reading or television. There is
a constant stream of thoughts about the deceased, and images of the
past are frequently conjured up. Eventually, the bereaved finds an
explanation that is adequate. There may even be several versions. "The
operation could have been a success, if his heart had been stronger."
"I guess he was ready to die." Of all the various explanations, one
eventually seems to emerge as the "official version," which satisfies
almost everyone.

The occurrence of nightmares and nondisturbing dreams is
probably another attempt at solving the puzzle of the death. The
mental changes just described operate as defense mechanisms for the
most part, protecting the bereaved individual from overwhelming
anxiety and fear (Raphael, 1983).

Psychiatric disturbances and illnesses have also been ascribed to
bereavement. But here the studies have been divided. For example,
childhood bereavement has been thought to be an antecedent to adult

depression (Brown, 1982) or even schizophrenia, but the latter finding has not been confirmed. On the other hand, psychiatric disturbances that follow immediately after the experience of the loss are usually described as pathological grief. In these cases, the patient reports feelings of worthlessness, self-reproach and recriminations, the need for punishment, and guilt, in addition to the usual symptoms of acute grief (see Chapter 4).

Emotional Symptoms

Emotional reactions to bereavement are continuous and variably intense throughout the grief process. These reactions include: (a) denial, (b) depression and sadness, (c) guilt and anger, and (d) relief. We shall briefly discuss the formation of bereavement reactions because an understanding of the underlying dynamics helps the caregiver in the management of them.

Denial.   When a person dies, the family often reacts with total disbelief. This is particularly true of a sudden or unexpected death. This form of denial assumes varying degrees of intensity. Sometimes, the bereaved behaves as if the deceased were still alive, continuing to speak of the deceased person's opinion, "John says that we should not invest in this venture," or of recent plans or preferences, "Morry does not like to take these kinds of vacations." Denial may also appear in other ways. A widow, for example, may continue to say "we," even though only she is involved. Or parents may maintain a child's room just as it was before the child died (Kalish, 1985).

Mild degrees of denial commonly exist in all of us. We often hear, "I can't believe it really happened." Yet, a part of us is able to accept the fact that something did happen, the reality slowly integrating into our overall conception of the relationship with the deceased.

Sadness and depression.   Reactions of sadness and depression are the most common and best understood. Everyone expects a person to be sad and perhaps even depressed after the loss of a loved one. In the early phases of grief, it is difficult to distinguish typical sadness and sorrow from clinical depression. One researcher speculated that the difference lies in the amount of social support received by the bereaved (Clayton et al., 1972). There is likely to be severe depression if there is loneliness and isolation. However, there is one characteristic symptom which does differentiate the normally bereaved from those with potential unhealthy complications. This symptom is described as a "persistent wish to be dead" (Parkes & Weiss, 1983) or the "Giving Up-Given Up Complex" (Engel, 1968).

Guilt and anger. Guilt and anger are two prevalent emotions, particularly when the bereaved has had an ambivalent relationship with the deceased. The survivor may feel guilty for having failed to take certain precautionary measures that could have prevented the death. Guilt over withheld demonstrations of affection may be expressed as "I did not hug him enough." Typically, guilt feelings are contained in all of the expressions that start with "If only I had. . . ." One hears, "If only I had not let him drive the car," or, "If only I had not given permission for the surgery." The guilt arises from the failure to take action when it was thought to be crucial. Or it can emerge when there is a feeling that the deceased was treated poorly and unfairly.

There are other sources of guilt, although they are less frequent. When a person inherits some money, acquires an estate, obtains a promotion or better position in the company, or otherwise benefits directly from the death, there may be some feelings of guilt. Not uncommonly, however, feelings of elation from the gains are mixed with feelings of sadness and can lead to guilt if the relationship with the deceased was ambivalent. Sometimes the survivor has to struggle with previously held death wishes for the person who died. On the other hand, the death of someone may provide for greater freedom of action, opportunities for new sexual activities, or freedom from certain restrictions in daily living, such as food preferences, shows, sports, etc. Feelings of ambivalence are present in all of us to some extent, inasmuch as they were present during the past relationship with the deceased.

Another source of guilt is what has been described as "survivor's guilt." It is often seen in military or veterans hospitals, when war veterans and heroes return without their buddies. These survivors often wonder why they were spared. Similar patterns of guilt reactions were seen in survivors of Nazi concentration camps and the atomic bombings of Hiroshima and Nagasaki.

Anger seems to arise out of two main sources. First, the bereaved may feel angry for having been abandoned by the deceased, suddenly feeling left alone. Sometimes there is even a feeling that the deceased contributed to the death on purpose, either by neglecting medical care or by actively seeking suicide. Secondly, as was true for guilt, anger can stem from the ambivalent relationship with the lost one. Grief therapists sometimes refer to the lack of closure of the relationship as "unfinished business." Ambivalent feelings of love and hate can be brought out by the use of several techniques, such as asking the bereaved to "talk to the empty chair" or to "write a letter to the deceased," saying all the things that had not been said and should have been.

Anger is sometimes displayed to other people. It is usually aimed toward other family members who are around the bereaved person and who may not understand what is happening. Even offers for help may be rejected in an angry manner, much to the surprise of those who want to help. At other times, anger can be directed toward God, the medical profession and, more specifically, toward a particular physician or hospital, or anyone who had something to do with the care of the deceased.

Relief.   After a lingering illness, it is common for the family to experience a feeling of relief akin to the expression, "Finally it's over!" There is the certainty of no more pain or suffering. During the terminal stages of an illness, the family feels helpless, tired, and exhausted from seeing their loved one deteriorate while exhibiting weakness, childlike behavior, and total vulnerability. When the death finally occurs, it is like a deliverance from the burden of responsibility for further care. Life can return to normal after so many months of interrupted routines. The person who took leave from work can resume employment; the child who interrupted schooling or athletic activities can begin again. There is a new feeling of freedom from what was perceived as a losing battle and a hopeless cause. However, this sense of relief is sometimes associated with guilt, particularly, as in the previous case, where there is gain from the acquisition of money, power, position, status, or potential for new relationships not previously available.

Behavioral Manifestations

The newly bereaved will frequently show a spectrum of behavioral changes. The most dramatic responses are the self-damaging behaviors, such as the start or increase of smoking, drinking, and drug abuse. Increase is more notable in previous users who have a pattern of handling crises in this manner (Glick et al., 1974). Crying and uncontrolled tearfulness can cause the bereaved to withdraw and avoid social occasions because of embarrassment. At times, the bereaved person feels restless and engages in aimless activity. At other times, there is avoidance of any reminder of the deceased, or, on the contrary, a fascination with objects, activities, or places associated with the dead person. This constant preoccupation with the bereaved has been referred to as "searching behavior" (Parkes, 1970). Such searching is also evident when the survivor experiences illusions (perceiving that strangers in the street resemble the deceased), hallucinations (responding to visions of the deceased appearing for a few moments in the same room) or recurrent dreams in which the deceased appears so "vividly alive."

The most prominent change of behavior is in social withdrawal. This is characteristic of the early phases. Later on, in the resolution phase, when the "letting go" takes place, the widow or widower may experience difficulty with resuming a normal social life, particularly if the previous socializing was done with couples only. This is also true for the elderly person, who finds it more difficult to make new acquaintances and friendships, and who ends up feeling lonely and isolated. These people sometimes use their visits to a doctor as a form of socialization. When this is recognized, a supportive discussion and encouragement to join a support group in the community is extremely helpful. This process can be facilitated if a social worker is available in the clinic or hospital setting.

The Ending of the Bereavement Process

There is no sharp end point to the bereavement process. Rather, a new level of adaptation is achieved with new feelings, perceptions, and behaviors. Some people speak of a recovery, as if one were expected to recover from an illness. This is an erroneous concept, because there is agreement that the process is no more pathological than a pregnancy. Furthermore, grieving can reoccur with lesser intensity at different times in life. Typically, it recurs at the time of anniversary dates such as birthdays, celebrations, or memorial holidays.

So, bereavement ending is not necessarily an ending of the symptoms as much as it is the beginning of other life phases for the individual. Time remains the most crucial dimension. However, there is no standard yardstick for the time necessary to go through the bereavement process. General estimates have been made from studies of large samples of bereaved, and in most general terms, bereavement can last from 1 to 2 years for the loss of a spouse, and from 2 to 5 years for the loss of a child. In some cases grief-related symptoms and behavior have lasted indefinitely (Zisook et al., 1982) but with some degree of adaptation (Goin et al., 1979). Therefore, it is important for health professionals to recognize that there is a great deal of individuality and variability.

The reactions described above apply primarily to adults. The clinical management of those reactions will be discussed in subsequent chapters. At this point, we shall review the reactions characteristic of bereaved adolescents and children, along with some guiding principles for the management of the symptoms.

Bereavement Reactions in Adolescents

The reactions that adolescents have in response to losing someone close are not very different from those of adults. They also experience feelings of guilt, and their relationship to the deceased may in great part determine the intensity of their feelings. There are some differences, however. For example, teenagers often wonder what impact the death will have on their futures, and whether any drastic changes will result. There may be financial pressures, wherein the surviving parent may need financial assistance and the teenager may have to go to work, drop out of athletics, and have less time with friends.

A teenager who loses a sibling may experience guilt for not having contributed enough. Some adolescents, boys more than girls, tend to grieve silently, showing very little outward manifestation of grief. This is sometimes interpreted as their taking it well, "like a man," or progressing well through their grief. This is a false assumption on the part of adults around them, because denial is often the predominant expression in teenagers. The lack of emotional display may reflect a fear of appearing different or abnormal (LaGrand, 1981).

Others tend to manifest troublesome behavior, acting out their grief through sexual promiscuity or by using alcohol, drugs, or tobacco. Unless the acting-out behavior is recognized as a manifestation of grief, receiving the proper attention by the family or a health professional, the situation may deteriorate into severe psychological and social consequences (Raphael, 1983; Rutter, 1966). On the other hand, when depression does occur, it is not usually associated with thoughts of the deceased, as grown-ups might be led to believe. The adolescent tends to worry about the future, preservation of the family, and the new responsibility thrust upon them. In fact, the bereavement experience is viewed by some adolescents not so much as a crisis, but more as a push to grow quickly into adulthood with all of its burdens and responsibilities.

Bereavement Reactions in Children

Although studies of grief in normal children are rare, it is generally recognized that the grief process in children is different from that of adults. It is beyond the scope of this book to review in detail the research in this area. Such details of many research studies are well covered in *Bereavement: Reactions, Consequences and Care* by Osterweis, Solomon, and Green (1984) and *The Anatomy of Bereavement* by Raphael (1983). We shall briefly review the salient points that are pertinent to the understanding of the grief process in children.

Children's reactions vary in intensity and duration according to their ages, their concepts of death (see Appendix A), and the types of relationships with the persons before death, whether parent, grandparent, or sibling. To understand the child's bereavement reactions, we must first have a knowledge of the child's concept of death as it relates to the stages of biological and psychosocial development. Prior to age three, the child is too immature to have any concept of death (Nagy, 1948). From ages three to five, the child believes that death is reversible, that the dead person is just less alive and usually in a state of sleep. From ages five to nine, children begin to grasp the irreversibility of death, but that it happens only to other people. It is only after age ten that the child understands the causes of death, its finality, and its effect on the body. Variations do occur, depending on whether the child's emotional and intellectual development is either retarded or advanced (Gartley & Bernasconi, 1967).

What is primarily different about the bereavement reactions of children as compared to those of adults is the fact that intense emotional and behavioral expressions are *not continuous,* but rather intermittent. This can be explained by the fact that the child's capacity to experience intense emotions is considered to be limited (Osterweis et al., 1984). A four-year-old can only be sad for a few minutes.

In the early phases, children under three will typically exhibit loss of speech and generalized distress. Children under five will respond with disturbances of eating, sleeping, bladder and bowel control. School-age children often develop school phobias, hypochondriacal concerns, learning problems, antisocial behavior, aggression, or withdrawal. Others become overly attentive and clinging. Boys typically show an increase in aggressive and destructive behavior, showing their feelings in this way rather than openly displaying sadness (Raphael, 1983; Rutter, 1966). This is due to social expectations which discourage the expression of sadness and tenderness by males, behaviors that can make the child a target for ridicule or embarrassment. Abdominal pain *without* any demonstrable organic cause has been reported as a presenting symptom of children in a bereavement situation. But this symptom is suspect as an attempt to gain attention from their grieving parents rather than being a grief reaction as such (Kaffman & Elizur, 1983).

As with adults, the symptoms of bereavement in children denote underlying concerns that must be understood by those who are in a position to help. There are essentially three areas that children worry about when they are in the bereavement crisis. These worries are captured in the following three questions:

"What did I do to cause this to happen?"

"Will this happen to me too?"

"Who will take care of me now?"

It is most important that all of these questions be answered in some manner, even if they are not asked by the child (Goldreich, 1977; Grollman, 1967). Moreover, the answers must be carefully checked out to make sure that the child understands clearly, so that misinterpretations can be avoided. If this is not done, the child might become more anxious, fearful, or angry as a result of these misinterpretations. The child must also be reassured repeatedly about the answers to the questions.

Children frequently will not show any overt expression of emotion following loss. This may be partly due to the denial that takes place, and partly due to their limited ability to experience intense emotions. But troublesome emotions and behaviors may appear months or years after the loss, not uncommonly during adolescence or at the time of anniversary dates (Cain et al., 1964). Another difference between children and adult bereavement reactions is that children tend to form new relationships more quickly after the loss. As a result, they may be out of synchrony with their bereaved parents (Committee on the Health Consequences of the Stress of Bereavement, 1984).

Some clinicians like Dr. Kliman, former director of the Center for Preventive Psychiatry in White Plains, N.Y., take the view that all bereaved children are at risk for future emotional problems, therefore requiring evaluation to prevent the development of chronic problems (Kliman, 1980). Those clinicians also believe that all children should not only be allowed to express grief but should be actively encouraged to do so. This is an issue that obviously needs more research. However, in evaluating a grieving child, the following areas should be carefully examined by the professional team member:

(a) How did the child relate to the parent before death?
(b) How did the death occur?
(c) How does the surviving parent perceive the loss?
(d) How does the parent speak to the child about the loss?

According to Zelman, current Director of the Center for Preventive Psychiatry in White Plains, N.Y., the last two questions are probably the most important ones in determining the bereavement outcome for the child (Committee on Health Consequences of the Stress of Bereavement, 1984). For example, if the surviving parent feels and expresses excessive anger about the loss, perceiving it as abandonment, the impact on the child may be negative and disturbing. Another troublesome factor responsible for complications in the bereavement process is when the death results from suicide or other violence rather than from an illness. Children in these situations should be referred for evaluation or counseling to prevent future emotional complications.

The child who is able to talk freely and openly in positive or negative terms about the dead parent will have a more favorable outcome than the one who cannot or the one who can recall *only* negative memories. The latter behaviors could foretell potential problems.

Another significant factor in the grief process is the impact of the parent's grief on parenting, affecting a period which can last from 1 to 2 years. The troubled parent will have a significant influence on the child's adjustment and development.

Management Guidelines

Before the family is advised about how to proceed with telling the child about a death, several decisions must be agreed upon. First, there must be agreement on who tells the child, the best timing for the news, and the manner in which to do so. To a large extent, the family's belief system will determine what they will do. Yet, when health professionals are asked for recommendations, caution must be exercised. The caregiver must get some history about the family's cultural and religious background, noting their preferences and inclinations (Vaughn, 1983). As pointed out above, it is critical to know the level of the intellectual and emotional development of the child. In some cases, the best approach is to discuss the matter with the whole family present. In others, it is most effective to have the first news of the death presented by a single significant person.

Given the above insights, what approaches should health professionals take with the bereaved child? In advising parents on how to deal with the reactions of the bereaved child, the following points should be kept in mind:

1. Most importantly, the news of the death should never be withheld. A child should be told the truth in simple terms that can be understood. For the younger child, the simple and early explanation is best. Questions should be encouraged to eliminate the development of fantasies and fears through misperceptions or misinterpretations (Chaloner, 1962; Plank, 1971).

2. If the parent is terminally ill, the child should be told that these events are beyond anyone's control and that everything will be done to preserve life as long as possible.

3. In cases of sudden death, any misinterpretations by the child should be quickly corrected (Furman, 1974).

4. The child should be reassured that he or she will not die in connection with the death. Relief is a very likely response.

5. The child must be reassured about not being responsible for what happened to the deceased (Reed, 1972).

6. It is wise to ask the child to repeat what is understood by asking him to pretend that he has to explain it again to a friend. Clarify any misconceptions and check understanding once again.

7. Regarding the child's attendance at the funeral, there is much uncertainty among families, the predominant feeling being that it might be upsetting or frightening. Most experts recommend that children be allowed to attend if they wish, but that they should not be forced to participate in the mourning rituals and funeral rites. If a child chooses to go, it may help with the acceptance of death, just as it does with adults (Grollman, 1967). But it is important, then, to prepare the child for the experience by describing what to expect to see and to hear before reaching the funeral service. A relative should always stay with the child. If the casket is an open one, the child should be given the choice about seeing the body.

Health professionals should be trained and equipped to deal with bereavement issues and questions when they arise in the hospital or clinic setting because families often turn to them to seek advice on how to talk to children about grief. Physicians, nurses, and social workers must be able to distinguish the normal from the pathological. Unlike other models of intervention in medicine where the main goal is to relieve pain, in the grief situation the health care team must work together to facilitate the painful process of grieving by acknowledging the pain. This is not a paradoxical position for the health team, but a difficult and exhausting one. However, through the sharing of cases and discussion among colleagues, the emotional burden becomes tolerable.

In conclusion, we feel that with knowledge of the signs and symptoms of the bereavement process, the health care team will feel more secure in recognizing and filling the needs of bereaved families in the hospital and clinic setting. In the next chapter, we shall discuss the differences between healthy and unhealthy grief.

Chapter 4

PATHOLOGICAL GRIEF

CRITERIA FOR PATHOLOGICAL GRIEF

There has been no universally accepted definition of what constitutes pathological grief. Generally, it is recognized that unresolved grief leads to pathological manifestations of grief. Some clinicians have referred to it when (a) the grief is prolonged or very intense, (b) the grief has been inhibited or arrested in one of the phases of the grief process, (c) the grief has developed into a full clinical illness such as a major depression or other psychiatric entity, or (d) the bereaved perceives difficulty in coping with the loss.

Given the above criteria for pathological grief, it is estimated that 10 to 15 percent of bereaved individuals go on to develop pathological outcomes following loss (Clayton & Darvish, 1979; Parkes & Weiss, 1983; Zisook & DeVaul, 1983). It is important for health professionals to be able to identify those patients with unresolved grief if preventive and therapeutic measures are to be taken. Pathological grief can lead to serious psychiatric problems, such as major depression, psychosomatic conditions (e.g., ulcerative colitis, asthma, rheumatoid arthritis), phobias, obsessive and anxiety disorders, drug and alcohol abuse, family problems, or even psychotic disorders. High morbidity, mortality, and suicide have also been reported (Bornstein et al., 1973;

Bunch et al., 1971; Clayton et al., 1974; Parkes et al., 1969; Maddison & Viola, 1968; Rees & Lutkins, 1967).

Differential Diagnosis

The distinction between normal and pathological grieving is not easy in the early phases of grief, because the symptoms are virtually identical. Even the *Diagnostic and Statistical Manual of the American Psychiatric Association* (DSM-III-R) (1987) defines uncomplicated bereavement as follows: "Uncomplicated Bereavement is distinguished from a Major Depressive Episode and is not considered a mental disorder even when associated with the full depressive syndrome. However, morbid preoccupation with worthlessness, suicidal ideation, marked functional impairment or psychomotor retardation, or prolonged duration suggests that bereavement is complicated by a Major Depressive Episode" (p. 333).

In other cases, anxiety and even panic attacks seem to be the most prominent symptoms. Belitsky and Jacobs (1986) have suggested that these symptoms can be understood in terms of a kind of "separation anxiety" as a reaction to the loss. Several studies have reported the persistence of panic symptoms as long as one year after the bereavement. Many of these patients seem overwhelmed and even report fears of "losing their minds," a fear characteristic of patients with panic disorders. Table 1 (see p.   ) summarizes the spectrum of symptoms seen in normal and pathological grief according to each phase of grief.

Despite the above attempts to differentiate between normal and pathological grieving, it is clear that symptoms alone are not sufficient to make the differential diagnosis. There are also predisposing factors (Shanfield, 1983).

Predisposing Factors

Additional criteria for pathological grief have been suggested by researchers and clinicians. These have included: (a) the presence or absence of feelings of worthlessness, (b) the severity of depressive symptoms, (c) the duration of the grieving process, (d) a history of multiple losses, (e) a history of difficulty in getting along with mother (Zisook et al., 1985), and (f) complaints of depression and physical distress.

Normal Grieving vs. Major Depression

Even with the above criteria in mind, there is considerable overlap
between clinical depression and normal grieving. In the Zisook bereavement studies, the authors suggested a set of guidelines that would
identify more clearly the distinction between Major Depression and
normal grieving. The following features taken from the guidelines
encompass several aspects of the clinical picture (Zisook, 1987).

Onset of Symptoms

In normal grieving, the onset of depressive symptoms occurs in
the first 3 months after loss, and it usually ends within a year. The
onset of symptoms in Major Depression, on the other hand, may start
any time, even 2 or 3 months after the loss.

Duration and Intensity of the Depressive Symptoms

Major Depression is a more likely diagnosis if the symptoms of
anhedonia, apathy, early morning awakening, severe psychomotor
agitation or retardation, anorexia, and excessive guilt persist beyond
6 months after the loss. The intensity of the symptoms, although difficult to gauge because of individual variations, can be another clue,
particularly if there is not improvement in the first year. Usually, according to Lindemann (1944), the depression is of the agitated type,
which includes symptoms of tension, agitation, insomnia, feelings of
worthlessness, bitter self-accusation, obvious need for punishment, and
suicidal ideation and behavior. Granting that differentiation between
symptoms of normal and pathological grief remains difficult, Shuchter
and Zisook (1987) use two criteria based on the nature of the depression itself:
    1) the depression has "a life of its own," referring to the obser-
vation that depressive symptoms occur regardless of the day-to-day
events or triggering emotions; and
    2) vegetative signs and symptoms of depression, such as insomnia,
anorexia, weight loss, low energy, fatigue, and agitation which persist
beyond 2 months after death.

Past History and Family History of Depression

A past history of mood disorder, or a family history of such a
disorder, is an important clue to the possibility of a predisposition to

a major depression, which tends to occur more frequently in individuals whose family members experienced an episode of depression (Clayton & Darvish, 1979).

Self-Perception and Insight

In normal grief, the bereaved do not perceive themselves as ill, even though they may request some help with insomnia and anorexia. On the other hand, patients with Major Depression may not even be aware that the grief is the basis of their depression.

Nature of Loss

The occurrence of a sudden and unexpected death can be a strong predisposing factor to Major Depression. So can the experience of losing a child. In these cases the bereaved are subjected to an overpowering blow, which probably upsets the entire psychological and biological equilibrium.

Relationship to the Deceased

If the grief is unresolved because of the intense involvement with the deceased, the bereaved may be predisposed to a Major Depression. This is particularly true if the griever had a very dependent or ambivalent relationship with the deceased (Lopata, 1983; Parkes & Weiss, 1983).

TYPES OF PATHOLOGICAL GRIEF

We shall now describe the various patterns that unresolved grief can take, keeping in mind that some overlapping does occur between the various types mentioned in the bereavement literature (Averill, 1968; Parkes & Weiss, 1983; Raphael, 1983). Generally, in pathological grieving, the bereaved use an excessive amount of denial of the loss or repression of the loss or the feelings connected with the loss. Pathological grievers with a particularly strong dependency on the deceased may experience feelings of guilt or ambivalence (Anderson, 1949).

Absent Grief

In cases of absent grief, the bereaved show no outward signs or feeling of grief (Deutsch, 1937). In fact, to the untrained observer, these individuals appear to be coping very well. There is a persistent denial that characterizes the total experience (Bowlby, 1980).

Subtle clues to this pathological process can be detected when the following observations can be made:

1. Excessive anxiety and discomfort are evident when recalling memories of the deceased.
2. Others are forbidden to make references to the death.
3. Expressions of sympathy or support are not accepted.
4. The behavior implies that nothing ever happened.
5. Episodes of irritability and tension occur from time to time without any reference to any particular situation.

Yet, as a prevailing symptom of absent grief, despite the above observations, these individuals give the impression that they are functioning quite effectively and coping remarkably well. It should be pointed out, however, that some denial may be adaptive. In fact, the early phase of shock is primarily characterized by denial. But when the denial continues and persists, it gives cause for concern and increases risk (Jacobs & Douglas, 1979). Such individuals are the least likely to seek help or be perceived as troubled since their return to full routine functioning causes little discomfort to others.

Somatized Grief

As in absent grief, manifestations of grieving are lacking. Instead there are numerous somatic complaints which serve as a substitute for depression. These somatic symptoms are referred to as *depressive equivalents* (Volkan, 1966). In such cases, depressive symptoms are just beneath the surface.

A few appropriate questions can easily elicit the feelings associated with the recent loss of a loved one. In the course of taking a history, the physician or nurse should ask about the causes of death in the family and whether a recent loss occurred. For example, "Have you lost anyone in your family in recent years?" "Did you experience the emotions of grief?" "Were you especially close to that person?"

Patients with somatic complaints frequently receive elaborate medical workups which focus entirely on the presenting symptoms. Although the symptoms should be treated with adequate medical intervention, a simultaneous approach of support and counseling is appropriate, if the physician can increase awareness in a supportive manner (DeVaul et al., 1979). Occasionally, a referral to a support group in the community or to a counseling program should be offered, if acceptable to the patient.

Delayed Grief

A grief reaction can be triggered months or years after the loss if the initial grief response was aborted, delayed, or sidetracked. The delay can occur if the grief is overtaken by other events, such as another loss, excessive responsibilities at the time of the loss, or the need to be strong and supportive of other family members. Months or years later, the individuals who have delayed their grieving may be suddenly reminded of the loss by another experience, such as the loss or illness of another family member.

There is a debate among clinicians and researchers as to whether or not such a condition is truly a delayed bereavement response or a new episode of mood disorder. The distinction is important to those who treat patients, some choosing to use antidepressant medications for affective disorders, others choosing to consider a psychological approach with grief counseling. The best approach is to consider the criteria of differential diagnosis discussed above in distinguishing between pathological grief and Major Depression.

Prolonged or Chronic Grief

When grief is experienced with the same intensity of emotions for months or years, it is considered pathological. It is the sign of inability to work through the various phases and tasks of healthy grieving, with the result of being "stuck" in the grief process. In many cases the grief is complicated by persistent and excessive guilt, anger, and self-blame, usually resulting from an ambivalent or dependent relationship with the deceased. Such emotions literally paralyze the bereaved in daily functioning and may require medical or psychiatric attention (Zisook et al., 1985). It is difficult to diagnose chronic grief because of the similarity to normal grief. The main clues about the chronic grief are in the persistence and intensity of the symptoms over a long period of time (Vachon et al., 1982).

Another sign of chronic grief includes resistance to any involvement in new relationships and a view of the future as meaningless.

Typically, the person may say, "What is there for me now?" There is more than the usual withdrawal from and apathy toward relationships. There is a resistance to "getting involved" again. It is as though there is an attempt to keep alive the relationship with the deceased because there is a tendency to idealize the deceased. The intense yearning associated with the intense dependency on the deceased often reflects the insecurity of the griever. Although literature on widowers is limited at the present time, it is estimated that 10 to 15 percent of widows meet the criteria for chronic grief by experiencing symptoms of such intensity more than a year after the loss (Clayton & Darvish, 1979).

Case vignette

> Rachel was a shy and insecure forty-five-year-old postal worker when she lost her husband after a long illness. Over the years she had devoted all of her time and energy to meeting her husband's needs, running the household, and caring for the children. After her husband died, she retreated from all social activities, kept to herself, ignoring the children, and spent much time alone drinking and watching television. She made no attempt to reach out to others at work or in her neighborhood. Five years later, she had made no changes in her life.

Unanticipated Grief

This variant of the grief reaction also occurs when it follows an unnatural death, such as suicide or murder, or a death resulting from an accident (automobile, airplane crash, drowning, fall) or disaster (fire, earthquake, flood, avalanche, war, bombing). These deaths are felt to be totally unnatural and premature. In such cases, the bereaved are not only totally overwhelmed by sudden, unanticipated loss, but also by extreme feelings of bewilderment and anxiety, all of which prevent normal functioning in most areas of daily living. The circumstances of the death seem inexplicable and unacceptable. The death seems "unfair" because it did not conform with the natural course of events. In these cases, the conceptual model of pathological grief due to inadequate defenses appears insufficient. The patient is simply in a state of total collapse. Although the reactions are extremely severe and long lasting, they may not truly represent a picture of pathological grief. More research and follow-up are needed to determine the true nature of these reactions and the therapeutic implications (Glick et al., 1974; Parkes & Weiss, 1983).

Let us now examine the causes of pathological outcomes of unresolved grief.

CAUSES OF PATHOLOGICAL GRIEF

In addition to the general factors that influence the grief reaction,
such as personality traits, ethnic and cultural background, levels of
maturity and intelligence, there are other factors that contribute to
the outcome of pathological grief (Lazare, 1979).

First, there is the question of the circumstances of the death itself.
If the death, as mentioned above, is socially unacceptable, as in suicide
or homicide, the bereaved will pull away from assistance and support,
feeling ashamed. Health professionals may find it particularly hard
to be empathetic or know what to say in those cases.

Second, in cases where the death is not socially accepted as a loss,
such as an abortion or a miscarriage, the necessary support may not
be activated if it is not sought or offered to avert the complications
of the grief response. The same may be true if the griever did not
receive an official notification of the death, as in the case of those
missing in action, kidnapped, or feared drowned.

Third, if there is a history of past unresolved or multiple losses,
there may be a case of "bereavement overload." In many such cases,
there has been the loss of an entire family, as in catastrophic accidents
or concentration camps. Not infrequently, the elderly experience the
loss of all family members and friends by outliving them. Such pain
is often too overwhelming to deal with (Kastenbaum, 1969).

Fourth, complicated involvement in the relationship with the deceased may result in excessive dependency, ambivalence, anger, or
guilt. For some patients, the inability to be present at the moment of
death can generate considerable guilt and retard the grief process,
especially if a promise made to the dying person was broken. This
last example attributes more importance to the meaning of the event
than to the event itself, thereby prolonging the grief (Rando, 1984).

Fifth, a history of alcoholism and/or drug addiction can produce
complicated clinical pictures of bereavement. This is especially true
for younger alcoholic males (Kraus & Lilienfeld, 1959; Murphy &
Robins, 1967).

Sixth, the symbolic meaning of the grief response to the bereaved
may play a role in some cases of suppressed grief. Some people, for
example, are afraid to show or experience their feelings for fear that

it indicates a loss of control or appears as a sign of weakness. On the other end of the continuum, there are people who will not give up the pain because, symbolically, it maintains the bond to the deceased (Jackson, 1957).

Seventh, the bereavement in some people may trigger latent images of themselves as bad, hurtful, or incompetent. These reawakened, distorted thoughts and feelings contribute to the development of pathological grief responses (Horowitz et al., 1980).

How to Identify Grievers at Risk for Pathological Outcomes

There are many determinants predicting a pathological outcome in the bereavement population. Determinants of the most practical significance for the clinician include:

(a) lengthy duration of the terminal illness;

(b) intense dysphoria persisting for months after the loss, especially in younger alcoholic males;

(c) persistent somatic complaints not substantiated by medical findings;

(d) a history of previous psychiatric problems, alcoholism, and drug addiction; and

(e) a history of multiple losses.

This list is not complete, but it alerts physicians and other health professionals to the easiest possible predictors of clinic visits or hospitalization (Glick et al., 1974).

Patients identified as showing signs of pathological grief can often be seen in the course of regular medical practice. It is estimated that up to 25 percent of patients seen in hospital psychiatric consultation have unresolved grief reactions antedating the onset of the medical problems for which they are hospitalized (DeVaul et al., 1979). As outpatients, many individuals with unresolved grief consult numerous physicians and health professionals. They often undergo lengthy and costly medical workups and demand much time from the primary care physician. Once the identification of unresolved grief is made, the physician can proceed with a plan (Zisook & DeVaul, 1983).

Let us now discuss various approaches to the management of pathological grief.

Table 1 Differentiation between Normal and Pathological Grief

Phases and Symptoms of Normal Grief	*Pathological Grief*

A/Shock
  Numbness, denial, disbelief
B/Acute grieving
  Crying, sobbing, guilt, anger,
  depression, anorexia, insomnia,
  irritability, fatigue, empty feeling;
  identification and preoccupation
  with thoughts of the deceased:
  transient mimicking of habits,
  mannerisms, and somatic symptoms
  of the deceased; social withdrawal:
  inability to maintain work and family
  responsibilities; preoccupation with
  health
C/Resolution
  Acceptance of the loss; awareness of
  having grieved; ability to talk about
  the deceased and recall memories
  about the deceased without intense
  pain; return to full social
  functioning and well-being
	1/Absence of symptoms
	2/Symptoms inhibited
	3/Symptoms prolonged
	4/Symptoms very intense
	5/Symptoms delayed
	6/Symptoms reappear suddenly at
	anniversary dates, special occasions
	(wedding, other funeral, graduation
	ceremonies)
	7/Symptoms of major depression
	develop
	8/Unusual somatic symptoms (pain
	under the sternum)
	9/Persistent overactivity without
	purpose
	10/Deteriorating health
	11/Social withdrawal and alienation
	12/feelings of worthlessness
	13/Excessive guilt
	14/Suicidal ideation
	15/Extreme dependency and
	ambivalence toward the deceased

Management of Pathological Grief

After making the diagnosis of unresolved grief, and if the physician finds no medical problems, management of the grief problem takes the place of treatment of the presenting medical complaint. The health professional should refer to Table 1, which lists signs and symptoms, noting whether or not symptoms correspond to the various phases of normal grief. If not, further review of the characteristics listed in the column for pathological grief will help to define the problem.

Some patients who are unable to proceed through the first phase should be carefully evaluated for the possibility of a psychotic disorder, particularly if the denial of the death is severe. At the same time, the health professional must expect some denial of the loss as a common form of unresolved grief.

The best approach for the primary physician or the health professional dealing with any form of denial is to facilitate the grief process by *active listening* and the avoidance of advice, leading the bereaved to discuss all aspects of the death in detail. One technique is to relate everything the patient mentions to the recent loss. Using this approach, the health professional must encourage the patient to experience the sadness, anger, guilt, and other emotions that are a normal part of the grief continuum. Once mobilized, the grief process may be able to continue through its natural course (DeVaul et al., 1979).

In the second phase, the patient with unresolved grief can become obsessed with suicidal thoughts. Agitated depressions are not uncommon at this stage, and they must receive psychiatric attention. When seen in the psychiatric clinic, these patients may be treated with verbal re-grief therapy, which encourages them to experience those emotions of grief that were not experienced in the various phases of the grief process. The process may be facilitated with the use of sedatives or anxiolytics for insomnia and restlessness (Hackett, 1974) or antidepressant medications (Schmidt & Messner, 1975).

Failure to resolve the phase of social withdrawal may lead to chronic illness and hypochondriasis. As stated above, these patients often make numerous visits to the physician's office, expecting medications and treatments for relief of their symptoms, often to no avail. Sometimes these patients escalate their complaints at the time of anniversary dates of the death or when they reach the age when the deceased became ill (Musaph, 1973). These patients must be told of the lack of medical findings in light of their medical histories. The relationships between caregivers and assigned patients must be redefined, and the health professional must be available in a continuing relationship. During subsequent visits, patients must be encouraged to resume social relationships or to accept referral to social support groups in the community. Sometimes psychiatric referral is accepted if the latter is not interpreted as a rejection or a substitute for a rejection of the relationship with the primary care physician (DeVaul et al., 1979).

When the bereaved fail to work through the phase of acute grief, they may report symptoms similar to those suffered by the deceased. Usually, such identification is transient, and these persons go to the next grieving phase. But individuals who remain stuck in a particular phase often develop what has been termed *grief-related facsimile illnesses,* which consist of constellations of symptoms of the terminal illnesses of the deceased. It is as if these patients feel that by suffering the same illnesses and experiencing the same symptoms, they are keeping the lost persons, rather than acknowledging painful losses. Such patients often get elaborate medical workups and procedures. It is therefore important to identify such patients as early as possible, usually by taking careful histories of recent losses and by following up with discussions of the deaths and their effects upon the bereaved (Zisook & DeVaul, 1976–1977).

Failure to complete the resolution phase may result in chronic grievers, and, sometimes, in chronic somatizers (Katon, 1982; Lieberman, 1978). These people do not succeed in reinvesting in new relationships, and they therefore lack adequate social support systems. By foreclosing such opportunities for social growth and adaptation, the results become further obstacles to the grieving process. These bereaved then perceive a hostile and unfriendly world during or after grieving. Such patients can sometimes be helped if they accept a referral to peer support groups in the community, such as those designed specifically for widows or bereaved parents.

In conclusion, the physician, nurse, and social worker can do much to help identify patients at risk of pathological grief through skillful observation of vulnerable individuals. Health professionals can outline a program of prevention and intervention by encouraging patients to resume the interrupted grief process (Hauser & Feinberg, 1976). The primary physician can usually get the patient to focus on the issue of the death by a directed discussion and by offering support through active listening. The intervention can be further reinforced and carried out with the help of other members of the health care team. Individual and joint awareness, knowledge, and honing of skills will contribute to the effectiveness of the team in caring for those who are temporarily immobilized by the pain of bereavement.

Chapter 5

BEREAVEMENT FOLLOWING
SPECIFIC LOSSES

Of all the determinants that affect the course of bereavement, the relationship that the bereaved has with the deceased is one that has a profound influence on the subsequent social and psychological adjustment. The loss of a spouse, for example, has a different impact on the deceased than the loss of a child, a parent, or a sibling. In this chapter we shall discuss the main characteristics and consequences of each loss on the survivor.

LOSS OF A SPOUSE

Holmes and Rahe (1967), in their research on readjustment to stressful life events, found that the loss of a spouse was one of the most stressful life events for most people. The experience of widowhood, however, is different for men than for women. There are many reasons for these differences, some purely sociological, others rather psychological. We shall review the loss from those two vantage points.

Widows

Much of the research on bereavement was done with studies of widows' adjustment after the loss of their husbands (Glick et al., 1974).

Most widows, depending on their ages, must face major social adjustments in their life-styles, including the handling of financial responsibilities, and decision making for the family. If there are growing children, they must shoulder the total responsibility for raising them, fulfilling the roles of both mother and father to satisfy the children's emotional needs.

While many women in traditional marriages limit their socializing to other couples, when they suddenly become alone and single, they find social mixing much less accessible or attractive. As a group, widows tend to be ostracized, sometimes stigmatized and shunned by other women who may perceive the widows as threats to their own marriages. In her book *On Becoming a Widow*, Start (1973) states that "grief teaches you that there are two kinds of people in the world, those who are available and those who are not." For many years, widows are often referred to as "someone's wife" and therefore do not have identities of their own. Widowhood thrusts upon them new roles, new responsibilities, and the need for new identities.

Managing the finances is probably the single most difficult problem in adjusting to widowhood. Interestingly, assistance with financial matters is often underestimated by the helping professions, who tend to emphasize the emotional and social needs. In most marriages, husbands take care of the bills and major decisions about finances. When the wife is suddenly faced with widowhood, the lack of experience and familiarity with the family finances are enough to throw her into a panic.

Reentering the social scene can be made even more difficult by the fact that most widows experience a loss of interest in sex during the first year of bereavement. This is particularly true for women of low income and education, but less of a problem for modern career women who are comfortable socializing on their own.

Perhaps the most gnawing problem in the years that follow the loss is the loneliness that comes from the loss of companionship. Unless the widow is young, wealthy, and attractive, remarriage is often difficult. Older widows frequently remarry someone who is grieving the loss of a spouse, thus finding sympathy and companionship combined with an understanding of each other (Clayton, 1971).

Other problems that older widows face are those associated with the normal problems of aging, such as deteriorating health, financial difficulties, and social isolation, all of which are often brought to the attention of the family physician in subsequent years after the loss. Increasing problems of that nature account for many outpatient visits and even hospitalization. It has been reported that as a group, widows are more likely to seek help from social workers, physicians, and other health professionals, whereas widowers are more likely to turn to family and friends for help (Glick et al., 1974).

Widowers

For most men the bereavement means the loss of a companion, sexual partner, and mother to their children. Responsibilities for running the household seem especially overwhelming, which prompts many widowers to seek help from available family members and friends. If they can afford it, widowers employ housekeepers and additional help if the children are young. Young children may not understand the plight of the grieving father, and they often make excessive demands to meet unfilled needs. Widowers tend not to show their emotions and become more quickly reinvolved in a new relationship. Yet, as with widows, the main problem for most widowers remains loneliness. Widowers tend to be particularly vulnerable to social isolation. Younger ones often turn to excessive use of alcohol (Parkes & Brown, 1972), while older widowers sometimes resort to suicide (Bock & Webber, 1972; Stroebe et al., 1981–1982).

In summary, both widows and widowers experience loneliness as their most important problem in the years following bereavement. For widows, managing the finances is probably the main issue in adjusting to new roles and responsibilities. In contrast, the most difficult adjustment for widowers involves taking over household duties and care of the children. All of these findings have major implications for intervention.

Management Guidelines

The following suggestions are based on the knowledge derived from the literature and from interviews with over 100 families.

1. Bereaved individuals should be told to postpone making any major decisions, such as moving, remarrying, selling a home, or changing careers, for a minimum of 6 months or, ideally, for a full year (Davis, 1984).

2. They should be reassured that they are not "going crazy" or "losing their minds" but are experiencing a whole spectrum of intense emotions which are part of the grief process.

3. The loss should be acknowledged directly, i.e., "I'm sorry that John is dead." If positive statements can be made based on knowledge of the deceased, this may prove to be helpful, i.e., "He was a kind, brave, and gentle person," "We enjoyed his friendly disposition," or "He was a good patient, and we all liked him a lot." The wording of the statements is not as important as the expression of concern and care, which is what will be remembered (Davis, 1984). It is best not to say "Let me know if there's anything I can do," if you, as a health professional, will not be able to follow through. It is better to arrange for follow-up help with community agencies, self-support groups, or social services.

4. In the hospital, bereaved persons should be offered some medication in the form of bedtime sedation only. The general feeling at this time is that in cases of "normal grieving," tranquilizers or anti-depressants may interfere with the natural process of grieving. This is still an area of controversy and more research is needed (DeVaul et al., 1979).

5. Facilitating normal grief is best done by offering some preventive counseling in the form of empathetic therapy and offering understanding, warmth, and a climate in which the bereaved person can feel permission to express feelings of sadness, longing, fear, guilt, and anger. Explanations should be given that these widely ranging and intense emotions are normal and part of a natural process.

6. Newly bereaved spouses should be referred to the hospital or clinic social workers. They should be assessed as to their immediate needs. If there are young children in the household, the need for their caretaking should be assessed with the bereaved parent. One or two family sessions should be offered to facilitate the expression of feelings by the whole family. It should be explained to all members of the family that grief is a very individual thing and that it will be expressed in different ways by each member.

7. Bereaved spouses should be referred to social support groups such as Parents Without Partners (PWP), a group called "They Help Each Other Spiritually" (THEOS), or Widow to Widow (see Chapter 12). They should be provided with information about what to expect in new family interactions. They should be told about the grief process in children, so that the entire family can proceed toward a healthy resolution of the bereavement process. The social worker should be alert to the different educational, occupational, and social skills of older widows and help redirect them into productive roles in the community.

Loss of a Child

The death of a child is probably the single most traumatic experience a parent can endure in a lifetime (Gorer, 1965). In the U.S. today, approximately 400,000 children under the age 25 die each year from illnesses, accidents, suicides, or murders, leaving 800,000 parents in grief (Donnelly, 1982).

What makes the loss of a child so painful is that it clashes with our whole concept of the laws of nature, with our understanding of the life cycle, and with our hopes for the future. It threatens our own quest for meaning and our own existence, because in the normal course of events, we do not expect to outlive our children (Raphael, 1983). Although guilt and self-blame occur in other bereavements, they are particularly acute and prominent after the death of a child (Miles, 1985). Somehow, parents often feel that the death could have been prevented and that they could have had a part in preventing it. Because the one variable which seems to differentiate the reactions of parents to the death of an offspring is the age of the child when death occurs (Macon, 1979), we shall address the question in separate sections.

Now, we shall review the main features that characterize the reactions of parents following a stillbirth, a neonatal death, a sudden infant death (SIDS) and the death of an older child.

Stillbirth

Whether the baby dies in utero or at birth, the experience for the mother is always traumatic (See Appendix B, Davidson, 1977). In both situations mothers report that they experience both a birth and a death simultaneously (Kirkley-Best & Kellner, 1982). Regardless of the cause of death, parents feel that they have lost part of themselves as well as their link to the future (Borg & Lasker, 1982). They also develop a fear that no one will remember their baby.

In order to best understand mothers who grieve after a stillbirth, it is useful to review briefly the steps of the attachment process during pregnancy and after the delivery. Klaus and Kennell (1982) described nine steps that occur in this process. These include: (1) planning the pregnancy, (2) confirming the pregnancy, (3) accepting the pregnancy, (4) feeling fetal movements, (5) accepting the fetus as an individual, (6) giving birth, (7) hearing and seeing the baby, (8) touching and holding the infant, and (9) caring for the infant. The first five steps occur before the infant's birth and might explain the parents' increasing attachment even before the birth. The more intense the attachment, the more intense the grief will be. When the infant dies at birth, the parents have a tremendous need to complete the last three steps. It is also important to allow the father to participate in the grieving experience so that there can be some synchrony of feelings between the parents. This is more likely to occur if the father is also allowed to see and hold the infant.

Following attachment, there must be a phase of detachment which consists of accepting the reality. During this process, mothers experience feelings of pain, anger, sadness, and hostility, all which must be worked through and gradually let go. They also experience feelings of guilt, shame, inadequacy, and lowered self-esteem. They blame themselves and wonder what is wrong with them because they could not produce a healthy baby. They doubt their femininity (Gilson, 1976), and they wonder what they did wrong, why doctors failed, and why family members tend to minimize the situation. The lost infant is gradually perceived more like a real person as time passes, especially if the parents were allowed to see and hold the infant, or if photographs of the infant were taken.

When hospital staff members feel uncomfortable, they may suggest to the mother that it is best not to talk about the loss and may offer sedation. This can be explained because they have not had the opportunity to form a bond with the infant, or may not even have acknowledged the event, by not talking about the death or referring to the infant, who may not yet have been named. However, research has shown that this attitude and approach may aggravate the situation (Wolff et al., 1970). The need for grieving and the intensity of the bonding has been underestimated in the past few decades, but now it is recognized that the bereavement process is facilitated if the parents are permitted to see and touch the dead infant.

Many hospitals today encourage parents to name the dead baby and to collect mementos, such as locks of hair, hospital bracelets, or photographs (Lewis & Page, 1978), as a way to acknowledge the child and facilitate the grief process.

Management guidelines. Both parents should be informed about the death of the infant as soon as possible. If the infant has not been baptized, the opportunity to have it done should be offered to the parents. It is a good idea to give the baby a name to help establish its identity. Parents should be offered the opportunity to see and handle the dead infant. Any abnormality should be carefully concealed if possible and draped so that the baby's appearance is acceptable (some parents prefer to hold the baby wrapped in a blanket). These experiences may be and frequently are difficult for the staff, but it should be remembered that they help parents accept the death as a real event. If parents become actually upset, it is preferable not to give tranquilizers, although a sedative might be offered for nighttime or when medically indicated. Prior to leaving the hospital, parents should be allowed some time to be together, undisturbed, so they can give each other support. If the mother is unmarried, she should be allowed to share this moment of crisis with a significant person of her choice (Davis, 1984).

It is important for the hospital staff to know about the policy regarding the actual disposition of the infant's body and the burial policy of the hospital in order to attend to the parents' concerns and to answer their questions. Otherwise, parents can imagine the worst, i.e., that their baby was put in a jar or discarded somewhere (Condon, 1986; Davis, 1984). Parents should be warned that it will be uncomfortable for them to deal with people who are unaware of their baby's death and that friends and acquaintances will ask them if the baby is a boy or a girl. Or they may simply ask, "How's the baby?"

Perhaps the most important points to be made about stillbirths are that (a) parents should be allowed to grieve as in any other bereavement situation (Lewis, 1976, 1979), and (b) they should *not* be reassured with the hope of having another pregnancy and another child to replace the loss, at least not immediately after the loss. It is most important *not* to offer reassurance by raising the hope for a "replacement baby." Do not say, "It was for the best. It would not have been normal if it had lived." It is better to encourage parents to acknowledge the stillbirth as a *real* loss and an actual death. Simply say, "We are sorry that your baby died."

To help parents move through the grief process, nurses can gather concrete memories of the infant, such as footprints, photographs, locks of hair, namebands, blankets, etc. Such mementos also assist other members of the family, such as siblings and grandparents, who must be acknowledged as grievers (Davis, 1984).

Parents should be reassured that their feelings are normal and that they should be fully expressed. In this regard, some verbal responses by the nurse can be especially helpful in giving the mother permission to grieve openly. "It's okay to cry," or "I know that this must be a very hard time for you," "It's all right to let it out" (Carr & Knupp, 1985).

If the nurse notices that the family seems to be blocking the mother's grieving reaction, she should openly discuss the problem with the family and reinforce her statements by giving the mother permission to continue her grieving fully and individually without overprotection from the family (Beckey et al., 1985).

After the initial shock, parents often search for meaning in the face of their tragedy. In addition to support given by a trusted nurse, they should be given the name of a booklet entitled, "When Hello Means Goodbye," issued by the University of Oregon Health Sciences Center. They should also be referred to the local parent support group of SHARE (Source of Support and Help in Airing and Resolving Experiences), which is dedicated to helping parents after a perinatal loss.

Some hospitals have found it helpful to use a checklist to insure that all steps are taken without repetition or omission, to improve communication, and to provide adequate documentation. The checklist shown in Appendix G is now being used for the orientation of nurses new to the unit.

Carr and Knupp (1985) at the Lancaster Osteopathic Hospital in Lancaster, Pennsylvania, have designed an outline for a hospital program for nursing intervention with parents after a stillbirth (see Appendix C). They noted that their protocol, outlining a series of support measures and hospital policies for the management of cases of stillbirth, provides the continuity of care and the need for structure by staff and by bereaved parents. In addition, the protocol enables the staff to reach a feeling of closure and the parents to regain a sense of control over their lives.

Soon after the loss, the question of having another child will be raised. Although still controversial, it is the consensus that the couple should wait until they have worked through some of the grief and are ready to "re-invest in new relationships" (Cain & Cain, 1964; Legg & Sherick, 1976; Poznanski, 1972; Stringham et al., 1982).

Neonatal Death

As with stillbirths, mothers and fathers who experience a neonatal death react with considerable guilt. Mothers, who usually feel that they are to blame, question their behavior during their pregnancy. In some cases, mothers enter a state of disorganization and yearning (Berezin, 1982). The bereavement process can become complicated by the fact that the family may have had to make difficult decisions about additional medical or surgical interventions, which might have prolonged or saved the life of the infant. Sometimes, they make treat-

ment decisions that cause them to feel regrets and conflicts if unfa-
vorable outcomes develop and the baby dies sometime later or continues to live its life a little longer but with severe handicaps.

Because the infant lives a short time in the hospital, the staff,
family, and friends get to know the baby and form some attachment.
Despite this fact, when the death occurs, people still tend to ignore
the loss, thus provoking parenting feelings of anger, ambivalence, and
guilt.

As in the case of stillbirths, it is important to let the parents view
the body of the infant, hold it, and spend time with it. Sometimes,
feeling that the experience would be too painful or detrimental to the
mother, the staff member whisks the infant away, gives some sedation
to the mother, and provides no information as to what happened to
the remains. Nothing could be more harmful (Benfield et al., 1978).
In fact, when the loss is not acknowledged, reactions of anger, guilt,
and ambivalence tend to be much more severe. Self-blame persists,
and the mother often thinks that life is unfair because "the child never
had a chance."

Management guidelines. (See Chapter 8—NICU).

Sudden Infant Death Syndrome (SIDS)

Between the ages of one week and one year the major cause of
death in infants in the United States is the Sudden Infant Death Syndrome. SIDS accounts for 8,000 to 10,000 deaths annually (May &
Breme, 1982–1983). It occurs most frequently between the second
and third month, and no one knows what causes it and which babies
are at risk. Some experts believe that these infants have some cardio-
respiratory complications while others believe that some neurological
difficulties are responsible. In general, environmental rather than genetic factors have been attributed (Mellins & Haddad, 1983). Many
suspected causes have been ruled out, however, and these include:
(a) birth control pills, fluoridated water, (b) suffocating, vomiting,
choking, breast feeding, (c) hereditary conditions, and (d) underlying diseases. A 1987 study has reported that there is abnormal
elevation in fetal hemoglobin after the birth, which accounts for the
subsequent lack of oxygen in the blood and eventual death (Giulian
et al., 1987).

What is most upsetting to parents is that death seems to suddenly
strike what appears to be a healthy baby. This leads the parent to
speculate that the baby must have suffocated, choked, or had an un-

diagnosed illness. However, no validation for these claims can be provided. To complicate matters, misunderstandings sometimes develop because the cause of death appears to be mysterious in view of the relatively healthy appearance of the baby. Later, however, the infant's body may appear to be bruised, and the suspicion of child abuse is often raised by law enforcement officers. In Washington, D.C. at the Childrens' Hospital National Medical Center, a program of training for law officers has been developed in cooperation with the District of Columbia Medical Examiner's Office. The program is designed to sensitize officers to the particular vulnerability of parents, to explain the problem of SIDS, and to teach them how to deal with the parents during the inquiry (Cohen, 1979).

The bereavement process is particularly complicated because of the unique aspects of the SIDS loss experience. Markusen and his associates (1977–1978) have given five reasons why parents tend to feel victimized and intensely guilty:

1. The loss is sudden.
2. There is no known cause or rationale.
3. The death was sudden, unexpected, and occurred at a time when there was strong mother-infant bonding.
4. The cause of death is unknown and comes under suspicion by the investigating authorities, with an insinuation of some act of commission or omission in the care of the infant. Eventually, the parents become obsessed with an endless search for the cause of death.
5. Siblings in the family, who may have had some ambivalent feelings about the new arrival, must now struggle with their feelings of guilt after the loss of their sibling.

Grief reactions after a SIDS death are usually very intense. The entire family is disrupted and there is a high incidence of divorce among these couples (Bergman et al., 1969). The mother reacts with anger, frustration, and irritability while the siblings are bewildered and confused. Family members do not understand why some show intense manifestations of grief while others remain silent. There is not only sadness, but much anger and implicit blame as well (DeFrain et al., 1982).

Management guidelines.   In cases of SIDS deaths, there are several specific staff interventions that can prevent complications and facilitate the bereavement (Reilly & Cohen, 1983).

First, after the infant is pronounced dead, the family should be offered the option to be near the baby, hold it, and talk to him or her. Although this approach remains controversial among medical staff, subsequent reports from parents indicate that denial of this alternative tends to create regrets later.

Second, because the family is puzzled by the possible causes of death, they should be gently and tactfully encouraged to obtain an autopsy. Morgan and Goering (1978) have suggested that the more acceptable term of "postmortem examination" be used in this situation. Sometimes, because the guilt feelings are so strong, the permission for autopsy is denied. But the physician requesting the permission may point out several important reasons for its consideration:

1. It is the last chance to know the facts about an illness or cause of death.
2. It is easier to accept the death when we know that it was inevitable and not anyone's fault.
3. The cause of death may be necessary to settle legal or insurance matters.

Fourth, it is of special importance that the physician explain what is known and what is not known about SIDS itself.

Fifth, the parents should be counseled as to what kinds of reactions they will experience during the bereavement process. This will help reassure them that they are not going crazy or losing control. Later, the family should be followed in the clinic and assessed as to their potential for complications. A SIDS Family Adjustment Scale can be used to rate and assess adaptive responses and tasks that the family is expected to accomplish in order to reach a successful readjustment (May & Breme, 1982–1983). This scale measures on a 5-point continuum the range of adaptive and nonadaptive responses in the family's subsequent adjustment.

Sixth, the family should be referred for counseling and a self-help group, such as a local chapter of the national SIDS organization, where they can share their feelings with others in similar circumstances. They can be encouraged to obtain more information about SIDS by writing to the National Foundation for SIDS (see Chapter 12).

Finally, several months later, parents who wish to consider another pregnancy should be warned that research has shown that mothers who have lost a child through SIDS often have difficulty becoming pregnant again (Mandell & Wolfe, 1975; Markusen et al., 1977–1978). However, parents tend to be hesitant and afraid about having another baby for fear of repeating the terrible experience. If the couple does have another baby, they should be warned that they will experience both joy and pain. They should be encouraged during pregnancy to take time out to talk about any issue of unresolved grief (Rando, 1987).

Loss of an Older Child

Losing an older child is one of the most painful experiences a family can endure (Clayton, 1980). Of all causes of death in children, 45 percent are due to accidents, whereas 18 percent are due to leukemia and other cancers.

As in other types of bereavement, parents experience shock, sadness, and despair; but guilt and anger seem more prominent and intense than in other types of losses. Frequently, an overwhelming outrage takes over the bereaved parents. The experience seems so contrary to all the goals, values, and beliefs of the family that the whole order of life's normal sequence seems to be totally shattered. There is something completely unnatural and untimely about the occurrence of a child's death (Kalish, 1985).

The guilt feelings are so pronounced that it has led some researchers to consider it as another form of *survivor guilt* as seen in disasters, wars, or catastrophic events. Others have attributed the guilt to other negative or ambivalent feelings toward children that cannot be expressed in our culture, especially after a death (Raphael, 1983). Other prominent and common manifestations of guilt are suicidal thoughts and somatizations. But the most common symptoms are loss of sleep and appetite (Miles, 1985).

Parents show considerable irritability and a low frustration tolerance. If they are supportive of each other, the communication and closeness may improve, but if they show little understanding and are unable to keep from blaming each other and from being critical, the communication breaks down, and a climate of tension and silent hostility develops. This is further aggravated by the fact that parents grieve in their own ways, at their own pace, and for different lengths of time. The result is a lack of synchrony in their mutual grief. The mother may not understand why the father is able to go work (he may be forced to do so, as most men are not expected to grieve for a long time) or even resume a daily routine while she finds herself incapable of functioning. Couples, therefore, are at high risk for marital strain (Burnell, 1984). It is estimated that 50 to 70 percent of marriages end in divorce after the death of a child (Kaplan et al., 1976).

In the few hundred families we have seen in counseling, we have observed that, in the period of 3 to 6 months after the loss, some couples go to extreme lengths to avoid the pain of grief. Some parents quit or change their jobs, while others escape into extramarital affairs or turn to alcohol or drugs (Burnell, in press).

Bereaved couples find that sexual intimacy is more difficult to achieve. While some women want the closeness, they prefer just to be held and cannot understand why their husbands wish to have sex. For the husbands, the sexual act represents a way to feel strong again and to regain a sense of control (Burnell, in press).

Mothers, who derive their sense of fulfillment and feelings of adequacy in life from the interaction with the child, may be especially at risk because of their negative self-concepts. The bereavement process seems to span a longer time period than for other types of losses, lasting from 2 to 5 years. Rando (1987) found that although the intensity of the grief reaction tends to decrease in the second year, it does surge again in the third year. The upheaval which the bereavement causes in the family accounts for the tremendous difficulty in meeting the needs of the other siblings, who may also show psychological symptoms and acting-out behavior.

Some studies have shown that families whose children die at home from long-term illnesses, such as cancer, seem to adjust better than the families whose children die in the hospital (Mulhern et al., 1983). The parents who selected the hospital seemed to be more anxious, agitated, depressed, defensive, and socially withdrawn, and had more interpersonal problems, somatic complaints, and irrational fears.

Factors that were associated with favorable adjustment for these bereaved families included:

(a) good communication and support between the parents,

(b) ability to explain and understand why the death occurred,

(c) a consistent philosophy of life that helped accept the diagnosis in cases of cancer deaths (Spinetta et al., 1981), and

(d)   the ability to derive support and consolation from re-
        ligious faith (Martinson et al., 1980).

The research for this type of loss is still limited, and most of the
data come from clinical observations rather than well-controlled studies. The following suggestions are derived from over 300 families seen
in counseling by the authors (Burnell & Burnell, 1986).

Management guidelines.   Interventions by health professionals in
the hospital can have significant impact on the subsequent course of
bereavement. The following suggestions have been made by parents,
who later were able to give feedback on their experiences in the hospital and who made suggestions on what they thought would have
helped them more.

Arrange for parents to be with the child at the time of death, if
they wish to be there.

Be sure that the physician and nurse who cared for the child are
available, as they should give the family permission to cry and express
feelings of despair, anger, and guilt.

Answer questions directly, honestly, and briefly, without reluctance to repeat information several times to parents who are often so
bewildered, stunned, and shocked that they do not hear the answer
the first or second time.

Reassure the parents that their grief reactions are normal and
that they are not losing their minds. Inform them briefly about the
bereavement process if possible, that grief will be experienced and
expressed differently by various family members and that it may last
a long time. Tell them that they will never forget the loss, that the
feeling of emptiness will remain, but that the pain will ease with time.

The physician should not hesitate to bring up two questions: (a)
permission for a postmortem examination which, he should explain,
could help the family later in their search for an answer, and (b) permission for organ donation, which may later give the parents the feeling that the child's life was not wasted and futile.

The social worker should refer the parents to the local chapter
of The Compassionate Friends or a similar peer support group for
help during the months ahead (Burnell, 1985)

Later, if the question of having another child is raised in the course
of an outpatient visit with the physician or the social worker, an answer

should not be given before an assessment is made. In this evaluation, the following issues (Rando, 1984) should be addressed:

> Has the couple achieved some resolution of the loss of the deceased child?
>
> Does the couple want another child to prove that they can be normal and produce a child free of disease?
>
> Is this another attempt to assuage their guilt?
>
> Is the wished-for pregnancy another way to avoid the pain of grieving?
>
> Do they perceive a new child as a "replacement" child or "surrogate" for the deceased child rather than a new unique human being with a new identity?

Arrangements should be made for parents to make a few follow-up visits to the physician and the social worker to assess the course of bereavement in terms of physical, social, and psychological adjustment.

Parents should be told that they can expect an increase in their pain at anniversary dates such as birthdays, anniversaries of the death, and holidays (Hanukkah, Christmas, Easter, Thanksgiving).

Loss of a Parent

Comparatively speaking, the bereavement reaction to the loss of a parent is generally less traumatic for most people. Several reasons have been given, but research data in this area are still relatively scarce.

First, it is generally expected that as our parents get older, they will die. This is a universal phenomenon in the history of mankind, and the only surprise is when it occurs at a relatively early age.

Second, the preexisting relationship greatly colors the grief reaction. As grown children get busier in their daily lives, their involvement and attachment to their parents is likely to diminish in intensity.

Third, the death of a parent may signal a new role and responsibility for the grown child, who no longer can fall back on the parent for emotional or financial support.

Generally, the course of bereavement is shorter and less likely to cause complication (Sanders, 1979–1980). However, recent studies have shown that bereavement following the death of a parent can be a "serious life event which can lead to a measurable degree of symptomatic distress" (Horowitz et al., 1981, 1984) and that the death of a mother can be more difficult to accept than that of a father. The nurturing role of the mother in earlier life might account for these observations.

Management Guidelines

Managing bereavement reactions following the loss of a parent in the hospital is probably the easiest situation for most health professionals to deal with. The older the parents, the more expectation there is for their dying, and the less likelihood of projecting blame or anger onto the medical or nursing staff. In cases where prolonged suffering, disability, or loss of function occurs, the grown children may experience a feeling of relief. As in other cases of bereavement, however, unfinished business, ambivalent or negative feelings, and previous unresolved conflicts may complicate the bereavement process. These factors may play a role if a decision to sustain or discontinue life-support systems becomes an issue during the hospitalization.

Sometimes there may be dissension among older children, and this conflict may interfere with a rational approach to terminal care. Guilt feelings and ambivalence can be so strong that they produce an attitude of "overmanagement in the medical care" of the patient. However, the medical and nursing staff should be aware of the motivation of the family members, while remaining supportive. The use of any measure should be carefully evaluated and discussed with the family to avoid subsequent regrets and negative feelings toward the staff and among family members.

Chapter 6

ANTICIPATORY AND UNANTICIPATED GRIEF

Grief can occur prior to death, as in terminal illness, after the death from a chronic illness, or after a sudden and unexpected death, as in accidents, suicides, murders, or heart attacks. Because the nature of the death greatly determines the course and clinical picture of bereavement, we shall discuss these two types of bereavement separately.

GRIEF DURING AND FOLLOWING TERMINAL ILLNESS AND GRIEF FOLLOWING DEATH FROM CHRONIC ILLNESS

Anticipatory grief can be defined as the grief process that takes place in anticipation of the actual loss. The term was coined by Lindemann in 1944, and further elaborated by another psychiatrist, Knight Aldrich, in 1963. It has become particularly appropriate today because people live longer, have longer terminal illnesses, and die more frequently of chronic diseases. Forewarning of death to families is therefore more common and leads to a state of anticipation referred to as anticipatory grief.

It is important for health professionals who work with dying patients and their families to understand the special problems raised by anticipatory grief, since clinical interventions can alleviate suffering and prevent abnormal grief in the post-death period (Aronson, 1959; Wanzer et al., 1984).

The grief process actually affects the family as well as the person who is dying and presents different problems for each (Schoenberg et al., 1974). Whereas the family loses one member, the dying person loses several. The interaction between the family and the dying person involves a complex set of feelings which vary in intensity depending on the length of time before the death. Some clinicians have reported that anticipatory grief starts from the time of learning about the diagnosis of terminal illness (Bowlby, 1980; Brown & Stoudemire, 1983; Bugen, 1977).

Most characteristic among the feelings of anticipatory grief are those of ambivalence and resentment, which, in time, lead to guilt (Aldrich, 1974). Sometimes family members tend to withdraw their attachment too soon and give in to a sense of hopelessness summed up in the phrase, "There's nothing more we can do" (Weisman & Hackett, 1961). In the hospital, already emotionally and physically drained, they wait for the last moment, standing in hallways or in the patient's room like hovering vultures. This situation has been described as the *Waiting Vulture Syndrome* (Davidson, 1975).

Feelings of resentment and guilt develop if the patient's death is delayed and dying seems to be unusually long. A corollary of this occurs when the person does not die, suddenly gets better, and undergoes a remission of the illness. This situation has been called the *Lazarus Syndrome* (Rando, 1984).

In other cases, the families become increasingly more involved, have more difficulty in "letting go" of the relationship, and tend to develop feelings of heightened loyalty and commitment. This situation seems to intensify the grief at the time of death. In this regard, studies of anticipatory grief have shown conflicting results. Some have concluded that the grief is facilitated (Lebow, 1976; Rando, 1983), whereas others have argued that the grief is intensified and that attachment behaviors are harder to give up (Parkes & Weiss, 1983; Vachon et al., 1982). Whatever the conclusion, it is clear that there are many determinants in anticipatory grief that affect the intensity, duration, and outcome beyond the usual symptoms of depression and separation anxiety (Fulton & Fulton, 1971; Futterman et al., 1972). These features include:

> an acknowledgment of the fact that the death is an
> inevitable reality;

a heightened concern for the terminally ill;

a rehearsal of the death state and post-death period
in which the griever tends to engage in what has
been described as the "work of worry" (Janis, 1958),
that is, a situation similar to that of a patient who
is about to undergo surgery for a leg amputation
and who tries to imagine what it will be like after
the loss, thus engaging in a form of anticipatory
grief through worry about the outcome;

a gradual detachment—a state of decreasing emotional involvement from the dying person;

an adjustment to the consequences of dying, whereby
the survivor tries to gain some perspective and make
some sense out of the impending death, perceiving
the life of the dying as having some purpose or util-
ity;

a process of memorialization by which the griever tries
to visualize the deceased in a way that will be remembered mentally after the person's death.

Whether anticipatory grief is viewed as desirable or undesirable,
it is a phenomenon that does occur. It allows the family to absorb the
reality of the dying over a period of time, and it helps them to resolve
whatever unfinished business with the dying person still exists. It allows
family members to resolve past conflicts and to express all that needs
to be said. It also raises a general awareness of the process of dying
and the precariousness of life.

Management Guidelines

The physician should announce the diagnosis of terminal illness
to the family in a clear, simple, and honest manner. It is important
to set some time aside to deliver the diagnosis calmly. The physician
should reassure the family that something will be done, explaining
treatment options, risks and benefits. It is desirable at that point to
set up a support program that will include an ongoing relationship
with a clinical nurse specialist or social worker in the hospital. The
family should be informed about whether or not the physician will
follow the case only through the course of hospitalization or through-

out the course of illness. Continuity may be very important to the family. Make it a point to find out what the family knows in order to eliminate all misunderstandings and myths about the illness.

Rando (1984) has outlined a long list of steps for caregivers who manage anticipatory grief in families. Only a few points of importance to hospital personnel shall be mentioned here:

Assess the family's needs; the evaluation should take into account the usual psychosocial variables of personality traits and ethnic, cultural, and religious background.

Help families overcome their fears and assist them in not distancing themselves too quickly from the dying.

Allow the families to experience intense feelings and relabel the reactions as "normal releases" rather than "loss of control" or "breakdown," stating that crying and being upset are expected in this situation.

Mention that suppressing feelings may precipitate a loss of control, emphasizing that it is more desirable to release a little emotion at a time.

Inform families gradually with only as much information as they can tolerate at any given time.

Do not react to anger and hostility expressed by the family, but instead identify these feelings as a manifestation of their grief and their ambivalent relationship to the deceased rather than a reaction to hospital personnel.

If guilt feelings are expressed, acknowledge that negative and ambivalent feelings towards the dying person do occur as a normal phenomenon.

Assess the energy level of the family and encourage them to get proper rest, so that they will not be totally exhausted at the time of death.

Do not attempt to change the basic communication style of families. Try to adapt to the family's style. If they are giving, spontaneous, and demonstrative, integrate the last moments of the dying by allowing them to be demonstrative and loving. If their styles are formal, distant, and reserved, arrange the last few moments to let them be formal and solemn.

Whenever possible, allow the family to be present at the time of the death, particularly if they have been keeping a vigil.

As the time of death approaches, some families may show panic, fear, and restlessness. They should be reassured by asking them what they think the patient would want. Their final attempt to rescue the dying person may be easier if it is recognized as an abnormal response which may not need to be acted upon.

Allow the family to spend time with the body of the deceased and encourage verbalization of feelings at this time.

Assist the family in making funeral arrangements.

Refer the bereaved to appropriate community support groups or to psychiatric professionals, if desired.

If there has been a meaningful relationship with the family, make a follow-up phone call to check on how the family is doing and to offer further help.

ANTICIPATORY GRIEF IN AIDS PATIENTS AND THEIR FAMILIES

Although AIDS (Acquired Immunity Deficiency Syndrome) patients and their families manifest the same signs and symptoms of anticipatory grief seen in other terminal illnesses, we shall discuss them separately because they present certain unique features that should be known by health professionals caring for such patients.

Knowledge about AIDS is of crucial importance because it is rapidly becoming a major health problem (National Institute of Mental Health, 1986). In fact, AIDS has become one of the top priorities on the country's public health agenda. The AIDS virus has been increasingly found among hemophiliacs, IV drug users, and heterosexuals (*Suzi's Story*, 1987, Appendix B). It will be expected that all health professionals become familiar with and prepared to deal with this dreadful and fatal disease in years ahead until a vaccine and cure can be found. At this writing, there have been 35,000 cases since 1981, half of whom have already died. All states in the nation are involved, with New York having 40 percent of all cases, California having 20 percent, Florida and Texas being next.

As in all terminal illnesses, the patient and the family, as well as other significant persons, go through the various stages of grief, although at varying periods of time. However, grieving usually begins as soon as the diagnosis of AIDS is made. As in other cases of anticipatory grief, the symptoms of the grief process are similar, except for the few differences which we shall discuss.

Grieving seems especially stressful in some AIDS cases because the family is given the simultaneous news of the terminal diagnosis and the likely homosexual or bisexual activity. In those the family feels stigmatized and isolated in addition to feeling shocked. The dying patient feels abandoned by all support systems and is brought into direct confrontation with the family which may have been avoided for years. It is not uncommon for most families to have denied or rejected the individual's life-style for a long time. In many cases the family had been living far from the dying person at the time of the diagnosis, thus requiring them to travel to be reunited after years of absence. So the grieving situation is further complicated by the fact that the family must come to grips not only with the dying of a spouse, a child, or a parent, but also with the life-style associated with the disease, whether it be homosexuality or a drug habit. Most parents tend to reject the "surrogate family" the patient has adopted in the intervening years.

Most of the patients with AIDS are young, in their twenties or thirties, and have never been ill before. The parents who come to be with them show a marked polarization in their reactions and attitudes, some being overprotective to the point of smothering, others showing disdain and a passive, subtly rejecting posture (Martelli, 1987).

Feelings and attitudes are differently expressed by mothers and fathers. Mothers tend to be overprotective, attentive, and forgiving, having no difficulty accepting their sons' life-styles. They readily offer their love and support. As one mother stated, "No matter what, he is my son. I'll be there until he does not need me anymore." By contrast, biological fathers have great difficulty overcoming the shame and sense of stigma which the disease brings to them. They are so immobilized that in some cases they have trouble even talking to their sons. This is not surprising, considering the likelihood that the relationships between fathers and sons had probably been virtually nonexistent or fraught with tension, animosity, and resentment for many years. Both fathers and sons find it difficult to forgive the hurt and rejection and to reach a comfortable level of intimacy at the time of death. Interestingly, stepfathers or adoptive fathers, by contrast, have little difficulty providing the needed support and they are better able to overcome their feelings of shame and hurt (Bridge, 1987). Sometimes mothers become angry with their husbands for not receiving support from them and for their withholding of support from their sons. As part of their grief work, mothers will sometimes offer to work as volunteers for the cause of AIDS, and they will readily join parent support groups in the hospital or in the community. Fathers, on the other hand, usually shy away from active participation, but they will offer money as their way of giving support. Sometimes, they will exhort their sons by saying, "Come on, put on a smile and fight this damn thing to beat the virus!"

The grieving families of AIDS patients, unlike other grieving families, cannot share their sorrow with friends, coworkers, and other family members, feeling that AIDS is an unspeakable disease and that it is best to keep this information in the "family closet." Another difficulty experienced by these grieving families is the "roller coaster" effect associated with relapses and remissions (Frierson et al., 1987). Guilt in most cases seems particularly severe, with parents feeling that they should have intervened even before the disease began. Not uncommonly, mothers want to relate to their son's lover, despite the family's warnings and disapproval. On the other hand, some families are willing to "bargain" in that they are willing to accept the life-style in exchange for survival of their sons.

Later, as the dying patient progresses through the grief, the family typically seems to lag behind. Whereas the patient may have reached a state of acceptance, others around him are still expressing denial and anger. Some parents' reactions are so extreme that they result in severe depression, suicidal behavior, or a full-blown psychosis requiring psychiatric hospitalization (Morin & Batchelor, 1984; Nichols & Ostrow, 1984). Surviving lovers, often rejected by their own biological parents, have a very difficult plight in their grief (Siegel & Hoefer, 1981). They may be subjected to embarrassment, shame, and possible exposure during the investigation conducted by the family, police, or medical agencies. Families may regard their grief as inappropriate and may reject their participation in mourning rituals (Nicholas, 1986). The social support system of surviving lovers may be inadequate, and if there is no one with whom they can share their grief, they may appear to be chronically depressed (Gonsiorek, 1982). Like family members, they also experience a very intense and painful grief. Following the shock and depression, they feel an extreme void and a sensation that time has stopped. Most of them feel intense guilt for having survived and that somehow they are responsible for the death. They often develop feelings of worthlessness and numerous somatic complaints including stomachaches, backaches, and headaches, or panic attacks with overwhelming anxiety and terror (Moffat, 1986).

Management Guidelines

As with cancer and other diseases, there is little question that health providers can do much to ease the emotional burden of AIDS patients and their families. But first, they must gain knowledge of the disease itself, a sense of the dynamics of grief in AIDS patients and their families, and then, they must take a series of steps in dealing with these special cases of anticipatory grief. We shall outline these particular steps in the form of recommendations and suggestions to the health care team:

1. Relate the diagnosis calmly, setting plenty of time aside for discussion with the patient and the family.

2. Immediately reassure the patient and family, plus other significant persons, that appropriate medical interventions will be made.

3. Refer the patient and family to support services in the hospital or community.

4. Find out the patient's and family's level of knowledge about the disease and correct any myth they might express.

5. Answer as many questions as possible and avoid oversimplified answers.

6. Make a psychosocial assessment of the family and surrogate family, taking into account the following:

   the prior relationship of the family to the dying person;

   the current occupational status of the patient;

   the patterns of coping with previous major stresses;

   the amount of social and psychological support available from others;

   the levels of anxiety, depression, and guilt;

   the presence of suicidal behavior.

7. Do not hesitate to seek out psychiatric consultation for the patient or the family, if there are neuropsychiatric complications such as dementia, suicidal behavior, or psychotic ideation in the patient (Holland & Tross, 1985).

8. Recognize the fact that it is typical for the health professional to experience varying levels of anticipatory grief along with feelings of frustration over the inability to change the course of the illness, es-

pecially with anger over the negative reactions of others.

9. When the patient develops dementia or delirium in the final stages of dying, be prepared to recognize these symptoms and adjust expectations about the patient's ability to adhere to procedures and treatment as mental capacities diminish (Faulstich, 1987).

10. Be prepared to deal with the stresses experienced by other staff members caring for AIDS patients and their families, and share in staff group support, education, and training programs.

11. Be aware that in dealing with AIDS cases, some staff members will experience fears of contagion and feelings of helplessess and futility that may interfere with the care.

UNANTICIPATED GRIEF

Unanticipated grief refers to the grief process that follows a sudden and unexpected loss. Sudden deaths include unnatural deaths, such as suicide, homicide, accidental death from automobile or plane crash, fall, drowning, fire, or from heart attacks. As shown in most studies (Parkes, 1975), these situations are all traumatic and require further understanding and special interventions.

Worden, an expert in the field of grief and loss, has drawn attention to several unique features that characterize grief after sudden death (Worden, 1982). We shall review these points briefly because they are important to all health professionals who make interventions with patients who suffer a sudden loss.

First, following a sudden loss, the survivor is left with a *sense of unreality* about the loss. The shock leaves the family numb and often confused, as if in a daze.

Second, although *guilt feelings* are common to all types of bereavement, in the case of sudden death, guilt feelingsare especially strong and intense. The bereaved person will often repeat incessantly, "My God, if only. . . ." or "If only I had been there" or "If only I had not let them go. . . ."

Third, the survivor has a *strong urge to blame* someone for what happened. The target for the blame can be a family member, friends, caretakers, or baby-sitters.

Fourth, sudden and unexplained deaths are often investigated by medical and legal authorities. This complication causes considerable stress and tension for those involved, particularly if the investigation moves slowly and leads to a trial. These proceedings can sidetrack the survivors in their grief process, so that the process becomes prolonged and unhealthy. Sometimes the legal proceedings can help the survivor in solving the question of suspicion and culpability, thus bringing some closure and resolution of the grief.

Fifth, the survivor experiences an extreme *sense of helplessness.* This feeling is so strong that it challenges the person's sense of autonomy and control. A frequent manifestation of this helpless feeling is through an outburst of rage and hostility toward those around. It is not uncommon in emergency rooms that the outraged survivor lashes out at physicians and nurses who gave the news of death and tried to be supportive. The threats even go as far as wishes to kill someone associated with the death, or they take the form of litigious statements. It is important *not* to respond directly and defensively to such threats, but rather to regard them as a cry for help and as a regressive response to overwhelming separation anxiety. Others react with extreme agitation and restlessness which progresses to an agitated depression.

Sixth, because of the circumstances of the death, *unfinished business* is a prominent feature. The relationship between the deceased and the family was severed without notice. Many things have not been said that should have been. Survivors express regrets for missed opportunities and for things that they never took time to do together.

Seventh, following a sudden loss, the bereaved has an especially strong need to explain and understand the events that led to the death. A strong *urge to know* and an almost morbid interest in the details of the death situation predominate the early phases of bereavement. Linked to the urge to know and to the lack of a satisfying answer is the need to choose God as the only available target. It is common to hear someone say, "I hate God" or "How could God do such a thing!"

We shall now discuss some points in the delicate management of bereavement following a sudden death.

Management Guidelines

The intervention in cases of sudden death consists of several distinctive steps: (1) notifying the family, (2) providing support while in the hospital, and (3) following up with the outpatient clinic (Dubin & Sarnoff, 1986).

Notifying the family. Generally speaking, families have a very difficult time accepting the sudden death of a family member. The process of notifying the family, which is the first step, becomes a delicate matter. The question as to whether the news of the death should be given over the phone remains a matter of controversy even today among medical professionals. Some contend that by giving the information over the phone, the family is prevented from rushing to the hospital and getting into an accident. Others argue that this approach will increase the risk of accidents. Some believe that it is best never to give all the facts over the phone, but to tell the family that their spouse (or child or parent) is in the emergency room and that "everything possible is being done" or that "the doctor is with her now." The last approach has the advantage of bringing the family into a more controlled environment when the news is broken. Davis (1984) suggests yet another approach, which is to let the family take the initiative after the nurse in the emergency room makes contact and verifies the relationship with the deceased before giving out any information. He gives the following example of this type of telephone exchange:

> *Nurse:* Hello, may I talk to Mrs. Brown? Mrs. Brown, this is Jane Smith, and I'm a nurse in the emergency department at Woodward Memorial Hospital. Is your husband's name Max Brown?
> *Relative:* Yes, What's happened?
> *Nurse:* Your husband has been brought to the emergency department by ambulance and we need for you to come to the hospital.
> *Relative:* What's happened?
> *Nurse:* Your husband apparently has had a heart attack. Would you like me to call someone to bring you to the hospital?
> *Relative:* No. I can call my neighbor. I'll be there right away.

The nurse responded to the wife's question and did not volunteer more than was asked. If the wife had asked specifically if her husband is dead, the nurse could have responded in the affirmative without giving any detail. Again, it is important to be brief, honest, and to repeat directions to the hospital. It is also wise to encourage the relative to get someone to provide transportation to avoid an accident on the way to the hospital.

Managing the family in the hospital. It is very important for a designated nurse or physician to be immediately available when the family arrives at the hospital. They should be made comfortable and given privacy in a quiet and pleasant room, away from the hustle and bustle of the emergency room. Until the attending physician arrives, the family should not be left alone. The relatives are usually anxious, tense, and apprehensive. The physician should be the one to talk to the family about the relative's death. This is to prevent suspicion or distrust and to provide reassurance that everything possible was done. Relatives need to hear such a statement to help them overcome their guilt feelings later. Also, in the case of an unexplained death, the family should be reassured that the autopsy, best referred to as a post-mortem examination, will be done with respect and dignity.

The family members should be given the option of viewing the body or part of the body. Before doing so, multilated parts should be covered. The room should be cleaned of blood, and tubes and drains should be removed from the body; but medical equipment should remain in the room as evidence that "everything possible was done." The viewing of the body, although traumatic, is believed by many experts to help the family overcome the denial of death, which can be very strong in many of these cases. However, the amount of pain the family is able to endure at the time will determine whether they can tolerate the confrontation with the display of their dead loved one.

At that point, support might be given by remaining in the room with the family. The physician, nurse, or social worker must be able to tolerate the acute grieving symptoms which are manifested. There may be crying, shouting, moaning, groaning, sobbing, or just quiet, confused stares and an appearance of bewilderment. The staff should refrain from statements of false reassurances and pseudowisdom, such as, "I know just how you must feel." It is impossible to know how another person feels, and to say so does not ring true. Do not say, "It was God's will," which will produce feelings of anger or guilt.

The family may ask many questions, such as, "Why did this occur?" It is best to answer honestly with "I don't know." They may ask, "Did he suffer?", "Did he say anything?", "Did he ask for anyone?" All questions should be answered directly and honestly. Often the be-reaved individual will repeat the questions in the midst of the intense emotional turmoil. It is important to repeat the answers several times if necessary.

Family members will sometimes manifest emotions of anger and hostility toward the staff, at times even blame. "Why did you let this happen?" "Why couldn't you save her?" Such remarks should not be taken literally or responded to directly. They should be considered a part of the acute grief manifestation, which does not require a direct answer.

Rather than offer false reassurance that everything is going to be all right, the most supportive stance is to legitimize and validate the family's feelings as they are being expressed. It is sometimes helpful to acknowledge, "It must be very hard for you."

Helping other family members with questions about the funeral arrangement is another supportive step. A bereaved person should not be allowed to leave the hospital unaccompanied. A relative, friend, or neighbor should be summoned to the hospital to drive the person home, and if possible, spend the night there. It is important to remember that there is a high risk of suicide following the loss of a lifetime spouse.

Whether bereaved families should be given any medication remains a controversial point in clinical practice. There is no adequate research to prove or disprove the advisability of medicating, but the general feeling in the medical community is that the normal process of grieving should not be interfered with. However, if the symptoms of tension, restlessness, fear, and agitation are extremely intense, the use of benzodiazepines might be useful in small doses. Most commonly, sedatives are used for a few nights if insomnia becomes so severe as to cause exhaustion and to interfere with grief.

Finally, the last step in the intervention by the hospital staff should be to make a telephone follow-up call or home visit to assess how the bereaved person is adjusting. If the person is isolated or is in need of further support because of lack of or insufficient support from the family, a referral to a support group is in order. Follow-up visits provide the opportunity for the bereaved to review unanswered questions and to fill the gaps which resulted from the confusion of the acute crisis (Vollman et al., 1971).

Although suicide is another example of sudden death followed by unanticipated grief, we feel that it deserves special attention because it presents unique problems for families and staff. It will be discussed in the following section.

GRIEF FOLLOWING SUICIDE

Of all the bereavements, the one following suicide constitutes the most difficult crisis a family has to face (Cain, 1972). Because suicide survivors number in the millions in this country, with 27,000 estimated suicides per year, Shneidman (1973) has stated that one of the major public health problems is "to alleviate the effects of stress in the survivor victims of suicidal deaths."

Health care providers are often the first ones to see survivors in the emergency room or in the office shortly after the suicide of a family member. For this reason it is important to recognize the essential features which characterize this situation in order to take effective and preventive steps. For one thing, survivors are generally more at risk for suicide themselves than the general population (Shepherd & Barraclough, 1974). They are also more prone to physical problems, especially spastic colon, ulcerative colitis, asthma, and rheumatoid arthritis (Stone, 1972).

The reactions following a suicide are particularly complex because the death is not socially accepted, carries considerable stigma, and brings heavy pressures upon the family from media and social circles (Schuyler, 1973). The question on everyone's mind is, "Why did he do it?" It should be noted, however, that there are many different types of suicides, and that the responses to them will vary greatly. For example, a number of cancer patients will choose to abbreviate a life of pain by making a conscious decision to end their lives (Danto, 1981). The impact of these suicides is not known; but it is wise to offer follow-up visits to families in order to answer their questions and offer assistance.

Suicide cases differ from other bereavements in that the reactions are more intense and have special features. We shall describe these features briefly.

Feeling of rejection. The most prevailing feeling of suicide survivors is that they feel rejected. In a way, this is the *ultimate rejection*. The survivor has no possibility of exploring with the deceased what the problem was. The underlying question about the reason for the suicide is really, "Why did she do it to me?" or "Why did he do it to us?" (Lindemann, 1972).

Anger. Angry feelings are very common and usually very intense because of the abruptness of the death, the unfinished business, and the feeling of abandonment. The reaction is especially severe in parents whose child committed suicide (Whitis, 1972). Sometimes the anger can be displayed toward the medical profession for having failed to recognize early clues about the contemplated suicide (Resnik, 1969).

Guilt. The emotion of guilt, which is exceptionally strong, may last for years. The guilt is promoted because there are no external causes for the death, and the survivor is left with attributing the cause to a psychological problem or a problem in the relationship with the deceased. For children whose parents committed suicide, the guilt may haunt them for years unless they are able to test the rationality of the event with the help of psychotherapy.

Self-blame. Survivors have a strong tendency to blame themselves for the suicide. It has been thought of as a form of survivor guilt similar to that experienced by those who survive an accident or catastrophic event.

Scapegoating. Survivors develop a strong tendency to look for scapegoats (Lindemann & Greer, 1972). Such scapegoating is often targeted at another member of the family, but it can occasionally be directed at strangers, such as health care professionals, including consulting psychiatrists in the hospital. For example, one mother, angry at the psychiatrist and the hospital staff, recalled that her twenty-seven-year-old son had just had a psychiatric consultation in the hospital the week before he jumped off the Golden Gate Bridge in San Francisco.

Shame. Because of society's critical attitudes, the death cannot be mentioned and readily talked about (Lazare, 1979). A strong sense of shame overtakes the whole family. This is further reinforced by the social stigma and the lack of support when friends, coworkers, and relatives pull away (Schuyler, 1973).

Pressures from the press, police, and investigating insurance agents add to the burden and stress of the family. These hassles contribute to increasing anger toward the deceased.

Denial takes on a peculiar form. The shame is so great that often the death is attributed to an "accident." It is interesting that the medical staff sometimes is also unable to deal with the family's pressure to conceal the death and will participate in the denial. This is even more likely to happen in the case of celebrities when the pressure from families and the media is so strong. In the case of parental suicide, children may later react with confusion if a conspiracy of silence develops into a family myth (Worden, 1982).

Suicidal ruminations. Survivors begin to wonder about the possibility of a hereditary aspect in suicide. Blachly's study (1968) of suicide by physicians confirmed the inherited tendency toward suicide. Another aspect of this rumination consists of the survivor's excessive identification with the deceased. The survivor then becomes frightened by his own impulse and ideation.

Management Guidelines

Clinicians should be particularly alert and sensitive to the dynamics just discussed. When a patient gives a history of suicide in the family in the course of a medical workup, certain precautionary measures should be taken (Welu, 1975). The following steps are considered desirable for prevention of further complications in the bereavement process:

1. After the family has been seen in the hospital or emergency room, they should be contacted within 48 hours for follow-up. Clergy or social workers attached to the hospital are the appropriate persons to perform this task.

2. An interview with the family shortly after the suicide may provide a therapeutic and cathartic experience (Worden, 1982).

3. When the suicide survivor is seen in the clinic, the following checklist should help in assessing the current status of the griever:

> Is there a history of self-destructive behavior, such as recent suicidal attempts, excess use of alcohol or drugs?
>
> Does the survivor harbor any suicidal thought or feeling? The physician should not hesitate to inquire, justifying the question to the griever by saying, "These thoughts are not unusual in persons who grieve after a loss by suicide."
>
> Does the survivor have physical problems or psychosomatic conditions such as asthma, spastic or ulcerative colitis, or rheumatoid arthritis?
>
> Is there any indication of social withdrawal from friends or neighbors?
>
> Does the survivor give any indication of excessive use of tranquilizers to cope with the grief?

Interventions by a primary care provider, although limited, can be crucial during the one or two follow-up visits. If the assessment described above points to more serious pathology and maladjustment, the survivor should be referred for counseling or psychotherapy. Self-help groups such as "Survivors of Suicide," The "Samaritans," "A Ray of Hope," or "Seasons" should be recommended to all survivors to facilitate the lengthy grief work (Check, 1985; Rogers et al., 1982).

Health professionals can do much to ease the emotional pain of families experiencing unanticipated or anticipatory grief. To do it effectively, the health provider must acquire some knowledge about the particular features of each type of loss and each type of grief. The team members must not feel competitive about giving support, because each one does it in an individual way. The physician, nurse, and social worker can all complement and support one another in the difficult but worthwhile task of giving support and meaning to the death and post-death situation.

Chapter 7

ROLES OF HEALTH PROFESSIONALS DURING BEREAVEMENT

Health professionals have a unique opportunity and responsibility in the crisis of bereavement faced by families during the period of terminal care or at the time of death. According to recent surveys, most professionals are usually perceived as being compassionate, honest, available, supportive, and willing to listen patiently to bereaved members of the family. Others, however, are seen as cold, impersonal, unconcerned, distant, and lacking gentleness (Davis, 1984). Regardless of the public image, the fact remains that most families turn to the doctor, nurse, and social worker for information, support, and guidance during the period preceding death and at the time of death.

Although the duties and roles of health professionals in patient care are well-defined, the same cannot be said of the responsibilities of each discipline with respect to the management of the bereavement situation. This probably occurs because each discipline faces different issues and problems that are getting more complex in an age of increasing technology and accountability. Tradition in medicine ascribes the role of case manager to the physician; yet there are times when the physician is not available or is too busy with other clinical matters to be able to provide the support and information needed by the family. In these cases, it would be advisable for the physician to designate either the nurse or a social worker on the health care team as the manager for family matters. The rationale for this approach is that the family should be viewed as the "unit of service" because it is significantly affected and traumatized by the patient's illness (Caroff & Dobrof, 1974). This model has been especially useful in such cases of terminal illness as leukemia and cystic fibrosis in children (McCollum & Schwartz, 1972) and chronic renal dialysis.

More recently hospitals have recognized that the well-being of families during terminal care or immediately after the death is important and should not be viewed as an obstacle to or interference with the medical care of the patient (Osterweis, 1984). These hospitals facilitate access of the family to the patient, arranging for privacy and even providing comfortable quarters during the dying period. The hospital staff is becoming more aware and sensitive to the needs of dying patients and their families, showing willingness to step back, to be less intrusive, and to answer questions and provide support.

In order to dispel the confusion that exists in clinical practice and in the literature with regard to the various responsibilities in the bereavement situation, we thought it would be helpful to discuss the role of each professional person on the team. Each discipline of medicine, nursing, and social work has different preoccupations and concerns in the pre- and post-death periods. In order to clarify the roles and responsibilities of each discipline, we shall discuss them separately.

THE ROLE OF THE PHYSICIAN

The tasks of the physician around the time of dying and at the time of death call for some specific skills for which there has not always been adequate training and education (Kutscher & Kutscher, 1974). These tasks include notifying the family, explaining the cause of illness and the cause of the death, requesting an autopsy and organ transplantation, discussing wills and life-sustaining measures, informing the patient and family of a terminal diagnosis, and providing support and guidance during the terminal care. We shall discuss the various problems and issues involved in each of these tasks.

Notifying the Family

The task of notification is always an unpleasant experience for the physician. Whenever the situation presents itself, the physician becomes concerned with issues of failure. Was everything possible done? Was something missed in the diagnosis or treatment of the pa-

tient? These questions are particularly relevant if the death was unexpected because the patient was in the hospital. Suddenly the physician must explain the unusual circumstances to the family.

Whether the death is expected or not, it is probably more acceptable to families to receive the news directly rather than on the
telephone. Although some physicians feel that in cases where the death
was expected, and where it is inconvenient for the family to come to
the hospital, the notification can be made by phone. In cases of terminal illness, it is best to arrange to have the family present at the
time of death. This is especially true for families of dying children
(Cohen et al., 1978; Engel, 1964).

The announcement of the death should be made in a clear, simple,
and direct fashion. "Your husband's heart became increasingly weak,
and he died at 3 A.M. I am very sorry." At this point, the physician
must behave in a way that is comfortable and appropriate for the
particular family. Of course, the relationship with the family greatly
influences the physician's behavior at this point. If he has known the
family for a long time, it will be more comfortable to show regrets to
a family with a longtime relationship than with family members who
are strangers, as is frequently the case in emergency rooms. It is desirable to have a nurse present during the announcement of the news
and the explanations of the cause of death so that later the nurse will
be able to repeat the physician's answers, which may not have been
heard by the family during the acute crisis. The nurse should remain
with the family after the physician leaves the room to provide the
necessary support.

Requesting the Autopsy and Organ Transplant

Despite the fact that a minimum autopsy rate is no longer required
by the Joint Commission on the Accreditation of Hospitals and that
increased accuracy in diagnosis exists through the use of more sophisticated diagnostic tools, the postmortem examination is still considered a key to diagnostic quality control, research, and education
(Scottolini & Weinstein, 1983).

Nevertheless, to ask a bereaved family permission for an autopsy
remains one of the most unpleasant and sensitive tasks a physician
must perform. The experience is generally delicate, awkward, and
worsened by the fact that most physicians do not receive adequate
training or preparation for dealing with this situation (Katz & Gardner,
1972). As a result, physicians develop an approach based on their

personal "on the job experience," on their prior exposure to death, if any, and on their own feelings and attitudes derived from their own personal losses. In the course of becoming familiar with this duty, most physicians have to overcome feelings of self-doubt, inadequacy, and failure.

To explain the circumstances of the death to the family and to answer questions about the illness often puts the physician in a defensive posture if death represents a personal admission of impotence and failure. The physician then becomes ill-prepared to weather the hurt, disappointment, and anger of the family in acute grief. Furthermore, this renders the physician unable to deal with the objections, arguments, and resistances put forth by the families. For example, what responses can be given to such comments as, "It's against our religion," "Hasn't she suffered enough already?," "We already knew what his condition was," "She wouldn't have wanted it," or "It won't help to bring him back." If the family has strong objections to an autopsy and organ transplant, these feelings should be respected. Generally, however, the manner in which the family is approached will usually determine whether they will accept or reject the request (Katz & Gardner, 1972).

The topic should not be brought up without an initial period of sympathetic listening to the hurt, anger, despair, and disappointment of the family. After this is done, the question of funeral arrangements may come up, eventually leading to the issues of the postmortem examination. The process is greatly facilitated if the physician already has a well-established and trusting relationship with the family.

Various reasons might be given to convince the family to consent to the autopsy. These should be chosen by the physician on the basis of an evaluation of the family's social and cultural background. A partial list of such reasons might include:

> to establish the cause of death;
>
> to facilitate the grieving process by providing some specific answers;
>
> to reveal associated conditions;
>
> to identify in the case of neonatal deaths genetic and hereditary factors that could affect future births;
>
> to help understand the illness for the purpose of future prevention.

In the case of a child's death, the autopsy request may be particularly delicate, but experience shows that parents frequently want the autopsy but are not sure how and when to ask for it (Berger, 1978). Sometimes, they may want to do it as a gesture of gratitude toward the hospital or as a way to help other children. Follow-up interviews have shown that parents usually do not regret having obtained the autopsy (Bergman, 1974).

There are times when it may be inappropriate and detrimental to pursue the consent for autopsy or organ transplant. This would be the case, for example, if the objection is definite and strong, when the postmortem will provide little new information (as in the case of a child who died after a well-diagnosed chronic illness) or when the parents seem conflicted and divided about their decision. Pursuing the permission in these cases may result in future marital discord, regrets, and remorse, and it may also undermine the future relationship with the physician. In such cases, it is best to accept the parents' refusal and to support them in their decision.

If the permission for autopsy is granted, it is important to plan a meeting with the family approximately 6 to 8 weeks later. At that time, the physician can discuss the result of the autopsy as well as other remaining questions about the death, the illness, or the hospitalization (Berger, 1978; Katz & Gardner, 1972; Reynolds, 1978). It is also an opportunity to reevaluate the family's progress in their grief work and to reassess their need for counseling. The practice of a follow-up meeting, however, is still unpopular because there are virtually no incentives for the physician to carry out the task. In addition to being again exposed to a most difficult situation with the bereaved family, the physician is further discouraged by the fact that there will be neither compensation by third-party payers nor allotted time if work is in an institutional setting. Until institutions and chiefs of service recognize the need in this area, the resistance to deal with these activities will continue to be significant (Osterweis, 1984).

Requests for organ donations should also be made at the same time as the request for an autopsy. The opportunity to make a donation of organs that might save another life usually makes families feel better and gives them the feeling that the tragedy of death has some potential for meaning (Gonda, 1972). In contrast to the autopsy, organ donations may help relieve guilt feelings and make the loss more acceptable (Christopherson & Gonda, 1974).

Another factor which discourages physicians from further involvement with the family is the fear of malpractice suits. The physician may feel that the autopsy may reveal errors of commission or omission, or raise further doubts about competence; later attentiveness to the family may even be viewed with suspicion (Rabin & Rabin, 1970). Many physicians have the feeling that families blame them for deaths, although there is no real evidence for this except the physicians' own feelings of guilt (Osterweis, 1984).

It is clear that in view of all the difficulties, administrators and chiefs of service should institute educational and administrative guidelines that will encourage and support physicians in the above activities. The fact that Congress is considering legislation requiring hospitals to make routine requests for organ donations will probably revive the interest in such guidelines (*The Honolulu Advertiser*, 1987).

Providing Support and Guidance

Physicians can often reduce the stress experienced by grieving families during or after a terminal illness. To do this they must be prepared to deal with feelings of anger, guilt, and helplessness. During a terminal illness the physician can ask a spouse, or an adult son or daughter: "Do you think you and your spouse (or parent) have any unfinished business you need to talk about? What are you going to do about that? Any unfinished business with other people? Does your spouse (or parent) leave a will? Is it current? Have you discussed funeral arrangements?" (Fuller & Geis, 1985).

THE ROLE OF THE NURSE

In contrast to physicians, nurses do get a solid grounding in knowledge about bereavement, grief, and loss during nursing school training. In addition, by virtue of their continuous contact with patients and their families, they develop a close and trusting relationship and remain more involved than other health professionals. They are usually perceived as sympathetic and supportive, although sometimes they can be viewed as cold and unconcerned (Davis, 1984). In most cases, the nurse plays a crucial role in intervention during the acute grief crisis. Martocchio (1985) has emphasized that the nurse can prevent further suppression and repression of feelings during the grief reaction, thus preventing an abnormal grief reaction later. In some hospitals, the nurse-counselor is expected to relieve anxiety and uncertainty in patients facing major surgery for cancer (Osterweis, 1984).

At times, families may be reticent about asking the physician certain questions for fear that their questions will be misinterpreted as loss of trust. In these situations, the nurse can help the family formulate and organize their questions and encourage them to be open with their physicians.

Most nursing textbooks cover the subject of nursing interventions fairly thoroughly, and we shall only mention a few aspects of special significance here.

As with the physician's role, the nurse's role in the management of bereavement encompasses the areas of education and information, emotional support, management of the acute crisis, identification of high-risk families, and assistance in their follow-up care (Giaquinta, 1977).

During the dying period, the nurse should be present when the physician tells the family about the terminal diagnosis and explains the procedures that are being considered (Engel, 1964). It is important that the nurse be fully knowledgeable in order to clarify questions asked later by the family. This may also prevent either future misinterpretations about what the physician said or self-blame for having misunderstood what was meant.

The nurse is in a unique position to help facilitate the grief process by giving the family permission to express strong reactions. If the death is anticipated, the nurse can offer support by encouraging the family to talk about their feelings before the loss (Freihofer & Felton, 1976; Rinear, 1975; Winder & Elam, 1978).

Nurses generally have more opportunity to share their feelings among each other, therefore working through their own grieving experiences when they lose a patient. The need to discuss these feelings is becoming increasingly recognized, and clinical psychiatric nurse specialists now offer support individually or in groups to nurses who are repeatedly exposed to losses during their service. Because repeated experiences with losses are very draining and interpersonally painful, supervisors are becoming aware of the need to rotate nurses and to provide them with some respite by assigning them to other duties with high gratification potential (Vachon, 1987).

Another area of nursing intervention is that of identifying high-risk families, e.g., those families who are apt to develop maladaptive coping patterns and eventually fail to resolve their grief. In this regard, it has been shown that the single most important factor in developing prolonged grief is when the family believes that the death was preventable (Bugen, 1977).

Finally, by using listening skills in the relationship with the dying patient and family, the nurse is ideally suited to maintain and restore a feeling of hope in the families who experience anticipatory or acute grief. In an individualized way, the nurse can encourage self-awareness, sharing, reality testing, and creativity (Adams & Proulx, 1975; Martocchio, 1985). It is important to remain comfortable with personal feelings about death and loss in order successfully to work through the personal grief process.

The following is an example of a dialogue between a nurse and the wife of a patient who died of cancer after a long course of illness.

> *Nurse:* This must be a very difficult time for you. (Nurse acknowledges the wife's pain.)
>
> *Bereaved Wife:* Right now, I'm just numb. I don't seem to feel that this is real.
>
> *Nurse:* These feelings are understandable. No matter how prepared you think you are, it must still be a shock and difficult to cope with. (Nurse validates feelings and gives permission to express more emotion.)
>
> *Bereaved Wife:* Yes, these last few months have been horrible. It seems that my husband had to suffer so much before he died. It was devastating to see this once independent man become so helpless.
>
> *Nurse:* This must have taken a lot of strength on your part. (Nurse offers no explanation for the death; instead she acknowledges that feelings were painful.)
>
> *Bereaved Wife:* Yes, at times I just got so tired of it all, and sometimes I wished it would be all over, then I'd feel bad for feeling that way.
>
> *Nurse:* Your feelings are understandable. It's only natural to have these feelings. (Nurse acknowledges guilt feelings and tries to decrease the guilt expressed.)
>
> *Bereaved Wife:* Yes, I guess so, but I wonder if somehow we couldn't have done more; I keep thinking if only. . . .
>
> *Nurse:* Feelings like the ones you are experiencing are not unusual. I believe that you and the staff provided the best care and treatment available, and everything was done that could have been done. I'm sure that he knew of your loving care. (Nurse continues to validate feelings, reassuring the wife that her feelings are not abnormal and that she is not a bad person for having such feelings.)

Bereaved Wife: Yes, I guess you're right. I have felt so much pain associated with my husband's illness that I hope I never see this hospital again.

(Red flag: Wife is beginning to feel some anger at this point, which she will need to express at a later time.)

Nurse: I feel concerned for you and your adjustment to this loss. I would like you to know that our social worker (or the co-ordinator of our grief counseling program) will be contacting you to offer you support services during the months ahead. We care about you and your health during this period in your life. (Nurse expresses concern but does not focus on the underlying angry feelings; instead she notes the need for follow-up and prepares the wife for further support. At this point, she uses nonverbal communication by gently touching the wife's hand or shoulder.)

Stuart and Sundeen (1987) offer a summary of the goals, rationale, and nursing interventions that are appropriate in uncomplicated grief reactions encountered within the hospital setting. Sometimes when a patient is hospitalized shortly after a bereavement reaction, a nursing care plan should be written up and implemented (see Appendix E).

Nurses and physicians often experience difficulties in dealing with the grief reactions of their patients' families. This can be explained by a variety of factors, relating partly to former training, and partly to the culture of the medical milieu. For example, the training and education of nurses emphasize the professional demeanor to the point where any show of emotion can lead to unresolved grief reactions. Yet nurses do experience attenuated but nonetheless real grief reactions following the loss of patients. In most situations a sensitive instructor or supervisor can help student nurses and staff nurses by giving them permission to grieve. Even then, the expressed grief is never completed because the next loss occurs before resolution is achieved. This probably explains why nurses tend to use avoidance as a coping behavior, thus asking for a transfer or moving from hospital to hospital where death cases are less frequent. Other nurses, however, choose to stay because they get sufficient support from the shared responsibility of the medical team, as in the case of those who work with leukemic children (Binger et al., 1969).

Both physicians and nurses have difficulties dealing with death and dying because each experience is frequently a compounding of several professional losses. For both, the inability to prevent or forestall the death of a patient is a reminder of failure, more for the physician than the nurse, as well as a loss of power and ability to control the situation. This is especially true when treating patients with cancer, kidney disease, or chronic and degenerative conditions (Vachon, 1987).

Another reason for suppressing all feelings connected with the bereavement is that the fear of making mistakes in the care of the patient might affect the health professional's life by leading to self-doubt and errors in judgment, a situation which is intolerable. Worse yet, negligent errors can lead to fears of malpractice liability and loss of respect by peers (Rabin & Rabin, 1970). For these reasons, many health professionals tend to suppress their feelings not only among themselves, but especially in front of their families. Occasionally, when the staff invests considerable time and energy in a particular patient, as in cases of chronic renal dialysis with their many ups and downs, there is an unusual degree of attachment to the patient. Then the emotional investment is in preventing the loss at all costs rather than in the emotional expression of grieving (Short & Wilson, 1969).

Much in these inhibitions and suppression of feelings can be alleviated through a team-building effort aimed at developing trust and mutual respect.

THE ROLE OF THE SOCIAL WORKER

Next to the nurse in the hospital, the social worker has the most continuous relationship with the bereaved family. Although social workers are part of the health team, they are not directly involved with medical treatment. To some extent, this may be an advantage in dealing with bereaved families. Social workers do not have to face the occasional feelings of anger and frustration directed toward the nurse and physician, therefore they may feel freer in their encounters with families (Phillips, 1972).

Social workers play a major role in dealing with families after bereavement. They are particularly well prepared because their training emphasizes the family as the entity needing care. Furthermore, the social work curriculum includes courses on dying, death and the various problems encountered at different stages of the life cycle (Mullaney & Fox, 1981). There is not much question that in most cases the family system is affected to varying degrees by the impact of the loss of a family member. As mentioned previously, some experts have gone as far as saying that the family should be considered the "unit of service" in the hospital setting because any life threatening illnesses constitute an assault on the whole family (Caroff & Dobrof,

1974). Others have emphasized the magnitude of the impact according to the type of death. They have conceptualized a "high grief potential" versus a "low grief potential," explaining that the degree or intensity of one's grief at the time of death is a function of the kind of death experienced" (Fulton & Fulton, 1971).

In anticipatory grief, social workers provide valuable support to patients as well as to families (Abrams, 1972). For example, they might assist other health professionals in running support groups for parents of dying children (McCollum & Schwartz, 1972) or they might help a family cope with the adjustment necessary after the death of a mother (Prichard, 1974). In addition to helping families and patients during terminal care, the social worker can encourage communication among family members, help them locate relatives, make burial plans, notify next of kin, arrange for homemaker services, and make contact with community agencies. Some social workers with special training will offer to do grief counseling and therapy to help the dying and the bereaved work through the grief process and restore personal and family equilibrium. Their coping with this difficult task has been amply described by Harper (1977). It is interesting to note that the interventions by social workers sometimes are taken so much for granted in the hospital setting that these interventions are not even recorded in the medical record. McCollum and Schwartz (1972) have recommended some guidelines to correct this deficiency.

The medical team *should know* the family's current stresses, resources, and problem areas, such as finances and care for the children. The social worker should be able to help the family make the necessary adjustments following discharge from the hospital. Following a death in the family, as in the loss of a child, the strain on the family can be so great as to disintegrate the entire family unit and lead to divorce, social isolation, and lifetime scars on the other children (Wiener, 1970). In these cases the social worker can play a crucial role in maintaining the family bonds and cohesiveness.

The duties and functions of social workers are generally well-defined in their training. Their philosophical orientation and responsibility are primarily directed toward the family unit as a whole. To them, bereavement is an attack on the whole family system and will require subsequent adaptation in terms of a readjustment of the whole family system (Ochoa et al., 1975). Therefore grief counseling consists of interventions with the family unit during the full span of the dying and death experience. Therapeutic goals include the following:

Provide crisis intervention for families reacting to severe trauma, shock, and sudden death in the emergency room and other parts of the hospital (Stromberg, 1987).

Maintain family relationships and communication during the terminal illness of the patient, at the time of death, and during the post death period (Abrams, 1972).

Help the family plan for a variety of services, such as funeral arrangements, financial aid, public welfare, legal services, homemaker services, and contact with other community agencies.

Lead or participate in support groups for bereaved parents or spouses.

Help locate relatives and help notify relatives in distant places.

Insure continuity of care for other family members.

Offer counseling and grief therapy, or help with the referral to mental health professionals, if indicated (Woodward et al., 1985).

It should become clear from the above discussion that hospital staff members should remain involved with families in the post-death situation and help them with the stresses of social isolation and readjustment during the bereavement period (Cohen, in press; Rogers et al., 1982; Stubblefield, 1977). Social workers, physicians, and nurses can all help families in their grief reactions to better understand their unique experiences as survivors. The professional team can also make significant interventions by recognizing early patterns of abnormal bereavement and make the necessary referrals when appropriate.

Chapter 8

BEREAVEMENT IN THE HOSPITAL AND THE CLINIC

IN THE HOSPITAL

This chapter will focus on bereavement as it occurs in various parts of the hospital setting. Specifically, we shall review and discuss the types of deaths that are characteristic of various units, the circumstances of the death, the reactions of the survivors, problems and concerns that are particular to the unit in question, and, finally, management guidelines especially applicable in the light of these specific considerations.

Managing bereaved families in the hospital setting has now become a major focus of attention, since the majority of people today die in hospitals. Instead of dying at home with all of the traditional comforts of warm family support, most people nowadays are taken to the hospital, admitted to a medical or surgical service or, if they suffer from an unexpected and urgent condition, rushed to an emergency room (Lerner, 1970). The hospital has become the setting where the family will interact with a dying member for the last few days and hours of life.

The survivors are subject to the normal dynamics of grief, and the staff is faced with its own internal struggles (Glaser & Strauss, 1968; Sudnow, 1967). The communications and subsequent interactions between staff and survivors in most cases influence the subsequent outcome of the family's adjustment to the immediate post-death situation (Freihofer & Felton, 1976; Hampe, 1975). The overall impression and feelings conveyed to the survivors at this point usually intensify either positive or negative reactions to the death, therefore influencing the subsequent outcome of the grief process.

In general, bereavement reactions in the hospital will vary with 1) the type of death, whether sudden, unexpected, or the result of a lingering illness; 2) the circumstances of the death, whether the patient's life was cut short or whether he had a long and happy life; 3) the family's communication system, whether loving family and friends are available at the time of death or whether the patient has been abandoned; 4) the amount of pain or mutilation at the time of dying; 5) the presence of surviving young children and, finally, 6) the amount of financial problems left for the survivors. All of these variables will significantly affect the dynamics of bereavement and should be taken into account as much as possible at the time of intervention (Hollingsworth & Pasnau, 1977).

In our interviews with physicians and nurses we followed a standardized protocol. We focused on the stressors mentioned above. In addition, we inquired about staff reactions, their coping strategies, personal experiences with loss and grief, current bereavement philosophy, and approaches to managing bereaved families.

Let us now review the special concerns and problems in the death and bereavement situation as they apply to the various units of the hospital. Although some terms are used interchangeably in practice and in the literature, we will attempt to bring some consistency to the terminology. For example, we will refer to a "service" as the broader delivery system as opposed to the more specialized "unit." We will also use "CCU" to refer to the Critical Care Unit only, using the complete description to refer to the Coronary Care Unit.

In the Emergency Room (ER)

The loss of life in the Emergency Room (ER) is particularly stressful because of the sudden development of events that precede the death. It is important to realize that the overall impression and feeling conveyed by the staff to the family of a patient who dies in the ER can intensify the reactions and memories experienced later in the grief process (Willis, 1977).

The Emergency Room is the one area in the hospital where most sudden and unexpected deaths occur. Today, with the development of high technology, most deaths are usually "coded" en route to the hospital rather than "pronounced" before arrival at the ER. This new practice, however, creates additional stress for the family because "false hopes" remain even though the patient might have already died before reaching the hospital.

Types of death. Most deaths in the Emergency Room fall into three categories:

1. Cardiovascular deaths. In these cases patients are usually elderly and debilitated. The expectation of the ending of life has no element of surprise. Most physicians feel that if they "give it their best shot," they will not experience feelings of guilt, failure, or regret. On the interpersonal level, there is virtually no emotional involvement in the relationship because there is no time to get to know the patient.

2. Trauma cases. The intensity of involvement is usually much greater with these cases. Physicians agree that they make a 100 percent effort in their attempts to rescue victims of accidents. Most staff members admit that they consciously choose not to get involved in their relationships with these patients, tending to cultivate an "emotional shield" to prevent close involvement. As one physician put it, "You 'build a wall' so you can function more effectively." This kind of practice comes only with experience. But at times it is difficult to stay neutral, particularly with cases in which the death results from the negligence of drunken drivers or the cruelty of a murderer.

3. Pediatric deaths. Most physicians and nurses have great difficulty dealing with the deaths of children or teenagers, as well as with the post-death situation of such cases. Frequently, they feel that the death could have been prevented if the responsible party had exercised better judgment. Feelings of anger are sometimes directed at the parents, who may be perceived as stupid or neglectful. Because of this resentment, the staff often has some difficulty providing the support needed by the bereaved family. Most professionals agree that this type of reaction is more likely to take place when the patient is younger than twenty years of age.

Management guidelines. Breaking the news of death is always an unpleasant task which the physician must face and carry out (see Chapter 6). In the Emergency Room it is a frequent occurrence. Yet it is never easy. Each case must be considered individually, based on as much knowledge as possible about the deceased and the family.

Generally, the family of the patient are not known to the ER staff.

Therefore it is not wise to break the news over the telephone. In most cases the family is told that the patient is extremely ill or has been hurt, that their presence is needed, but that there is no need to rush to the hospital (Davis, 1984). This is to avoid any emotional upheaval that might be responsible for causing an accident on the way to the hospital. When the family members get to the hospital, they should be taken to a private room and made as comfortable as possible. Shortly thereafter, the physician who took care of the patient should advise the family of the death, breaking the news in a straightforward and direct manner. Sometimes a brief explanation of the events that led to the demise might be helpful: "Your husband became very weak, his heart muscle gave out, and he died shortly after. Everything that could be done was done."

It is advisable to have a member of the nursing staff present so that support can be given after the physician leaves the room. At this point, it is best to watch for any reaction, wait for the questions, remain supportive, and wait silently for a few minutes (Davis, 1984). Reactions at this point tend to be predictable. Families react with shock, disbelief and numbness, denial, anger, a deep sense of pain, and sometimes guilt. At that moment, it is important for the staff to understand that they may be perceived as (a) the bearer of bad news, (b) incompetent people (e.g., "you could have done more if you were good enough"), or (c) uncaring people (e.g., "you could have done more if you cared"). Nevertheless it is best for the nurse to remain with the family, even if the target of some verbal assaults.

The nurse should be prepared to answer further questions about the death immediately after it is announced in order to repeat and clarify previously given information, which is frequently not heard or understood the first time. Encourage viewing the body, if so desired, but without pressure on the family, especially if there is strong objection. It is also helpful at this time to alleviate any concern expressed about funeral arrangements.

Offer a sedative to the bereaved survivor for a few nights only, if it is desired. Tranquilizers, however, should be avoided except in cases where the bereaved is known to have a medical condition, such as heart disease or high blood pressure, and an undue amount of stress on the organism must be prevented. If the nurse is unable to stay, a social worker, chaplain, or trained volunteer should remain with the family to help them by listening and making supportive comments (see Chapter 10 on Do's and Don'ts), making phone calls, offering coffee or anything else they might request. But before leaving the family with another member of the support team, offer to be accessible to the family at a later time, should they have any further questions. Better yet, call the survivors a couple of days later to check on their condition, offering to see them if they wish.

To summarize, the most important consideration for the management of bereavement reactions in the Emergency Room is to have a well-organized support system in place. Roles should be well-defined in advance. Physicians must accept the responsibility to provide the initial support to the family and insure that the transition for continued support is made smoothly and when the family is ready. The nurse should be readily available to provide the continued emotional support, answer questions, and make arrangements with other members of the family. The social worker should be available, if needed, and the clergy should be on call and readily accessible as soon as the family's religious preferences are known. When all of these conditions are met, a sense of orderliness prevails, and the crisis can be managed effectively by the entire staff.

Malpractice fears.   Bereavement situations in the Emergency Room are sometimes complicated by the fact that families will engage the hospital in a legal suit (Vachon, 1987). The staff has been sensitized over the years by the publicity over litigation and by the fear of being blamed by families for what might have developed while the patient was dying. This state of affairs further inhibits any demonstration or expression of feeling from the staff for fear that it might be misunderstood or held against the treating clinician. Sometimes, the anger displayed upon news of the death gets channeled into legal threats. It is best not to respond to such threats in a personal manner or in a literal sense but to accept them as part of the acute grief reaction at the time.

In the Neonatal Intensive Care Unit (NICU)

Deaths in the Neonatal Intensive Care Unit do not occur frequently. Nationally, the death rate is 4 to 5 deaths per 1,000, and some hospitals average an even lower rate. Some units have a higher rate because they serve as a regional referral center for seriously ill newborns. For example, the NICU at the Children's Hospital National Medical Center in Washington, D.C. has approximately 600 admissions per year, of which approximately 60 result in death (Committee on the Health Consequences of the Stress of Bereavement, 1984). At this center, two guiding principles have emerged from the experience of working with parents whose babies have died after admission to the NICU. First, the parents must be thoroughly informed about all aspects of the care given to their baby. Second, the parents must be given emotional support from the day the infant is admitted to the NICU.

Types of death. In all cases of impending death a tense drama develops, involving both parents and the staff throughout the unit. In general, deaths tend to occur in a matter of hours or days, the majority of cases involving premature babies or high-risk babies with "anomalies syndrome."

Circumstances of the death. Occasionally a baby lingers between life and death for several days or weeks. In that situation both physicians and nurses tend to become attached and develop what has been called "special baby relationships" (Vachon, 1987). When the baby dies, the staff experiences acute grief and shares the sadness with the parents. In over half the cases with impending death, a deliberate decision is made not to continue giving active treatment, so as not to prolong an inevitable death.

In all of these cases, considerable discussion takes place among the staff about the advisability of discontinuing treatment, while the physician keeps the parents informed and attempts to involve them in the decision. If the parents disagree, a nurse and social worker should continue to meet with them in order to share and interpret new medical information and to talk about their feelings concerning death. When life-support systems are discontinued, some parents opt to hold their babies while it is dying. Others prefer to be reassured that a nurse or doctor was holding the infant when it died.

Parental reaction in the immediate post-death situation. The immediate response of the mother after the infant's death is to ask herself, "What did I do wrong?" and "What could I have done to prevent this?" Later, both parents may express feelings of irritability or even anger at the staff. The anger may be directed at the physician, nurse, hospital, family, or even friends. This behavior should be recognized as a "normal response" of the grief process rather than a problem of coping with the crisis (Hildebrand & Schreiner, 1980).

In most instances parents experience a period of confusion and bewilderment, feeling totally overwhelmed (Seitz & Warrick, 1974).

Shortly after hearing the announcement of the death, they are virtually incapable of absorbing any more information. For this reason, the physician and nurse should plan another meeting before discharge from the hospital, thus providing an opportunity to go over what took place, to answer questions, and to give further information about what to expect during the bereavement process.

Management guidelines.   The most salient points about dealing with parents whose baby is dying must be reemphasized here. It is of utmost importance for the NICU staff to understand and agree on the principle of *open communication* with parents from the very beginning. A staff member must be designated to be available to give continuous emotional support from the day of admission (Schreiner, 1984; Schreiner et al., 1979).

For the following guidelines we have drawn heavily upon the recommendations made by the staff of the Children's Hospital National Medical Center in Washington, D.C.

When a decision to discontinue life support is *contemplated*, the parents should be informed and invited to participate in the decision with knowledge of all the medical facts and consequences as they progress in the course of the hospitalization (Cohen et al., 1978). In general, it is recommended that in cases of infants on ventilators beyond 6 weeks, medical and nursing staff should meet to discuss a strategy about discontinuing treatment.

If there is a disagreement, further meetings should be scheduled with a designated nurse and social worker to explore feelings about death, prior experiences, the meaning of the pregnancy, and the expectations about the infant.

At the time of death, parents should be allowed to be with the infant, to hold it, and to take pictures.

If the baby is deformed, the deformed parts should be judiciously covered with a blanket, although some parents do not object and even find some "beauty" in their deformed infant.

Both parents should be involved in the decision-making about the disposition of the body. Traditionally, fathers have been expected to make all the arrangements, but experience shows that mothers frequently end up resenting the fact that they were left out of the decision.

Parents should not be given any sedatives or tranquilizers while viewing the baby so that the experience does not become clouded, thus potentially fostering the denial of the death.

In the case of a loss of multiple births, such as sextuplets or septuplets, it is important for the medical staff to shield the parents from the media in order to prevent interference with the grieving process (Burnell, 1977).

When the mother takes the wheelchair ride before leaving the hospital, she should be allowed to have an "empty arms package," consisting of mementos, such as locks of hair, photographs, a sample of the infant's footprints, a blanket, or nursery bracelet. She should be told that "This is going to be a very difficult time for you, and you are going to feel like crying, and that's all right."

Parents should be told that they will feel a strong sense of guilt, and that it is a common and normal feeling to have in these circumstances. The guilt should be equated with the feeling of helplessness. Prescribing a ritual sometimes can help, or channeling the guilt into a creative pursuit connected with the baby can provide much relief, such as working as a volunteer for a community cause.

It is important to recognize red flags indicating which parents are at high risk for complications in their bereavement and who will need referral for professional counseling or psychiatric consultation (Turco, 1981) (see Chapter 12).

Parents should be referred to self-support groups such as SHARE or The Compassionate Friends (see Chapter 12) (Forrest et al., 1982; Burnell & Burnell, 1986).

The attending physician who took care of the infant should call the parents in the first 2 weeks following the death. If an autopsy was done, the result should be discussed with the parent after about 3 months after the death. This will provide an opportunity to discuss genetic counseling and check on how the parents are getting along. It should be remembered that the cause of death is usually an important issue to the parents, who will be grateful for the information received. The information should be direct, honest, and factual.

Even if permission for an autopsy was not granted, a meeting with the parents 2 or 3 months after the death is good practice. It serves to clear up any questions about the infant's medical condition or care. It should be remembered that parents are usually too upset to remember all the answers or explanations given at the time of the death.

In the Critical Care Unit (CCU)

This section on the Critical Care Unit (CCU) includes discussion of the Intensive Care Unit (ICU) and the Coronary Care Unit.

Types of illnesses and deaths. Most patients admitted to the CCU tend to be persons in their sixties or seventies suffering from cardiovascular or pulmonary complications. Younger patients in their forties and fifties for the most part are admitted with a diagnosis of myocardial infarction. When death occurs it tends to come within a matter of days. Occasionally a patient may linger for weeks while on life-support systems, ventilators, or transfusions.

Circumstances of the death. The main problem involving many CCU patients is the decision regarding the "code status," the code being what determines the behavior of the staff in case there is a need for resuscitation. A "code red" carries the order for total effort toward resuscitation, whereas a "code white" means that no intervention will be made for resuscitation. Although these determinations are made by physicians, they present a problem if patients themselves, nurses, or family members are in disagreement with the decision of the physician.

To avoid such conflicts, it is best to combine sound medical judgment with the wishes of the patient and family. When a consensus is reached, nurses usually feel at peace and are therefore better able to meet the emotional and physical needs of the patient. The bereavement situation which follows a conflict-free death is less likely to develop into a crisis or a conflict for the survivors. On the other hand, when the medical and nursing staff are divided, nurses feel frustrated, angry, and helpless. Their feelings often get transmitted to the family, who feel equally frustrated and angry with the physician (Campbell, 1980).

Management guidelines. Team conferences can be very useful on a periodic basis to discuss issues of death, dying, and bereavement. In cases of a prolonged course of life support, the CCU supervisor should anticipate potential conflicts and schedule such team conferences. The consensus, when reached between the staff and the family, constitutes a strong supportive measure to facilitate the bereavement process in the family which is not burdened with unresolved feelings of resentment against the hospital staff. On the other hand, the failure to recognize or anticipate conflicts can inhibit or complicate the grief process in the survivors and the nursing staff. Therefore, physicians and nurses should become aware that their own death anxiety is usually at the base of the conflict and the troubled communication (Campbell, 1980). Vachon (1987) has reviewed extensively the various communication problems of nurses and physicians in the Intensive Care Unit. These should be studied by supervisors and nurses interested in planning programs that would facilitate death with dignity for patients and an uncomplicated bereavement process for the survivors (Gentry & Parkes, 1982).

In the Oncology Unit

In the majority of cases, families work closely with an oncologist prior to the patient's death, so that a close relationship has developed by the time of the bereavement (Wahl, 1973). Therefore communication at that time is really a continuation of a dialogue that started weeks or months before the terminal phase of the illness. During the period of treatment the oncologist is perceived as a powerful, kind, empathic, and supportive person. Nurses, too, form close bonds with patients in the unit and become important sources of support for the family (Marks, 1976).

By the time the patient dies, the staff has made a fairly good assessment of the family's needs, strengths, and weaknesses. Staff members are in a good position to establish an appropriate approach to the family. If the family has accepted the death, the grieving proceeds without any difficulty; but if there has been conflict over the decision to choose between active and passive treatment, the family may react with strong feelings of guilt and regret. Typically, they will say, "We should not have put him through this ordeal if he was going to die anyway." The guilt seems even more intense if the patient was in conflict with the family's decision to pursue treatment when he himself did not want to be treated.

Sometimes, the conflict is between the physician and the family. Passive treatment may be suggested by the physician, that is, treatment aimed at relieving the symptoms rather than the underlying condition; but the family is unable to accept this alternative and continues to seek other opinions and treatment elsewhere (Annas et al., 1981). But even if the family agrees to stop aggressive treatment, there may be some problems for the nursing staff in accepting such a course of action because of their own personal and ethical convictions (Davis & Aroskar, 1983).

Management guidelines.   In all cases it is important that the physician work with the family of the dying patient, because cancer is not just an individual's illness but an illness that has profound impact on the whole family (Hansen & Frantz, 1984; Kosten et al., 1985). This approach will facilitate the management of bereavement and subsequent grief reactions. It will also reduce the guilt experienced by the family, as well as the potential for litigation.

A follow-up visit with the survivors is recommended because it offers the opportunity for closure. It enables the survivors to ask questions about the illness that they did not remember to ask at the time of death. It also allows them to reminisce with those who cared for the patient at the moment of death, an experience that can have lasting memories for them.

If the survivors appear to be struggling in their anticipatory grief during their visits before the death, or even after the death, they should be referred to support groups in the hospital (I Can Cope program) or to a support staff person, such as a clinical nurse specialist or a social worker.

Oncology teams should discuss in advance the way in which they will choose to interact with the family at the time of death (Clark & LaBeff, 1982).

Because the burnout rate is high among oncology staff, there should be some institutional support with periodic structured conferences, workshops, and occasional educational programs available to the staff (Fawzy et al., 1983; Mount, 1986).

Just as families grieve in their own ways, so do nurses and physicians after the loss of patients. Physicians work through their grief by resolving their feelings of responsibility and their survivor guilt by attending mortality rounds and "postmortems" (Vachon, 1987). Nurses, on the other hand, have their various ways of grieving. Some find satisfaction in keeping a "Last Moments Book" in which they record and capture the precious moments spent with the patient at the time of death. Others prefer to hold Psychosocial Autopsies in which they discuss the circumstances of the death, including the psychological and social dimensions of the patient's life and that of the family (Weisman & Kastenbaum, 1968). We recommend that the staff find some mutually agreeable way to structure some discussion of each death within the unit. Before this can be done, the administration must recognize the high risk for burnout and endorse support programs as a preventive of further staff attrition and as a valid program for continuing education (Koocher, 1979; Rainey et al., 1983).

Pediatric Service

This section on Pediatric Service includes discussion of the Pediatric Oncology Unit and the Pediatric Intensive Care Unit (PICU).

Types of illness and nature of death. Except for SIDS deaths, which are usually seen in the Emergency Room, most children's deaths result from leukemias, brain tumors, solid tumors, cystic fibrosis, or neuromuscular degeneration. The course of illness is usually chronic, and death may not occur for several months or years. But bereavement after the loss of a child following a long illness cannot be understood without knowledge of the reactions and events that precede the death.

The reaction following bereavement depends in great part on the management of the various phases of the child's illness, from the time of diagnosis to the last few moments before the death. This is an intense period in the family's life, during which the health team has a unique opportunity to intervene and neutralize the terrible impact of this calamity and the resulting burden on the parents. This can be done, as we shall see, by offering empathy, professional guidance, and consideration for the family, and by making them as comfortable as possible (Friedman et al., 1963; Richmond & Waisman, 1955; Sahler, 1978). Communication with the family is an essential and critical element in the treatment of the dying child, and any conflict that may arise in this communication can lead to complications in the grieving process (Heller & Schneider, 1977–1978).

The nature of the death may vary according to the locale of terminal care. If the children die at home, they are more likely to die from a hemorrhage, whereas if they die in the hospital, they are likely to have a complicated and lengthy demise. The reason for this is that the house staff often feels obligated to continue the care by ordering all sorts of tests and procedures while maintaining the child with intravenous equipment, transfusions, and life-support measures such as ventilators. The child, although faced with an inevitable death, has to endure the available technologies of modern medicine before eventually dying of sepsis or other complications. As the locale of the death seems to influence the type of death the child will have, so the type of death in turn has a profound impact on the subsequent bereavement reaction. Dying at home in a warm, supportive, and comfortable environment with familiar surroundings is far easier on the child. Complications are less likely to occur, and the death is more apt to be quick and painless.

Parental reactions. From the time of referral by the pediatrician to the oncology specialist, the parents begin a saga of pain, anxiety, and fear. Immediately after hearing the diagnosis of terminal illness, they react with shock, numbness, and disbelief. This reaction of denial is protective, since at first there is only so much that the family can absorb. The denial will gradually give way and completely drop by the time of death (Easson, 1980).

As the reality sets in, the family sometimes becomes critical of the referring physician for not having referred the case earlier. This tendency to scapegoat is not unusual and could be considered part of the coping process which involves giving way to anger. Nevertheless it often leaves the referring physician feeling helpless and frustrated (Pakes, 1979). From then on, parents go through the various phases of anticipatory grief as described in Chapter 6. In this section, we shall not repeat the various features of this type of grief, but we shall point out certain elements which characterize grieving for a dying child.

Besides feeling helpless and out of control, parents experience several other characteristic reactions. Guilt is particularly prominent in all cases (Miles & Demi, 1986) and can be overwhelming in some parents. This reaction leads to an extreme overindulgence toward the dying child, which must be curbed by the staff, because the child then begins to behave in unhealthy ways. Some parents believe that the illness came upon the family as a form of punishment for bad deeds and wrongdoings of the past (Rando, 1987). Sometimes, the illness waxes and wanes, the death appears imminent, then gives way to temporary improvement. When this occurs repeatedly over a prolonged period of time, the family sometimes gets detached prematurely, as in the "Lazarus Syndrome" described in Chapter 6. Subsequently a new form of resentment develops (Rando, 1987). In cases where parents watch in pain as their child dies a slow death from neuromuscular degeneration, they entertain some wishes and fantasies about killing their child in order to spare him and themselves further pain and suffering (Holroyd & Guthrie, 1979).

Another characteristic of the parental coping process is the need to search for some meaning in their child's illness (Craig, 1977; Miles & Demi, 1985). This search may go on for weeks or months and should be considered part of the grief process. Parents who find some meaning in a philosophy of life or religion generally make a better adjustment before and after the bereavement (Martinson et al., 1980; Spinetta et al., 1981).

Next to guilt, the most prominent emotion expressed by parents is that of anger. Not infrequently this anger will be projected onto the medical and nursing staff members, who become targets of their attacks. It is most important for the health team to realize that such anger is a nonspecific response to the stress of the illness, and that the anger is expressed to the nearest caregivers as the stress is being experienced (Easson, 1980; Goodell, 1980).

There is a wide spectrum of reactions among parents of dying children. We have only mentioned the most prominent and most significant to health professionals. For further details on parental reactions and coping, we recommend the studies by Binger et al., (1969), Kemler (1981), Kerner et al., (1979), Kreuger et al., (1981), Kupst et al., (1982), Lewis and Armstrong (1977–1978) and, specifically for cases of cystic fibrosis, Bywater (1981).

Management guidelines. It is most important to be open, honest, and direct with patients and their families from the beginning. Both parents should be included in all sessions giving vital information. There should be no secrets. Expect the family to express denial at first, absorbing the information in due time, as it becomes tolerable. The denial will gradually wear off and eventually be dropped by the time of death.

At the time of the initial diagnosis, it is advisable to encourage the family to get a second opinion. This frequently helps the family gain more confidence in the treating physician. It also reduces their guilt and anxiety by giving them the feeling that they have done everything possible within their power (Easson, 1970).

A feeling of hope must be maintained throughout the illness. This is not hope in the sense of expecting a cure, which would be unrealistic, but, on the contrary, in the sense of helping the family adopt a more realistic appreciation of the time remaining. It allows the family to develop an awareness of quality time and gives meaning within the context of ending the relationship with the child. This can best be done by keeping the family informed and promoting the appreciation of life remaining in new ways (Adams & Proulx, 1975; Foster et al., 1981). As one physician said about the feeling of hope, "I never give up before the patient does." This seems especially true for teenagers, who are totally future oriented. One teenager was still kidding about "going to the game next weekend" the day before he died.

Just as you tell the family what to expect before the death, you need to tell them what to expect after bereavement.

Attendance at the funeral by a member of the staff is always greatly appreciated and usually has a profound impact on the family. Some hospitals have encouraged this practice. It also helps the staff gain some perspective over the situation and bring a sense of closure. The reliance on some spiritual framework or personal life philosophy helps greatly. As one physician was reminded by his wife one day when he had lost several patients, "Who do you think you are? Remember, you just work in the vineyard!"

A follow-up visit should be offered between 3 to 6 weeks after the death. About half of the parents will respond to the offer. Sometimes they will bring gifts to the nurses in a gesture of gratitude. Others will come back to ask questions about the illness or simply reminisce with those who cared for the child. Others still will avoid the hospital completely. The follow-up visit can be extremely supportive and important for the subsequent grief process. It also enables the physician to make an important assessment as to how the grief work is progressing.

Bereaved parents should be told about self-support groups such as the Compassionate Friends (Burnell & Burnell, 1986).

Pediatric Intensive Care Unit (PICU)

Except for children dying of cancer, most of the cases admitted to the PICU are in danger of dying from one day to the next, many of the deaths resulting from trauma or complications from congenital anomalies. In many of these cases, there has been no time to work with the family, who are in shock from the time of admission. The level of uncertainty is intense, and the emotional demands placed on the staff are extreme (Vachon, 1987). One of the most difficult decisions to be made is when to stop life-support measures on a child whose chances for living a normal life are minimal. In all cases it is most important to remain in close communication with the family in order to avoid subsequent misunderstanding and conflict.

The best approach is to continually involve family members in the decision-making process (Evans, 1968; Green & Solnit, 1959). Even then, when the child's condition becomes clearly irreversible, the pediatrician is sometimes faced with the difficult task of telling the parents of the poor prognosis. The physician's position has been compared to the plight of Cassandra, the mythical Greek prophetess of doom who was cursed to see into the future and not to be believed. This has been referred to as the *Cassandra Prophecy phenomenon,* which is observed as in the prophecy, when the parents show an intense denial coupled with almost total disbelief, sometimes even displaying animosity toward the medical and nursing staff (Waller et al., 1979). In these cases, the staff will observe that when the parents are told of the child's poor chances, they "don't seem to hear or understand." An example was that of an eight-month-old infant with multiple congenital anomalies, who was being maintained on mechanical ventilation. Despite the child's deteriorating condition, the mother kept her conviction that medical science would produce a "cure." Both parents were determined to help the child "conquer" the problem, a goal that the medical and nursing staff considered totally unrealistic.

To prevent and to manage these difficult situations, the authors have suggested a set of guidelines as follows.

Management guidelines. Information concerning prognosis is best given when parents request such information. The staff should make a point that no one, however, can be certain about the future.

If parents are not asking for the information, but the medical staff feels that the family should know some information about the child's deteriorating condition, this should be presented tactfully and with sensitivity. At this point it is important to promise a therapeutic commitment "that everything possible will be done" and to insure continued communication.

When parents ask for further information, they should be asked what they already know and have heard from others. Then, the questions can be answered by building gradually upon their existing knowledge.

Should the denial expressed by parents continue to be strong, other members of the health team, such as nurses, social workers, or consulting psychiatrists should get involved.

The staff should become aware of their own impatience and become more tolerant of parents who suffer while watching their child die.

Sometimes, when the situation becomes hopeless, as in the case of a child who is declared already dead, or can only be maintained on a respirator, the parents continue to express denial by insisting on continued life support. It is important to maintain communication with gentle confrontation and avoid a court ruling. The goal is to reach an eventual consensus between the PICU team and the parents. It is only when careful attention is paid to these interpersonal relationships from the beginning that a working alliance can be achieved with the possible result of a mutually satisfying outcome (Waller et al., 1979).

Obstetrical Service

Types of illnesses and deaths. Acute grief reactions in the Obstetrical Service occur in the context of stillbirths, neonatal deaths, fetal deaths, or malformed infants. For a full discussion of grief reactions following stillbirths and neonatal deaths (Lewis, 1979), the reader is referred to Chapter 5 on Specific Losses. In this section we shall discuss only the reactions following miscarriages, abortions, fetal deaths, and the birth of a malformed baby.

Miscarriages.   Most physicians and nurses do not have any difficulty handling a patient after a miscarriage. The most common approach, however, is to remain at a purely intellectual level, giving details about the statistical probability of a recurrence versus a future successful pregnancy. However, that is not what the patient wants to hear in most cases. Future pregnancies certainly remain a concern for most women, but it may just ignore the most important aspect of the experience: the fact that these women have experienced a loss or an actual death. The reaction is likely to be particularly intense if the pregnancy was planned, the expectations were high, and the announcements to the community were loud and clear. In cases where the pregnancy was not planned or was unwanted, the miscarriage may precipitate feelings of guilt or relief. In any case, it is not therapeutic to minimize the experience by focusing on future pregnancies.

A miscarriage does involve the loss of a person, and therefore a certain amount of grief work must be done. In some cases, women take such an event in stride as "something that just happened" as an act of nature, readily accepting the miscarriage without further elaboration. In cases where a formed fetus has been expelled, there is mixed opinion as to whether or not the parents should be allowed to see the fetus. In some cases the experience enables the parents to focus on the reality of the loss and helps them say good-bye when they see the unborn baby (Worden, 1982). In other cases, just talking about the loss is sufficient, and this may be done in the clinic a few days after discharge from the hospital.

Abortion.   Although a grief reaction occurs in about 10 to 20 percent of women after an abortion, there is a tendency for most women to avoid discussing their feelings with anyone and to want to forget the whole experience (Burnell & Norfleet, 1987). There are many reasons for this. First, abortion remains even today as an unmentionable loss because of the persistent social stigma. Second, the experience reactivates feelings about a troubled relationship and about emotional conflicts with spouses, lovers, or parents. In the case of teenagers, they show a strong reluctance to talk about it. The pregnancy usually reflects a conflict in the mother-daughter relationship, in that the adolescent is having a difficult time in accepting her dependent status on the parents and is using the pregnancy to achieve independence (Bright, 1987). Later, these teenagers seem to express their feelings by replacing the loss with another pregnancy (Horowitz, 1978). Much can be done to address the emotional concerns and conflicts by providing a support program, using a group format or assigning a support staff person to the adolescent during labor and delivery (Daniels & Manning, 1983). Sometimes, post abortion counseling can be very helpful (Burnell et al., 1972).

Fetal death. The course of a normal delivery is straightforward and uncomplicated. The mother is well prepared, receives simple and direct instructions and education, then gets support in the delivery room, on the ward and at follow-up. But in the case of an abnormal delivery, such as a known fetal death, the mother will require more extensive help and support.

Despite the conscious knowledge of the fetal death, the mother will maintain some hope for a normal, healthy infant. This denial will be maintained until the dead baby is born.

Whether the mother should see the dead baby is still an area of controversy. In general, if the baby is not grossly deformed, it is desirable for her to see the baby (Lippman & Carlson, 1977), and if the mother is hesitant, she should be gently encouraged and informed of the importance of this experience. She should be prepared to meet with a variety of people, including personnel from the Office of Decedent Affairs, the Pathology Department, and the funeral home. Nurses and physicians should provide continuous support for both parents during the grief process, making arrangements for follow-up by social workers in the outpatient clinic. If the cause of fetal death had a genetic etiology, arrangements for genetic counseling should be made.

In the case of teenagers, nurses can be especially helpful by providing emotional support and forecasting the typical responses to loss that the adolescent and family might have, including rage and guilt. The tendency for parents to blame the adolescent for such a loss is very common, despite education about pregnancy loss and grief; but it can be greatly diminished by a nurse's presence and support. By predicting such "blame the victim" responses from the teenager's mother, the nurse can help the adolescent immunize herself against feeling a loss of control usually provoked by the blame (Worlow, 1978).

Malformed infants. The same issues of viewing the infant and giving support to the parents apply in cases of a distressed or malformed infant. But in the case of a distressed baby, the situation is more complex because the infant may live or die. Staff members usually experience more stress because of the additional demands put upon them. Monitoring of the mother's responses is a delicate task. She cannot be allowed to venture too far in her anticipatory grief or in her belief that her baby will be dead. After delivery of a malformed, yet viable baby, the mother will grieve the loss of the normal infant she expected.

In the delivery room the staff must be prepared to deal with the high level of tension and anxiety associated with the delivery of a malformed baby. The news of a well-formed baby is not announced, and the parents begin to grieve as soon as they suspect something is wrong. The diagnosis of a tragic birth should be made in the delivery room. Both the father and the mother should be given the most concrete and accurate information available at the time. The physician who gives this information may have to repeat it several times before the mother leaves the hospital. Frequently the information is not heard and not registered fully by the mother in shock. Therefore the information should be simple and straightforward, such as, "Your baby is small and has an atypical heartbeat; that is all we can tell you now; we need to do further diagnostic testing; we will get back to you; and as soon as we know something more we will tell you" (Lippman & Carlson, 1977).

When back on the obstetrical floor, it is advisable to have a nurse designated and assigned to give further care and emotional support as well as help to coordinate and interpret all the information given to the mother. This nurse should create an atmosphere of open communication with both parents, providing additional education as needed. Thus she can facilitate ventilation of grief feelings and discussion of problems centering on the infant (Hagen, 1974).

In all of these cases the mother will require additional education, open and honest information, and further psychosocial support by medical, nursing, and social work staff. Later referral for further care and counseling may be necessary (Lippman & Carlson, 1977; see Appendix D).

Medical Service

In the Medical Service, deaths occur at a fairly significant rate, depending on the type (public versus private) and the size of the hospital. In most cases the families turn to the staff for information about treatment, causes of death, and mostly for reassurance that "everything that could be done was done" (Green & Goldberg, 1986).

Circumstances of the death. In the majority of cases there are warning signs and clues about impending death several days and weeks before the critical period (U.S. Dept. of HEW, 1978). Theoretically, this should enable the physician to prepare the family for the potential outcome of death and provide the staff with many opportunities to intervene with those who are to be bereaved (Osterweis, 1984). How much a family can be helped at this stage usually depends on how comfortable the staff is in dealing with the immediate post-death situation. Health professionals undergo a certain maturation in their attitudes and responses to death as they work with dying patients over the years, gradually becoming immunized against the initial trauma of losing patients and increasingly aware of the need to interact with the families. This is particularly true for the family practitioners, who are well aware of the importance of maintaining a relationship with the family in subsequent years.

Generally, deaths that occur suddenly and unexpectedly in the Medical Service always precipitate a crisis (Glaser & Strauss, 1968). The fact that the death was not anticipated immediately raises many questions among the staff and family. There is a prevailing feeling of defeat, a sense of inadequacy and, not infrequently, some guilt feelings. The fear of malpractice always looms in the background. With all of these feelings and conflicts, it is not surprising that the behavior toward families is somewhat inhibited and lacks spontaneity and warmth. A demonstration of caring after the death is thought by some professionals to represent an admission of guilt for negligence. This explains why some physicians are reluctant to telephone or write to the family, again thinking that this additional step might raise suspicion about their level of concern. However, our experience tells us after talking to hundreds of families over the years that the follow-up telephone call or office visit is greatly appreciated by the survivors.

In cases where dying is slow, gradual, prolonged, and difficult, as in hopeless medical conditions, the experience is equally stressful for families and staff members. When death finally occurs, everyone feels a sense of relief.

Management guidelines. In addition to the general guidelines mentioned in previous chapters, the following specific suggestions apply to the Medical Service.

It is wise to keep in close communication with the family while the patient is terminally ill. This will facilitate any interaction with the survivors at the time of death. Whether the death occurs gradually or suddenly, it is now considered good practice to offer the survivor a follow-up appointment to discuss any questions or feelings surrounding the care or the circumstances and causes of death (Osterweis, 1984). In some cases, where circumstances prevent the family from coming in, or if there is some reluctance or objection to scheduling a visit, a telephone call might be appropriate and helpful.

In cases where the decision to turn off the respirator has been made, it is often helpful for the physician or nurse to remain present in the room for 5 or 10 minutes and to hold hands with the family while remaining quiet.

It is usually desirable to give a brief explanation of the circumstances of the death without elaborating in great detail. Something like the following is sufficient: "Your wife died 15 minutes ago; she had some chest pain, her heart stopped, and she died without suffering." After the explanation, it is best to stop, observe any reaction, and provide emotional support with attentive listening.

Obviously, each case will be different and will call for judgment, timing, and sensitivity. These guidelines only serve as basic reminders about a few essential points. They are not a substitute for the professional's judgment, empathy, and sense of timing.

Surgical Service

Deaths in the Surgical Service fall into two large categories, those that are unexpected and those that are expected. Among unexpected deaths are cases involving severe trauma, cases of surgical complications such as massive intractable bleeding, and cases of elective surgery that run into anesthesia problems. Among expected deaths are those of cancer illnesses with metastases and those of postoperative complications developed after trauma.

Many surgeons will admit that they do not feel comfortable dealing with death because, as one surgeon said, "For us, death is the enemy." Death represents a reminder that one has failed or has been defeated (Vachon, 1987). Feelings of inadequacy and failure probably account for the surgeon's anxiety in dealing with the death and bereavement situation. Surgeons speak of an "acceptable mortality rate" for various types of surgical interventions as a way of dealing with their feelings surrounding death cases. For example, the acceptable mortality rate for most intra-abdominal surgeries is between 3 and 5 percent, and for pancreatic cancer surgery it is around 20 percent. In the bereavement situation the surgeon comes face-to-face with another reminder of failure and, sometimes, the feeling that the family has been let down. Most surgeons, however, are very careful about warning and preparing families for all possible risks before the surgery. In cases of cancer, many patients are often reported to have an "intuitive sense" about the outcome of the surgery when they ask the surgeon about the results. In response to a surgeon announcing, "I'm sorry, Mrs. Smith, we found that the tumor spread to your liver," the answer will often be, "I thought (or I knew) you'd say this."

Dealing with a patient's family is never easy. Some surgeons refer their cases back to the family physician or to an oncologist for follow-up before the death occurs. Others insist on staying with the case to provide some support to the family. In most Surgical Services there is little or no opportunity to talk about the psychological or social circumstances of the death cases or bereavement problems. Mortality rates or autopsy findings are the most common ways of referring to a death.

Nurses do not as a rule discuss their feelings about losing patients in surgery except on an informal basis among themselves. They do not feel competent or responsible for approaching bereaved families, leaving this task to the surgeon. However, it has been noted that families have difficulty communicating with surgeons and are often afraid to ask questions, fearing that their confusion or questions will indicate a lack of trust (Osterweis, 1984).

One attempt to solve this problem was tested at the Memorial Sloan-Kettering Cancer Center in New York where a nurse-counselor met with patients the day before surgery to determine what information patients want their families to know. During the day of surgery the nurse served as the link between the surgeons in the operating room and the families in the waiting room. This kind of communication reduced fears and misconceptions which family members can build up and store about the illness and the surgery, thus getting further clarification on what the surgeon had already told them (Watson & Hickey, 1984).

When surgery for life-threatening conditions is performed, families wait anxiously. At those times, a nurse functioning as a liaison communicator between the surgical team and the family can be very therapeutic in allaying fear, anxieties, and hostile feelings.

Several surgeons who were interviewed volunteered that they would welcome an opportunity to discuss death and bereavement

problems as well as management guidelines at departmental conferences. It is our feeling that with the increasing awareness about these
issues, surgical departments may eventually become more receptive
to presentations of death and post-death reactions during their departmental meetings.

Management guidelines.   The staff dealing with expected deaths
should refer to the guidelines on anticipatory grief in Chapter 6. For
assistance in dealing with unexpected death, refer to the section on
unanticipated grief also in Chapter 6. In rare cases of death in surgery,
the nurse coordinator described above may be very effective in helping
the surgeon manage the acute grief situation (Watson & Hickey, 1984).

Geriatric Service

Not all hospitals have a Geriatric Service. However, the following
observations and recommendations would apply to the general medical
ward where elderly patients are admitted for acute and subacute care.
Many of these patients are admitted as transfers from institutions such
as nursing homes or retirement communities. Women for the most
part tend to be widows who rely on adult children or friends for emotional support and help before and during the dying experience.

Types and circumstances of deaths.   Most of the deaths that occur
in Geriatric Service result from the complications of chronic conditions
such as heart disease, cancer, stroke, kidney or lung disease. Because
death is an expected event in old age, families do not usually react
with surprise or shock as they do when younger people die (Kalish &
Reynolds, 1981; Weisman, 1972).

When elderly patients are admitted in a terminally ill condition,
they are frequently confused or comatose. This makes communication
very difficult, and as a result there is relatively little or no communication with the staff, who may then feel resentful for having to give
so much care without receiving any gratitude or recognition for their
efforts (Kalish, 1985). In a way, these patients are functioning as
"nonpersons," and the general feeling from relatives, friends, and staff
is that they have outlived a useful life. Furthermore, these patients
are often perceived as having little or no social value left in the re-
mainder of their lives, therefore making life-sustaining measures at
this point less critical for them than for younger people (Kalish, 1985).

For these reasons, the staff may not wish to apply heroic measures of resuscitation, and when families are consulted about this issue, they usually will agree to recommend a DNR (Do Not Resuscitate) order in case of cardiac arrest.

Reactions of survivors. The most important feeling that adult children can convey to their dying parents is that they are not being abandoned at the time of dying. However, expressed reactions and feelings vary a great deal.

The death of a parent has many meanings for adult children. For some, the loss of a second parent seems to be particularly more difficult to bear. One speculation is that it reactivates the loss of the other parent and seems to carry a certain feeling of finality and transition in one's life (Horowitz et al., 1984). For others, there is relatively little reaction or grieving because a certain detachment has already taken place over the last few years, and current jobs and responsibilities do not allow much time for grieving (Owen et al., 1982–1983; Sanders 1979–1980).

In view of the above studies and observations, the staff should expect a spectrum of reactions varying from what might appear to be a relative absence of feelings to a surprisingly intense reaction. Sometimes, family conflicts and rivalries emerge at the bedside of a dying parent. These conflicts may have been dormant for years, and therefore it is not realistic for the hospital staff to get involved and expect some resolution of these tensions because of the special circumstances of a dying parent (Osterweis, 1984).

It is feasible and reasonable to be sure that everyone is notified, that all family members have an opportunity to say good-bye, and that they have a part in the decision-making process when possible. However, the staff should not put too much pressure on family members to resolve issues about DNR orders or questions about autopsies and organ transplantation. It is important to be as diplomatic as possible and to treat each family member with as much flexibility as possible. This approach will help mitigate further tensions and reduce the potential for hostility and anger displaced toward staff members.

Home care. A few words should be said about the increasing trend toward home care for the elderly. The home care nurse and public health nurse are now being assigned to patients who prefer to die at home. Both patients and families have great expectations and make heavy emotional demands on these nurses during the period of anticipatory grief.

The nurse must retain a sense of control and competence through knowledge of grief dynamics. This involves remembering to conceptualize the care of the patient in terms of a family illness, which by definition must include all members of the household. An assessment of the family dynamics and communication system must be made. Usually there is time to make such an assessment because the patient's terminal illness lasts several months (Turnbull, 1986).

If the family is in conflict with the dying patient, there is an opportunity to intervene and resolve any unfinished business before the death and bereavement. This may require meeting with other members of the family, separately at first, then jointly with the dying patient. The family must be educated about the potential impact of unfinished business after the death experience. It is therefore in the interest of all of them to accept supportive assistance in dealing with unfinished business during the remaining months to reach some sense of peace before death occurs (Jacobsen, 1984).

The premise for the home care nurse to keep in mind is the need to resolve unfinished business so that anticipatory grief can proceed along its normal course to prevent an outcome of pathological grief for the wife or any other family members.

Management guidelines. Whenever possible, all family members should be invited to be present at the time of death. Most physicians see their role as notifying the family, providing a brief explanation, and conveying their feelings of regret. Most of the support is likely to come from the nursing and social work staff who have been present during the preceding period. Family members are especially appreciative of assistance with keeping the patient well-groomed during the dying period, keeping the patient as physically comfortable as possible, and staying with the patient to avoid the feeling of abandonment at the time of dying. Otherwise, family members expect to have their questions answered honestly.

What has been said in the guidelines for the Medical Service also applies here. A follow-up phone call to the family will very likely be appreciated, particularly if the physician has an ongoing relationship with the family. The social worker is also a valuable support member when assisting with appropriate referrals to community agencies for legal, fiscal, and administrative help during the days immediately following the death.

IN THE CLINIC

Assessment and Support of Bereaved Patients

Bereaved individuals are seen in the physician's office under two sets of circumstances. In the first instance, a bereaved person may be seen in a follow-up visit at the invitation of the physician, usually 2 to 6 weeks after the loss of a family member. During the visit, the doctor will encourage the patient to ask questions about the illness or the death, or findings of the autopsy. The physician will also assess the progress of the grief process and perhaps reminisce a little bit about the patient who died.

Another circumstance that brings a bereaved person into the physician's office is when that person presents multiple somatic and psychosomatic complaints, and when a history of bereavement occurred in the preceding 3 years. Sometimes, the complaints and symptoms coincide with the anniversary of the death. This may be more likely in certain ethnic groups of the working class in which somatization of the grief is culturally approved. Extensive workups for such patients are generally unnecessary and sometimes even harmful (Kleinman, 1982). It should be noted that in many cases the patient may not volunteer the history and that it is up to the physician to be alert enough to raise that possibility. A few pertinent questions during the comprehensive history will elicit the grief process, such as "Have you lost any member of your family in recent years? If so, whom?" When a history of loss is elicited in the absence of positive organic findings, the primary care physician must decide whether or not to continue seeing the patient with the goal of relieving the complaints and symptoms with a counseling approach or whether it is more appropriate to refer the patient for follow-up counseling (see Chapter 11 on When and Where to Refer).

If the physician decides to follow the patient in subsequent visits, the doctor-patient interaction must be redefined with an explanation to the patient that there will be further inquiry about the history of loss (DeVaul et al., 1979). In the course of these visits, the physician can encourage the patient to discuss all aspects of the loss (a method which has been called re-grief therapy), an approach which will encourage the patient to relive the experience of the loss cognitively and emotionally (Volkan, 1975). Contrary to what is usually believed, these sessions do not have to take much time, particularly after the relationship is established. In fact, patients will usually adapt to whatever time frame the doctor chooses.

The main technique used is *attentive listening,* a method which consists of encouraging the patient to talk about the loss, including circumstances of the death, the illness, and the characteristics of the deceased. This task is probably easier for a physician who was not the one caring for the member who died. It is important to allow the bereaved patient to feel the sadness, anger, guilt, and any other emotion that may be associated with the death so that eventually the patient can acknowledge and accept the reality of the loss (Schmidt & Messner, 1975).

Once mobilized by these emotions, the grieving process can proceed on its own toward resolution with continued supportive listening (DeVaul et al., 1979). The number of sessions may vary, but they are usually limited to five or six over the span of a few weeks. Referrals to self-support groups in the community should also be encouraged. If it appears that the bereaved patient becomes "stuck" in the grieving process, seemingly unable to show any improvement or remobilization with this approach, then a psychiatric referral should be considered.

Medications for Bereaved Patients

The use of medications for the bereaved remains a matter of controversy. Although in clinical practice grieving individuals often receive sedative/hypnotics for insomnia and anxiolytics for restlessness and agitation (Hackett, 1974), a panel of experts has recommended caution and restraint (Consensus Panel, 1984; Goldberg et al., 1986). They specifically warned against the prolonged use of sleeping pills and long-acting benzodiazepines in the elderly, who are prone to developing problems of confusion, disorientation, memory impairment, motor incoordination, and loss of balance (Solomon et al., 1979). When drugs are used, they should be used for a short time, no longer than 3 weeks, preferably intermittently, with skipping of nightly dosages after one or two good nights of sleep. Only the smallest effective dosage should be administered (Hollister, 1972).

There are no good studies to date that prove or negate the usefulness of drugs in bereavement, whether on a short- or long-term basis. While some experts reject the use of medications (Lindemann, 1944; Morgan, 1980) for the pain of normal grief on the grounds that it might inhibit, impede, or delay the grief process, others feel that if the symptoms are severe enough to be incapacitating and to warrant a diagnosis of clinical depression, the use of antidepressants might be quite helpful (Shuchter, 1982; Shuchter & Zisook, 1987). The problem remains of deciding when the symptoms are severe enough to warrant such a diagnosis (refer to Chapter 4 for criteria of pathological grief and differential diagnosis). Assuming that the bereaved patient has a full depressive syndrome, aggressive treatment then has several major effects. First, it prevents future medical problems, such as psychosomatic illnesses. Second, it enables the bereaved to better cope with the grief process, thus preventing further immobilization and dysfunction. Third, it relieves the characteristic acute and intolerable separation anxiety at the beginning of the grief process.

Management guidelines. In the initial phase of bereavement, a short-acting sedative, such as triazolam, might help with severe insomnia, prevent a state of exhaustion, and avert cardiovascular complications in susceptible individuals.

When using a sedative/hypnotic, it is best to use the smallest dose possible, recommending intermittent use for no more than 2 or 3 weeks (Hollister, 1972).

In the elderly, it is best to choose drugs that have more rapid elimination in the lowest possible doses.

If the criteria for clinical depression are met, treat the bereaved with antidepressants (Jacobs, 1982) or refer for psychiatric consultation.

Chapter 9

SPECIAL ISSUES AND CONCERNS ABOUT TERMINAL CARE, DEATH, AND BEREAVEMENT

Attitudes and behaviors of health professionals toward the death experience have been noted to have an impact on the subsequent course of bereavement (Lindemann, 1944). Whether they like it or not, physicians and nurses have become the "masters of death-of-the-moment," and in this process, they control not only the circumstances of death but also the attitudes of patients and survivors (Aries, 1974). They come to expect from patients an "acceptance style of living while dying" with the accent on "acceptable." An acceptable death is a death that is accepted and tolerated both by survivors and professionals. The less emotional display is witnessed, the more it is acceptable.

However, the dying experience, especially with today's advanced technology, triggers some strong emotions and conflicts in both survivors and caregivers. In many cases the end result is a shirking of an "embarrassingly graceless dying" so that dying becomes a solitary and shameful experience (Aries, 1974). The bereavement reaction that follows is dominated by guilt which is often heard in statements like, "We should not have put him through all this" or "We should have let her die in peace."

Concerns and issues that play a role in pre-terminal phases of dying are different for families and health professionals. Initially, all are concerned with the saving or prolonging of life. But as the patient's condition worsens, each professional begins to think and react in different ways, depending on past experiences, values, and knowledge about the death experience.

Because of advances in medical technology and increasing longevity in the last few decades, health professionals are increasingly faced with difficult decisions and choices in treating their patients. These decisions and alternative choices have given rise to specific issues and problems which cause both stress and conflict. The way in which health professionals solve problems and resolve conflicts will influence their intervention with bereaved families (Kasper, 1959). For this reason, it is important that they understand the underlying issues faced by each discipline in the pre- and post-death period. We shall discuss these concerns under the following subheadings: 1) Ethical Issues, 2) Legal Issues, 3) Personal Concerns and Conflicts, and 4) Burnout and Coping Strategies.

ETHICAL ISSUES

People today live longer than at any other time in history. Some live on respirators or on kidney dialysis machines, while others linger on with transplanted organs, artificial hearts, or chemotherapy. Others simply become terminally ill or live on with little or no brain function as their bodies continue to age.

In the case of the terminally ill, the physician is faced with increasing demands by patients and their families to provide care with procedures that are beyond what is necessary or, in some cases, desirable. Most of these patients will die, but not without first receiving aggressive medical interventions.

The general feeling from the public is that death can be avoided indefinitely if a patient is given the proper medical treatment. This attitude is often reinforced by health professionals themselves, who generally feel that "to care for" is "to cure." However, it is this attitude that often leads physicians to feel helpless in their treatment of the terminally ill patient. To overcome this feeling of helplessness, physicians and nurses overtreat their patients, using machines, drugs, and procedures rather than engage in personal contact with patients. Anything that will avoid confrontation with death is deemed more desirable (Beauchamp & Perlin, 1978).

Difficult decisions cannot be put off and must be faced by dealing with patients and families. Physicians themselves demonstrate their fear by showing their reluctance to tell a patient about a terminal diagnosis, even though, according to the law of informed consent, they are supposed to do so (Humphry & Wickett, 1986). The doctrine of informed consent sets a dual responsibility for the physician: 1) a duty to disclose to the patient the nature and ramification of available treatments, and 2) the duty to obtain the patient's consent to any treatment prior to its administration. But recent judicial decisions have gone further, extending the responsibility of the physician to inform the patient adequately about treatment alternatives as an integral part of the informed consent (Humphry & Wickett, 1986).

The problems associated with extended life continue to increase each decade as longevity increases. In 1949, 50 percent of the population died in hospitals, medical centers or nursing homes. In 1958, this figure rose to 61 percent. In the 1980s, 80 percent of chronically ill patients died in institutions (President's Commission for the Study of Ethical Problems in Medicine and Biomedical and Behavioral Research, 1983).

While the dying patient clings to life, many questions arise for staff and families. "When should the patient be told of a terminal diagnosis?" "At what point does he have the right to refuse treatment?" "How long should life-support measures be continued?" "When are innovative treatments applicable and appropriate?"

Even when answers to the above questions are clear, who makes the decision? There are no fixed guidelines at present.* And in the case of a patient lingering between life and death, this limbo state can be prolonged. "For as long as [the machines] circulate, oxygenate, and cleanse the patient's blood, his organs will continue many of their normal functions" (Kelly, 1958). Although there is more to a person than organs and brain function, the point of death has been officially defined in biological terms. The most recent proposal for a definition of death, the Uniform Determination of Death Act, does not take into account such things as personality, memory, and emotions, much to the dismay of ethicists (Humphry & Wickett, 1986). For health professionals to rely solely on technology and to make decisions based primarily on biological function is to disregard the social and emotional aspects of life that give a true and unique meaning to existence itself. The physician and hospital staff who struggle with these decisions

---

*In Canada official guidelines have been published in Law Reform Commission of Canada. Report on Euthanasia, Aiding Suicide, and Cessation of Treatment (1982), Ottawa: Ministry of Supply and Services Canada.

must be knowledgeable in these areas if they are to be of help to patients and their families. For further in-depth coverage of these subjects the reader is referred to the works of Abrams and Brucker (1983), Barnard (1980), Humphry and Wickett (1986), Kapp (1982) and Kelly (1958).

Legislation regarding Living Wills was passed in California in 1976. The Natural Death Act now exists in 36 states. A new piece of legislation is currently being introduced in California, enlarging on the Natural Death Act. It is currently referred to as the *Humane and Dignified Death Act*. It retains the safeguards of the California Natural Death Act, but it adds the provision that the patient may make a voluntary, competent, and informed decision to request that a physician aid in his or her death in the least active manner. It also stipulates that two physicians must certify that the patient is terminally ill and will die within 6 months, that he must be competent, and while competent, he must have named an agent to effect the request for aid-in-dying. There are provisions built in to prevent intervention by family members. The act will protect physicians from civil or criminal liability if they exercise mercy at the patient's request.

More recently, the New Jersey Supreme Court has ruled in three separate, simultaneous decisions that hospitals and nursing homes *are required* to stop life-prolonging treatment to honor the wishes of a dying or hopelessly comatose patient or the wishes of a qualified family member (*Medical Ethics Advisor*, 1987). The three patients involved in the rulings were Nancy Ellen Jobes, Hilda M. Peter, and Eileen Farrell.

Briefly, the Jobes case is that of a woman who was involved in an automobile accident that injured her and killed her fetus. During the operation to remove the fetus, Jobes sustained a severe loss of oxygen and blood flow to the brain. She never regained consciousness and suffered what the court called "massive and irreversible damage to the part of her brain that controls thought and movement." She remained comatose for more than 6 years before she was allowed to die by withdrawal of food and water supplied by tubes. Like Jobes, Hilda Peter, a sixty-five-year-old woman in a nursing home, had been in a coma since suffering from a stroke in 1984, a condition which, according to the doctors, could go on for years through an artificial feeding device. Eileen Farrell, thirty-seven, suffered from amyotrophic lateral sclerosis, also known as Lou Gehrig's disease. She was living at home, was competent, and wanted to have her respirator discontinued. While on the respirator, however, she died while the court was still reviewing her case. Nevertheless, the Supreme Court decided to proceed with her case "because of the extreme importance of the issue." The Court held that the patient's rights outweighed the four traditional state interests in such cases, namely, preserving life, preventing suicide, safeguarding the integrity of the medical profession, and protecting innocent third parties. Because of the widespread influence of the New Jersey Supreme Court in right-to-die issues, one famous precedent being its landmark decision in 1976 in the case of Karen Ann Quinlan, it is expected to have major significance on the national scene.

Despite all of the legal and ethical problems connected with allowing a person to die (passive euthanasia), public opinion and courts are now agreed that, in general, it is inhumane to keep people alive when they are in a hopeless condition, when they are suffering, and when they wish to die (Humphry & Wickett, 1986). Nevertheless, there is considerable restraint and reticence about discussing the subject in daily clinical practice. However, discussions should take place in multidisciplinary conferences in an open atmosphere. Medical staff members should become knowledgeable about current and local requirements of Living Wills in their states so that they can answer questions from patients and families (Storch, 1982).

Another thorny question that plagues physicians and nurses is when to issue an order for DNR (Do Not Resuscitate). The problem is to decide when to forego or forestall life-sustaining measures. In this regard, families will ask many questions about informed consent, duty, privacy, and death itself.

As far as patients are concerned, it is important to remember that they want a death with dignity, a death without prolonged suffering and humiliation; in other words, they want "a good death." And so do their families. If the death is uncomplicated, their grief will be greatly facilitated because they will not experience the pain of guilt and remorse. The physician and his assistants have a duty to help families in reaching a realistic and mature decision. Whenever possible, the professional staff can rely on their knowledge of the patient's wishes and intents. When that is unclear, they should inquire about decisions made by responsible family members. Sometimes the problem becomes complicated if various family members disagree on the best course of action in deciding on permission to use or not to use a DNR order. When that happens, the best course of action is determined by what the patient's wishes were, as expressed to family members.

Another concern in recent times is the increasing cost of care and the necessary monitoring of the utilization of hospital beds. Added to this is the limited amount of resources in certain areas of care, such as kidney dyalysis and heart transplantation. The questions faced by clinicians and administrators are extremely delicate. "Who shall receive the treatment if it is limited?" "How long should the treatment be available?" "Who shall decide?" The responses to these questions become a "painful prescription for rationing hospital care" and a direct confrontation with another aspect of the euthanasia problem (Aaron & Schwartz, 1984; Davis & Aroskar, 1983).

A physician who senses the potential for malpractice liability would do well to contact the hospital risk manager or attorney and inquire how to use the hospital chart to document statements that would protect against liability (Rando, 1984). Such written documentation should include justifications for *why* and *how* the decision was reasonable and acceptable.

Ethical and legal questions are continuously raised by staff members and families dealing with death and dying issues. These questions undoubtedly have an impact on subsequent grief reactions, particularly if they are not dealt with in an open and knowledgeable manner. These questions are a good basis for further discussion in case conferences as well, since they do not have an absolute black-and-white answer. Rando (1984) and Veatch (1977, 1981) have grouped the typical questions as follows:

As They Relate to the Patient.

1. Should the patient be told about his/her terminal diagnosis, and if so, when?
2. Does a patient have a right to die and a right to refuse treatment?
3. Does a patient have the right to actively end his/her own life? (commit suicide)
4. How binding is the Living Will, the Natural Death Act?

As They Relate to the Family.

1. Under what conditions can the family make treatment decisions for the patient?
2. Should families be put in the position of making decisions that will result in guilt for them?

There are no easy answers to the questions. But the more the staff knows about the patient's family, its beliefs, its dynamics, its strengths and weaknesses, the more they will be able to arrive at a consensus with the family and the patient.

As They Relate to Health Professionals.

1. To what extent should health professionals be involved in the decision making for orders of DNR?
2. Should hospital staff members be involved if the family chooses to have passive (or active) euthanasia?
3. Under what circumstances should health professionals agree to withhold treatment?
4. Is the Living Will easy or difficult to interpret? (Eisendrath and Jonsen, 1983)
5. Can an order for DNR stand if a conflict exists on religious or philosophical grounds?

The staff can use these questions to promote open discussion and to help resolve some of the differences on these issues. This practice will also prevent conflicts from being internalized and from resurfacing at a later time. But it does require an awareness and an acceptance that sharing diagnostic information and taking the time to reassess staff expectations in terminal cases are as important to patients as taking care of their physical needs (Hamric, 1977).

As They Relate to Institutions.

1. What is the hospital responsibility in preserving and maintaining dignity in the dying patient?
2. What is the hospital responsibility in responding to the patient's wishes for euthanasia or refusal for treatment?
3. How do terminal care or ethics committees function in allowing or declining life-sustaining treatment? Are patients' wishes and interests overshadowed by the committee's "group think" mentality? (Lo, 1987)
4. What precautions does the hospital provide to protect the health professional in matters of life-and-death decisions?

LEGAL ISSUES

Most physicians today are acutely aware of the potential for malpractice liability in cases of death in the hospital (Rabin & Rabin, 1970). This awareness plays a role in the attitude assumed toward families at the time of death and during the post-death period. Physicians are frequently haunted by thoughts about whether all that could have been done and should have been done was in fact carried out. Fears about errors of omission or commission remain a concern. Such fears can create doubts in the minds of the best physicians. This is especially likely to occur with the death of a young patient or with an unexpected death.

As has been noted, physicians sometimes feel that if they demonstrate an overattentive or solicitous attitude toward a grieving family, they might become suspect of wanting to cover up some deficiency in the treatment of the patient. Nurses do not share these concerns and therefore feel freer in their attempts to reach out to families at the time of death and during the post-death period. But these concerns should be shared between nurses and physicians to promote more effective communication with the families. Most physicians, however, do not have a problem in extending their warm feelings and in giving support when they know the family well.

PERSONAL CONCERNS AND CONFLICTS

In cases of unexpected death or the loss of a young patient when death could not be predicted or prevented, physicians often develop feelings of inadequacy or incompetence, as well as the sense of having lost control and power (Vachon, 1987).

Shifts of feelings among medical and nursing staff are not uncommon in cases where there is a downhill course, where the medical management is precarious and delicate, as in advanced kidney disease, cancer, or deteriorating chronic conditions (Benoliel, 1974; Stedeford, 1983).

The medical staff sometimes feel that the family blames them, even if there is no evidence for this, except for their own guilt feelings. This mental attitude, along with the fear of liability, can inhibit the process of reaching out to the family, whether by phone or by letter. Yet, despite these understandable reservations, contacts and telephone calls are extremely important to the family because they demonstrate concern and have an important function in helping the family cope with the post-death situation (Osterweis, 1984).

Physicians have also learned to protect themselves by "not getting involved," instead adopting an attitude of "detached concern" that they have learned in the course of their medical training (Fox, 1957). In the case of elderly patients who have not been known for a long time, that is not difficult to do. But in cases where the family and the patient are well known to the physician, it is more difficult to remain uninvolved. Yet, it is healthy for the physician to allow the display of some feeling. This is especially true in dealing with parents of dying children. By virtue of an authoritative position, the physician is often put on a pedestal. If this posture is accepted, the family learns to expect Godlike actions and miracles (Spikes, 1979; Spikes & Holland, 1975). It may be easier for physicians to admit that, at times, they do not know the answers about the prognosis or the reasons for the death (Connerford, 1974).

Nurses, too, tend to distance themselves and avoid contacts with dying patients and their families by moving from job to job or by transferring from one service to another (Quint, 1967). On the other hand, some nurses find reward in working in situations where death is a frequent occurrence, as in the ICU, leukemia, and kidney dialysis units. But they too develop a strategy of maintaining a significant social distance in their interaction with dying patients and their families (Glaser & Strauss, 1965).

Both physicians and nurses experience feelings of futility and failure in dealing with patients during a prolonged dying situation that has demanded considerable time, energy, and clinical effort. This is partly explained by the fact that their medical and nursing training has emphasized the saving of lives at all cost rather than the comfort and emotional well-being of patients and families. It is also explained by the fact that they do not have sufficient knowledge to deal with the anticipatory grief of dying patients and families.

There is also the fear of losing professional respect and competence if they engage in negligent behavior or if they make errors in judgment. These errors are even more likely to occur in life-and-death situations where critical decisions have to be made quickly and continuously (Vachon, 1987).

Another source of conflict occurs when physicians and nurses have to deal with uncertainty. Davis (1966) described two kinds of uncertainty: one he calls the *real uncertainty*, which is uncertainty associated with the facts of the clinical picture; and the second, which is the *uncertainty conveyed to the family* despite the known facts of the patient's condition. For example, parents of a dying child may be told that "we don't really have the clinical evidence required for an accurate prognosis." This statement serves to avoid involvement with the family, given the rationale that there is no time or energy to devote to the family at the time. The real questions are: "When should the family be told? When should the patient be told?"

The telling of the prognosis, according to Glaser and Strauss (1965), opens up a new context of awareness that sets off new types of interaction between patients, families, and staff. Thus, the authors have described four types of awareness depending on whether:

> the patient is not aware but others are (closed aware-
> ness);
> the patient suspects others know, and he tries to con-
> firm it or invalidate it (suspected awareness);
> both the patient and others know, but both pretend
> that they are unaware (mutual-pretense awareness);
> and
> both patient and others know and acknowledge their
> awareness, acting openly and appropriately (open
> awareness).

It is easy to see how all of the above situations can lead to more or less comfortable feelings among health professionals, patients, and families just before the death situation. For example, for patients who are unaware, noticing that their families are grieving too early can be very distressing. When the patient becomes aware, he is then plunged into the stage of dying as described by Kubler-Ross (1960).

BURNOUT AND COPING STRATEGIES

The stress created by dealing with frequent deaths and repeated grief reactions can lead to a burnout syndrome (Kalish, 1985; Shubin, 1978; Vachon, 1987; Worden, 1982). Typically, the syndrome consists of symptoms of irritability, insomnia, anorexia or overeating, a negative and cynical attitude, a tendency toward being argumentative, fatigue, loss of concern and feeling, or an attitude of hostility toward patients and their families, all of which can result in a state of physical and emotional exhaustion. Additional personal stresses can add to the burnout syndrome, which frequently starts insidiously, without awareness, and is often denied or attributed to external circumstances or lapses of effort. It has been repeatedly shown that professionals who take their problems home and rely on families for support are likely to develop serious problems in their personal lives (Gribbons & Marshall, 1982; McCue, 1982; Sargent et al., 1977).

It is not always easy to treat burnout, particularly if afflicted individuals will not admit to it. Taking a leave of absence and receiving some support may help individuals who are receptive. But the best approach to the problem of burnout, both for the individual and the institution, is to adopt a program of prevention and monitoring (Vachon, 1987).

Most health professionals working with repeated death situations and frequent exposure to grieving families will be subject to burnout if no "breaks" or "time outs" are taken. It is most important to make arrangements for vacations, take time to relax, and maintain a program of exercise, good nutrition, and regular rest and sleep. Equally important is the attention devoted to personal growth, enjoyment, and the needs of one's family. Occasional rotations of assignment can also be helpful.

Perhaps the best way to avoid burnout is to have a set of coping strategies. There is no simple cookbook approach. We shall not suggest a list of steps to be followed. Only a few important points for developing a coping strategy will be mentioned.

The health professional who encounters death and grief in the work situation can find some personal answers and meaning in life and death issues, either through personal insights or organized religion (Feifel, 1977; Frankl, 1959; Lifton, 1977; Weisman, 1977). Another aspect of coping is the ability to *reassess and readjust expectations* during the pre-death situation in dealing with patients and families. To that effect, support conferences can be very helpful in bringing about a more realistic perspective on the amount and level of care given. When a grieving reaction is experienced by a health professional, it should be allowed, acknowledged, and supported, rather than suppressed or inhibited (Weiner, 1981).

Another good coping strategy for health care providers is to keep up with the current knowledge and research in the field of thanatology and bereavement literature (Harper, 1977). This practice contributes to giving the practitioner a sense of competency and control over future situations.

This healthy attitude and feeling is best maintained when hospitals develop a system of monitoring staff stress responses in order to prevent burnout reactions (Vachon, 1987). In this regard, it is important for clinical administrators to recognize that working with dying patients and grieving families requires not only training and support systems, but personal and professional maturity, underscoring the need for such attributes in recruitment of new staff members (LaGrand, 1980; Mount & Voyer, 1980; Vachon, 1987). To create an atmosphere of support, administrators would encourage sensitivity to burnout issues by setting aside time for periodic meetings to discuss concerns and share feelings about terminally ill patients, deceased patients, family grief reactions and complications, including staff questions about any of these areas. A psychiatric liaison staff member can be very helpful in setting up such a program of supportive conferences (Beszterczey, 1977).

When the nursing staff takes the time to listen to patients and their families, they often find that it is as therapeutic as ministering to the physical needs of patients. Nursing supervisors can create an atmosphere that encourages sharing, training, and support on a continuing basis, especially in services where death tends to occur frequently or suddenly (Vachon, 1987). In palliative units (PCU) the stress from organizational and administrative pressures has been identified as a significant obstacle to the health professional who is attempting to cope. It has also been shown that when nurses in these units do not share feelings about the dying patients and their grieving families, they experience significant levels of stress (Vachon, Lyall & Freeman, 1978). This is even more likely to occur when nurses did not receive any previous training in this area, thus leaving them with a feeling of inadequacy and helplessness. Similarly, Harper (1977) has described the various stages of anxiety that social workers experience in their work with dying patients and their families.

In conclusion, it is important to recognize the need for an interdisciplinary approach to support when death is a frequent occurrence (Vachon, 1987). Even when death occurs occasionally, a staff "closure conference" of review and shared feelings will be beneficial (Rando, 1984).

Chapter 10

SUGGESTIONS FOR HELPING SURVIVORS

In this chapter we shall discuss the myths commonly held by survivors and the health professionals who help them. Although many of these notions have already been dispelled by studies mentioned in previous chapters, further discussion of specific attitudes and beliefs encapsulated in common expressions might prove useful to the health team. In the second part of the chapter we shall review some do's and don'ts in the clinical situation with bereaved families.

Myths have always played an important part in societies ranging from the primitive to the sophisticated. They have functioned as attempts to explain some of life's mysteries as well as to enforce moral and social order. There are aspects of present-day myths that are remnants of past practices that had their origins in well-intentioned advice. It is our purpose to identify such commonly held beliefs as myths that in fact serve as obstacles to a healthy grieving process. They fall into several general categories that indicate the common need to deal not only with issues of appropriate mourning, but more often with the powerful emotions and sense of helplessness associated with death and dying. Since myths can influence thinking and behavior, health professionals need to increase their awareness of the expressions which they may hear from surviving family members or even among members of their own professions.

DISPELLING OLD MYTHS ABOUT BEREAVEMENT

Myth #1 "Time takes care of everything."
The implication of the first myth is that time is the only thing that will heal. Therefore if the griever waits long enough, the wounds will be healed and everything painful will be forgotten. Actually, time does help greatly in the healing process. But as Phyllis Silverman (1974) said, "You don't really get over it, you just get used to it."

Individual variations among grievers must be recognized and respected. Sometimes people who believe the myth of time face their grief years later when another experience reactivates the dormant feelings (Rando, 1983).

Myth #2 "Grief lasts 6 months to a year."
Although it is true that many people can return to normal social functioning within that period of time, it is important to remember that grief is a highly individual experience that can vary in intensity and duration. It has been found in recent studies that the grieving that follows the loss of a spouse or a child can last from 1 to 5 years or more (Osterweis, 1984). The duration of the grief experience varies with the personality and temperament of the bereaved. It is also affected by a past history of emotional difficulties and by the nature of the relationship with the deceased (Osterweis et al., 1984; Rando, 1984).

Myth #3 "It's less painful not to think about the loss."
Avoidance of the pain of grief, denial of the loss, or suppression of the various feelings of bereavement can lead to complications in the course of the grieving process which is so important for final resolution. If the griever begins to show signs of avoiding the pain by not thinking about the loss, the health professional should gently encourage that person to deal with the painful thoughts. However, the helper should be sensitive to the amount of pain that the griever can tolerate, avoiding persistent confrontations (Lazare, 1979).

Myth #4 "It's more helpful to the bereaved person if the loss is not mentioned."
Well-meaning people sometimes feel that bringing up the loss in the course of ordinary conversation is either tactless or asking for trouble. More often than not, the mention of the loss is perceived as a sign of caring which is welcomed by the bereaved. It represents an opportunity to express some genuine feelings of caring and sympathy which can be very supportive to the griever. Do not hesitate to use the name of the deceased in your communication with the bereaved. This will facilitate the grief process (Rando, 1984).

Myth #5 "Anger and guilt occur only in abnormal grief reactions."

The two powerful emotions of anger and guilt occur predictably in almost all cases of the normal grief process. However, if these two emotions persist for an unusually long period of time and begin to immobilize the griever, then they can play a role in leading to abnormal grief reactions (Glick et al., 1974).

Myth #6 "People who cry and talk about their grief are having a more difficult time than people who show less emotion and never discuss their loss."

People who appear not to be upset and seem to be "taking it well," as shown by their outward manner of normalcy and their obvious avoidance of any discussion of the loss, are more likely to be avoiding any expression of their feelings out of fear of what it might mean. This is particularly true for men, who commonly equate expression of feelings with weakness or loss of control. The work setting does not tolerate open expression of sadness through tears, thereby pressuring the individual to suppress such feelings and to avoid any mention of the loss. Yet, talking about the loss and allowing the expression of feelings has been shown to facilitate the grief process. Sometimes the griever must be encouraged to find an appropriate setting for expressing such feelings in order to avoid embarrassing situations. The health professional must be sensitive to the individual's competing needs (Lazare, 1979).

Myth #7 "Grief brings a family closer together."

The grief experience can have a profound impact on the family dynamics. If relationships prior to the loss of a child, for example, were generally supportive, it is likely that the grief experience will be another opportunity to express such support. On the other hand, because grief produces such diverse reactions in different family members, it can often lead to temporary tensions, dislocations, and withdrawal from each other (Kaplan et al., 1976; Kupst et al., 1982; Lansky et al., 1978).

Myth #8 "Children are too young to understand death, so it's best to wait until they are older to discuss this concept with them."

This common generalization is dangerous because it may lead to the avoidance and suppression of the natural grief felt by children. It is important to know the age-related concepts of death for children, so that the family can be guided in dealing sensitively and appropriately with their children during bereavement (Raphael, 1983). (See Appendix A.)

Myth #9 "It's usually easier for the survivors if they are spared the experience of viewing the body of their loved one."

The viewing of the body has been thought to facilitate the initial phase of denial in the grief process. Therefore it is generally thought that the viewing of the body should be encouraged, but not forced upon the survivor. If the person expresses strong resistance or aversion, those wishes should be respected. In cases of unnatural deaths (suicide, murder, accidents with disfigurement), no undue pressure should be applied, and the person should never be left alone with the body. In cases of disfigurement, only parts acceptable for viewing may be shown, as was the case in war casualties, victims of the Holocaust, sudden deaths by drowning, plane or automobile accidents (Committee on the Health Consequences of the Stress of Bereavement, 1984).

When viewing is not possible, symbolic rituals with some physical representation enable the family and friends to pay their respect and say good-bye to the loved one. For example, one might use a favorite article of clothing in a gift package and burn it in a bonfire with significant people in attendance. Other possibilities would be the reading of a favorite piece of poetry or a passage from a book, followed by a ritual burning. Ashes from the ritual can then be scattered on the ocean, in the mountains, or at a private place.

If a traditional funeral is not feasible for any reason, the family should be encouraged to have some sort of symbolic ritual to facilitate the grief process (Raether & Slater, 1977).

Myth #10 "Drugs and alcohol can ease the pain of grieving."

Although mild sedation can help in a few selected cases, such measures usually delay the grief process. However, prolonged insomnia, exhaustion, and lack of nourishment should be avoided. If present, they should be evaluated clinically. In those cases, appropriate medications will help.

For most individuals the use of drugs and alcohol leads to undesirable complications, including physical deterioration, self-reproach, family disapproval and rejection, and physical dependence. If the griever persists in the use of chemicals as a means of coping, he or she should be referred for grief counseling or psychiatric consultation (Parkes & Weiss, 1983).

Myth #11 "Grieving too much can make you lose your mind."

Some grievers experience disturbing emotions and mental changes. They experience a loss of concentration, irritability, and unexpected temper outbursts.

These reactions are not unusual in the early stages of grief, which can last a few weeks. Sometimes, if long-standing ambivalence and conflict existed with the deceased, such reactions can progress to pathological manifestations, such as depression or psychosis. However, these extreme reactions tend to be rare. At times, prolonged or delayed grief can develop, in which case it should receive the attention of a counselor or a psychiatric therapist. Intense emotions, no matter how strong, do not correlate with subsequent clinical outcomes. For most individuals, the intensity of their emotions will subside in due course (Osterweis et al., 1984).

Myth #12 "People who have anticipated grief should have an easier time with the grief process."

This assumption is not necessarily so. Research has shown that families' reactions during the terminal illness of a loved one sometimes duplicate the sequence of emotions of the grief process. Although some say that the dying patient has a tendency toward gradual detachment, others say that there is an intensification of the emotional bond, particularly between spouses (Parkes & Weiss, 1983).

Myth #13 "Bereaved families are too upset to discuss the question of an autopsy or organ transplant."

Interaction with the family over a request for an autopsy or organ transplant offers an opportunity for a therapeutic experience for the survivors. In the case of an organ transplant, the family may not have thought about this option in the midst of the crisis. They may be grateful to the physician later for having helped them make a contribution, feeling that the death was not in vain. This may be particularly true in the case of a child's death. The organ donation may also help relieve the guilt and feeling of senselessness about the tragedy (Osterweis et al., 1984). Since relatives often welcome the chance to talk with their physician, they may be receptive to the request for an autopsy or organ transplant.

Myth #14 "Anger is not a normal emotional response in grieving and its expression should not be encouraged."

Clinical experience does not support this myth. Angry feelings toward dying or dead persons for "deserting" their loved ones are very common and understandable. The finality of death makes it impossible to resolve past conflicts which, when appearing insignificant at death, reinforce the feeling of guilt for not having made peace earlier. It is important to encourage the expression of such feelings and to reassure the survivors that they are normal. If allowed to express these feelings, the survivors are less likely to experience severe guilt and depression later (Worden, 1982).

Myth #15 "A rapid and quick acceptance of the loss of a loved one is an indication that the person is mature, strong-willed, and has adequately worked through the grief process."

In rare instances the griever shows a relatively quick recovery from the loss. This may be related to a lack of closeness in the relationship with the deceased. Or it may reflect the intellectualized manner in which a particular individual chooses to deal with the pain. Such people are prone to delaying their grief, which can manifest itself months or years later in the form of somatic problems (Osterweis et al., 1984).

Myth #16 "*Widows who continue to communicate with their spouses are using a pathological mechanism in coping with their grief.*"

Research has found that widows who maintain ways of "communicating" with their dead spouses cope more easily with their losses (Shuchter & Zisook, 1987). This coping mechanism helps to relieve the pain of the loss and does not interfere with the sense of reality. Health professionals should recognize this as a healthy and effective coping mechanism, reassuring survivors that it is both common and helpful (Rees, 1975).

Myth #17 "*One should not bring up the subject of suicide in talking with suicide survivors.*"

It is true that families who are faced with the tragedy of suicide are burdened with guilt, shame, and stigma. The latter can be overwhelming, and denial is a frequent occurrence. However, the avoidance of the subject or even the word "suicide" reinforces the stigma and denial. Such avoidance often represents a reflection of one's own anxiety and discomfort. Families need to talk about their experiences and their feelings toward this unnatural situation. They should be offered the opportunity to see a counselor or therapist to assist with the difficult aspects of suicide (Worden, 1982).

The beliefs described in the above myths have strong roots in our culture. Ironically, for the most part they seem to relieve the anxieties of the helpers rather than the grievers. It is important for health professionals to be able to tolerate a certain amount of discomfort and to share some of the pain expressed by the survivor. A sense of empathy will go a long way in helping the family in grief.

Do's and Don'ts in Dealing with Survivors

The immediate experience of grief is a crucial time, when the death occurs and the news has to be broken to the family and loved ones. This is when doctors and nurses can be very helpful. The following suggestions are derived from the archives of The Compassionate Friends, an organization of bereaved parents, from interviews with hundreds of families who had experienced comfort or discomfort in the medical setting, and from the literature on bereavement.

Always be truthful.

It is best not to shield the family from pain by withholding information. Tell the family member everything you honestly know. Be honest about what you do *not* know. Be equally supportive to each member of the family. Men need as much support as women, although it is generally not acknowledged.

Do not "hit and run" by breaking the bad news and leaving the room shortly thereafter.

Always allow some time to be with the family after giving them the bad news. If it is not possible to spend a reasonable amount of time with the survivors, arrange for some other skilled and sensitive professional person to be there before you leave (Davis, 1984).

Expect some denial to occur.

You may have to repeat details several times, and it is good to do so as often as necessary. The denial mechanism functions like a tape which has been accidentally erased and is hard to understand. If you tire of the repetition or run out of time or patience, be sure to arrange for an assistant to take your place. Remember that the denial serves as an emotional shield. It will disappear when the individual is ready (Worden, 1982).

Speak in terminology that can be easily understood.

Doctors and nurses frequently speak to families by using medical or surgical terms. They are poorly understood by lay persons. The bereaved may even be too upset to ask for clarification at the time the information is given. Only later does the family remember the terminology which then requires further explanation (Rando, 1984).

Prepare family members for what they will see before they see it.

Explain beforehand the use of machines, tubes, needles, catheters, monitors, or complicated equipment. Clean and bandage all you can before bringing the family into the ICU, CCU, or OR suite.

Reassure the family that "everything possible was done."

It is very comforting for the family to hear and to know that everything within the current state of technology and knowledge was done to save their loved one. Even if it seems obvious, it is important to mention it. Families will not automatically know or assume that.

Always refer to the loved one by name after death.

It hurts to hear a loved one referred to as "the body" or "the remains." In doing so there is a dehumanization quality to the cold, stark coroner's language. It has a chilling effect on families. It is best to speak of the deceased patient by name. If it is a young person, it is appropriate to use the first name. If it is an adult or an older person, it is respectful to use the last name. It is as important to convey respect as it is to express a sense of caring and compassion.

Answer questions about suffering and fear.

Be prepared to answer the two most frequently asked questions concerning the loss of a loved one: "Did she suffer?" and "Was she afraid?" Although you may or may not know the answers to the questions, try to answer as honestly and as supportively as possible. Remember that families will judge you by your *caring level* as well as your medical skills (Rando, 1984).

Allow as much time as the family needs to be with the loved one after death.

Allowing adequate time immediately after death is considered very important in the healing process of the acute grief reaction. Sometimes medical personnel are in a hurry to clear the room or the Emergency Room, thus bypassing an important step in the grief process.

Because each situation is unique, it is important to allow the loved one to have as much time as needed to be with the deceased. This is the beginning of the grief process and an important part of the leave-taking experience, which should not be curtailed or aborted. Sometimes it is erroneously thought that this experience is too painful and should not be unduly prolonged. Actually, when it is abbreviated by medical personnel, it is often resented by family members at a later time.

The surviving loved one must be allowed to be alone in the room with the deceased. This is an essential opportunity for the surviving member to have one last chance to communicate some meaningful message to the deceased. This final communication may serve to relieve guilt or resentment previously experienced with that person (Kubler-Ross, 1974).

The child who wishes to be with a family member at the time of death must be prepared ahead of time.

The child must be told what to expect and what will be seen. The information must be geared to the age of the child (see Appendix A for Age-Related Concepts of Death for Children). In general, most children over age ten are ready to accept explanations which you are prepared to give. However, the child's intelligence and previous experiences will affect the way in which the information is received. In any case, you might want to offer help to the family in making a sensible determination, including intervention with the child, if you and the family feel comfortable in doing so (Raphael, 1983).

Be prepared for expression of anger at the medical staff.

It is not unusual for families to express anger at nursing or medical personnel. Sometimes this anger is displaced onto the staff, and sometimes it is justified. In any case, it is important to allow ventilation of such feelings through outbursts or other expressions and to analyze the basis for the anger at a later time. This is not a time to be defensive, to rationalize, to distract, or change the subject. It is best to listen, to provide support, and to focus on the person's pain and sorrow (Worden, 1982).

Do not give explanations or rationalizations about why the death occurred.

It does not help to say, "Your son would have been a vegetable if he had lived; he's better off," or anything else of this nature. Many families cannot accept any explanation that would justify the deaths of their loved ones, no matter how rational it sounds to the scientific community.

It is not a good idea to use "at least" statements, such as "At least she didn't linger," "At least you didn't bring the baby home from the hospital," "At least he is with God," or "At least you have each other." It is also neither helpful nor appropriate to offer the explanation that "It is God's will," because the latter does not explain anything and may clash with the family's religious and cultural values. Furthermore, it frequently triggers more anger and frustration in the survivor. Although these common statements are meant to be soothing to the griever, they contribute to making grief more difficult. Health professionals have been taught to help patients feel better. They do not want to see them cry or make them cry, and they feel that crying is not therapeutic. They have not been taught to face grief in the clinical setting. They want to help the bereaved get through it with as little pain as possible, yet their efforts only succeed in relieving their own anxieties while often slowing down the grief process. Unlike any other situation in medicine, here the professional can best help by sharing in the experiences of pain without the usual attempt to alleviate it.

Validate the bereaved person's emotions of grief.

Sometimes family members become frightened by their own emotions and believe that they are losing control. They do not realize that expressions of anger, resentment, guilt, and brief feelings of wanting to join the deceased are within the normal range of the grief process. They need to be reassured that this is a process and that it will run its course.

Don't ever say "You'll get over it," referring to the loss.

Rather than saying "You'll get over it," when referring to the loss, it is more appropriate and caring to say that "Time will ease the pain." Don't say "I know how you feel," because you don't. Instead, say, "It must be hard for you." Here again it is important to acknowledge the griever's pain. To say that the pain will go away, when you don't know the nature of the relationship with the deceased may increase feelings of guilt, inadequacy, remorse, anger, or resentment.

Give the bereaved permission to cry.

Here is a helpful quote from a nurse to a woman whose husband died tragically:

> "Of course you feel pain and devastation; you have experienced a great loss. Go ahead and cry."

Do not view extreme emotions as pathological grief.

There are two instances that usually bring on pathological grief. The first one occurs when there is an absence of emotional expression at the time of death and during the grieving period. It is not unusual to see the appearance of an array of somatic complaints and symptoms in these individuals. The second instance occurs when the feelings of depression and suicidal thoughts persist and immobilize the grieving person. In both instances, when this is clearly recognized or suspected by other family members, a referral for psychiatric evaluation is appropriate. But the expression of intense emotions, uncontrollable sobbing, moaning, and lamenting may simply represent the acute phase of a normal grief reaction. Only if it persists for several weeks without any sign of letting up should a consultation with a mental health professional be offered (Zisook, 1987).

Physical touching may be very comforting.

Touching the survivor by putting your hand on an arm or your arm around a shoulder can be very comforting. It is probably the most basic and responsive form of communication, but it is also the most powerful and supportive (Davis, 1984).

Do not automatically offer medication.

This is an area of controversy because there are no conclusive studies that show that it is beneficial to medicate survivors in acute grief. The challenge is to be able to distinguish between true sadness in grieving and clinical depression. This is not always possible in the early stages. Even in acute grief, however, a mild tranquilizer might help and could be offered, but it should not be strongly recommended or urged (Osterweis, 1984). (See Chapter 8 on Medication of Bereaved Patients.)

At the appropriate time, after the initial shock, and usually during the early phases of grief, the following specific suggestions, when carefully selected, can be helpful (Segal et al., 1986).

"You will need time for the grieving process. Do not be in a hurry to get over it. Allow nature to take its course."

"Get plenty of rest."

"Continue or resume your busy routine whenever it is comfortable again."

"Remember that your powerful and overwhelming feelings of pain will ease with time."

"Share your pain with those you feel comfortable with and accept support when it is offered."

"Surround yourself with plants, animals, and friends."

"Use mementos to help your mourning."

"Avoid major decisions, and do not rely on alcohol, tobacco, or drugs."

"Keep a diary and record your memories of feelings about your loved one, past struggles and successes."

"Prepare to meet new friends, make new relationships, and use creative urges to write, build, paint, play music, plan a long trip, reorganize or redecorate your home."

"Make peace with yourself and others, remembering that what follows is part of the healing process."

"Expect holidays and anniversaries to be difficult for awhile as they will bring up painful feelings and memories."

CONCLUSION

The above suggestions must be appropriately timed and selected in a sensitive and caring manner. They are most effective when made at *variable intervals* at the time of death and during subsequent visits with the bereaved in the office setting. It is not unusual in the weeks following the death for bereaved persons to develop non specific somatic symptoms and complaints. It is only then that the physician, internist, pediatrician, or surgeon should make it a point to schedule a return appointment with the next of kin, who may return with a constellation of symptoms at a later date if early complaints are ignored. During the appointment several weeks after the death it will be easier to determine how the grief is progressing. It will also be more accurate then to assess the impact of the death on the physical health of the survivor and to decide whether further counseling or psychiatric consultation is indicated.

The above suggestions provide a general blueprint for how to approach the family in grief. But, as in any professional practice, experience becomes the best guide to action.

These caveats and recommendations are but a few of the most obvious do's and don'ts for physicians, nurses, and social workers. They emerged from hundreds of observations and reports shared by grieving families seen in clinic and hospital settings over several years. They are intended to serve as valuable reminders even for the most sensitive and caring professionals. They cannot substitute, however, for the genuine caring which, in the end, is the true medicine for grief.

Chapter 11

TRAINING AND SUPPORT PROGRAMS

RATIONALE FOR TRAINING AND SUPPORT PROGRAMS

In their work with dying patients and their families, health professionals assume enormous responsibilities and burdens which make heavy emotional demands upon them each day. For some it is the burden of making the right decision for a patient on a life-support system; for others it is the feeling of defeat when a patient dies. For still others it is the confrontation with an angry family after the death. Working with the critically ill, the dying, and the bereaved requires considerable patience, maturity, and coping skill. But even that is not enough.

Representatives of all disciplines have amply documented the struggles experienced by physicians (Artiss & Levine, 1973; Hollingsworth & Pasnau, 1977), by nurses (Benoliel, 1976; 1985), and by social workers (Harper, 1977). Anxieties, fears, uncertainties, doubts, and depression have been expressed and experienced by all, although not openly admitted (Vachon, 1987). Few health professionals have had the opportunity to work through their own feelings about death and dying. Yet they are expected to help others face and confront anxieties and fears which they themselves have never completely mastered (Rothenberg, 1967).

Physicians and nurses as a group have extraordinary fear and anxiety about death (Kasper, 1959). Studies have shown that despite the fact that nursing schools have an adequate curriculum on issues dealing with death, dying, grief, and loss, up to 35 percent of nurses feel unprepared to deal with the dying and bereaved families (Doyle, 1982; Poppoff, 1975). Physicians, on the other hand, get much less training and education devoted to these topics, and after medical school most of them feel totally unprepared to deal with the demands of their practice (Artiss & Levine, 1973; McCue, 1982). Even social workers, who receive a solid grounding in individual, group and family dynamics and interviewing skills, only get a limited number of lectures on death, dying, and bereavement (Mullaney & Fox, 1981).

Since the 1960s, however, there has been an increasing interest in and awareness of the need for more training and better coordination of the various members of the health team in dealing with issues and problems of death and grieving. There is no longer any doubt that more knowledge is needed by all disciplines, and that more training and support must be provided by institutions if the needs of families are to be met and if staff burnout is to be prevented (Roskin, 1980; Osterweis, 1984; Vachon, 1987).

The most desirable outcome is to achieve *a sense of balance between skills and stress*. However, for this to happen, three conditions must be met: people must *believe* in their work, they must not *do too much* of it, and they must have *a sense of success* in it (Todres et al., 1974). In working with the dying and the bereaved these conditions are generally difficult to meet; at least without some *reinterpretation* of the meaning of this type of work. The staff must obtain new sources of information and support in order to be able to meet the demands of dying patients and grieving families. For those in clinical practice, this can be achieved by way of programs offered in continuing education or through in-service training programs. For those still in medical, nursing, and social work schools, the goal can be reached by incorporating into the curriculum more information and training in these areas before graduation.

In their recommendations for improving the effectiveness of health professionals dealing with grieving families, the Committee on the Study of the Stress of Bereavement suggested a series of guidelines. They felt that additional training for all health professionals working with the bereaved should include development of the following skills:

   Observing the physical and emotional clues associated
   with the grief process;

Attentive listening so that the bereaved can be helped by understanding what is happening in the grief process and by allowing them to express their concerns and feelings;

Conveying empathy to the bereaved so that even non-medical concerns and questions can be addressed freely and openly;

Learning to establish and maintain a relationship with the bereaved so that follow-up and necessary referral can be made smoothly and appropriately.

TYPES OF PROGRAMS

In general an institution should not undertake a support and training program without surveying the particular needs of its staff (Miles, 1980). This survey can be done by using questionnaires or through informal inquiries of the staff members of the various units. For purposes of discussion we shall outline the elements of educational programs first. The reader should be aware, however, that much overlapping occurs in the sense that support is provided through some of the educational framework, and, in turn, education is transmitted through the support programs.

Educational Programs

Seminar format.   The seminar model seems to work best with medical students and house staff (Artiss & Levine, 1973; Bertman et al., 1982; Fox, 1957; Marks, in press). During the sessions, the following topics and issues are discussed:

The dependency relationship dying patients develop with their physicians and the realization that patients often set up unrealistic expectations from their physicians, who often become seduced by patients' flattery and praise, falling into the trap of trying to deliver a "larger than life" performance. The trap is encapsulated in this kind of statement by the patient: "Between you and God, we'll make it, won't we, Doctor?" At this point, the doctor is caught off guard, and, without some awareness, falls into the trap the patient set up. The eventual outcome is a patient who is disappointed, resentful, and angry at the physician for having been "let down."

The denial used by patients and their families when they are told about the diagnosis of cancer. Physicians often find this denial frustrating, often thinking that patients are unwilling to accept reality. These physicians often get angry, but later feel guilty because they wonder, "How can I be angry at a person who is dying?"

The question of how to interact with patients who continuously change their reality perceptions, their affect, their rage, their paranoid manifestations, and euphoric elation. The physician's unspoken complaint about their patients goes something like this: "Why don't my patients just die and not bother me with all their psychiatric problems?"

The profound social implications of the diagnosis of cancer and its impact on the family and community of friends. The health team must realize that including the family in the treatment program is an increasing expectation today (Tietz et al., 1977). To ignore it may lead to conflicts and frustrations at the time of death and bereavement. It is also very important not to underestimate the power of the following words to the family of a patient who is dying: "Everything is being done that can be done." This absolves the family of all sense of wrongdoing, neglect, or responsibility in the eyes of the community because "the mighty doctors at the renowned hospital" are doing "everything possible" (Artiss & Levine, 1977).

The importance of giving information to the family without being defensive or suspicious about the family's questions.

The need that families have to talk about their sense of guilt when their child is dying of cancer, and the reluctance that physicians sometimes have about letting parents "open up" for fear that there isn't enough time to deal with an outpouring of feeling. The truth is that time can be controlled with a little practice and training. The real issue is the reluctance to experience the discomfort of dealing with painful emotions.

Ways of coming to terms with one's own mortality before being able to deal with dying patients and their families.

The seminar format is attractive not only to medical students and house staff, but also to psychology, nursing and, social work students. It functions best on a weekly basis for a few weeks or months, depending on the curriculum.

Workshops in continuing education.   All-day workshops and courses on death and grief dynamics have been found to be very effective (Miles, 1980). These programs seem to be better received by nurses and social workers. An all-day program with one or two formal presentations by experts in the field seems to be the most workable arrangement in many hospitals. The coordinator for such programs can design questionnaires to raise awareness in the various areas of death, grief and loss.

Role-playing sessions. Role-playing techniques have been very useful in teaching concepts and interviewing skills for dealing with dying patients and families (Barton, 1977; Barton & Crowder, 1975). Physicians and nurses often have to learn *what not to say* in situations of bereavement (see Chapter 10 on Do's and Don'ts). Comments like "You must be so relieved" or "It's better that way" should be unlearned. In role-playing exercises, health professionals learn to use their own emotional responses as diagnostic tools along with their stethoscopes (Vachon, 1987). Another advantage of this approach is that it provides a safe opportunity for staff members to gain practical experience and to increase their feelings of competence without fear of making a terrible mistakes.

Research projects. Research activities are often as welcome for the interaction they stimulate among the staff, patients, and families as they are for the findings they produce. Research projects frequently sensitize the staff to issues previously submerged by the frantic course of clinical activities. They occasionally stimulate a new approach to patients and families.

Educational materials. A well-equipped hospital gathers resource materials for workshops, staff conferences, and student teaching. Among these materials are audiovisual materials, lists of community resources, and bibliographies on the subjects of death, dying, and bereavement (Chigier, in press; Rando, 1981; Wass & Corr, 1984; Wass et al., 1985) and physicians' families' personal accounts of dying and bereavement (Weinman-Lear, 1980). Materials are usually well received by a multidisciplinary staff. Films on death, grief and loss can be used as a stimulus for discussion at staff meetings, seminars or classes for medical, nursing and social work students (see Appendix B).

Support Programs

There are two types of support groups that can meet the needs of the staff: the support conference and the closure conference (Rando, 1984). The support conference is focused on the needs of the health professional, whereas the closure conference is about the death of a given patient and the aftermath.

Support conference. These group meetings seem to work best with nurses, social workers, and members of the clergy. They are aimed at exploring feelings about working in a particular area such as the ICU, the Oncology unit, etc., or about dealing with a specific family. Sometimes the conference focuses on eliciting opinions and feelings about an ethical dilemma such as the use of life-support measures in a given case (Vachon, 1987). The sessions can be scheduled regularly or on an ad hoc basis. They are extremely useful for relieving work stresses and burnout in units of high tension such as the ICU, the NICU, the PICU and the Oncology Unit (Hay & Oken, 1977).

Support conferences are most effective when led by an experienced and psychologically sophisticated staff member who can keep the communication focused on the work experience rather than on general self-exploration. Aims of the group process are:

> Encouragement of ventilation of intragroup feelings of frustration and suppressed anger;
>
> Sharing of feelings of doubt, fear, and uncertainty;
>
> Provision of some emotional release of feelings that were suppressed in the work situation and could not be expressed because of work demands;
>
> Exchange of views and ideas on innovative techniques and approaches with patients and families;
>
> Admission that minor mistakes are all right and inevitable, realizing that guilt and shame can be relieved by this kind of sharing;
>
> Finding of ways to communicate conflicts and solutions to problems to the administration (Kornfeld, 1969).

One of the most common themes in these meetings is the expression of feelings of inadequacy and fears of mistakes and failure. Perhaps the most important thing health professionals should remind themselves of during these meetings is that they often have unrealistic expectations in dealing with the dying (Spikes, 1979; Vachon, 1983) and that they need to regain a sense of perspective. But most important, they must realize that they are very much needed after the death by the families, and that just "being there" is as important as "keeping busy" or "having things to do" (Vachon, 1987).

   Closure conference.   A closure meeting is aimed at bringing a sense of completion to the process after a death or several deaths. It is especially useful if the involvement with a patient was long and intense, as in the case of a long terminal illness of a teenager who died from a malignancy. As in a funeral or therapy session, the closure conference enables the staff members to review the relationship, remember the critical and the good times with the patient, and confront unresolved questions and concerns (Rando, 1984). Sometimes support groups and closure conferences are merged into support conferences, where both kinds of agendas are brought up at different times (Lippman & Carlson, 1977).

   Informal sharing between coworkers.   Sharing one's frustrations over a cup of coffee or lunch can be very effective and helpful in easing the stress level of staff members. The advantage is that it is more readily available and easier to schedule because of its spontaneous nature. Such informal sharing should be encouraged in services with high-risk patients.

CONSULTATION SERVICES

   Periodic meetings with a psychiatrist or a clinical nurse specialist in mental health can be very helpful to the staff burdened with many deaths and difficult families (Rahe, 1975; Strain & Grossman, 1975). Sometimes the meetings may focus on the professionals' feelings in dealing with stressful situations, whereas at other times the focus may be on how to deal with problem cases (Baker & Lynne, 1979; Beszterczey, 1977; Hollingsworth & Pasnau, 1977). The aim of such consultation is to resolve conflicts among family members of dying patients, conflicts between nurses and physicians, or conflicts between staff and families (Lieberman & Jacobs, 1987). These situations tend to arise when there is a divergent point of view on the issue of life-support measures for a dying patient. The role of the consultant then is to raise the staff's awareness of their own death anxiety and to show them how this death anxiety is motivating their perceptions of situations and their resistances in dealing with the issue of dying and grief.

Chapter 12

WHEN AND WHERE TO REFER
BEREAVED FAMILIES

Another major responsibility in working with bereaved families is knowing when and where to refer them for professional help or when to suggest a self-support group in the community. In this chapter we will discuss indications for referrals and give the clues or "red flags" that denote high-risk individuals. We will also discuss the value of self-help groups and give a list of community resources for the bereaved.

REFERRING FOR GRIEF COUNSELING OR PSYCHIATRIC TREATMENT

It is not always easy to determine what is the best intervention for a bereaved individual in need of additional help and follow-up. In addition to certain risk factors, one should take into account other factors such as the receptivity to such a referral, the psychological sophistication of the individual, the ethnic and religious background, the economic status, and the prior experience with counseling or a support group.

Checklist of Risk Factors

The risk factors to be considered prior to a professional referral include any one or a group of factors in the following list.

Absence of grief;

"Unfinished business," especially after sudden death, when there is insufficient time to resolve feelings or past conflicts;

A history of violent death (suicide, murder, accident) or multiple deaths;

A history of disturbed relationships with the deceased;

Presence of feelings of worthlessness, excessive guilt, ambivalence, anger, rejection, or alienation;

Continual self-blame, low self-esteem, and changes in self-image;

Persistence of depressive symptoms for more than a year;

Occurrence of extremely intense depression with vegetative signs and symptoms including anorexia, G.I. problems, weight loss, insomnia, menstrual changes, or headaches;

Onset of severe and recurrent anxiety attacks;

Recurring painful fantasies, nightmares, and reliving of the dying experience;

Dependence on alcohol, illicit drugs, or medications;

Acting-out or antisocial behavior, including suicide attempts, accident-proneness, and risk-taking behavior;

Onset of chronic medical problems such as psychosomatic disorders, vague somatic complaints, or cardiovascular disturbances (Melson & Rynearson, 1982);

Total avoidance of mention of the deceased, removal of all objects belonging to the deceased and photos of the deceased;

Continued and prolonged social withdrawal associated with intense grieving as a way to keep a link with the deceased;

Personality changes and radical changes in life style.

"Red Flags" for Parents Who Lose a Child

A number of specific clues that seem to predict a troubled outcome in bereaved families who have lost a child should be noted by the hospital staff shortly after the death (Fletcher, 1984). Parents who are at risk for problems will exhibit the following behaviors:

> They will not make any eye contact and will not speak to each other or hold hands.
>
> They will decline any return visit to the hospital after the death of the child.
>
> They will become tearful at the mere sight of the physician even before a conversation takes place.
>
> They will show no evidence of any social support in the community.
>
> They may have a past history of sleep and eating problems.
>
> They may have a past history of psychiatric problems.
>
> They may have a past history of drinking and marital discord.

WHEN TO REFER THE BEREAVED FOR PROFESSIONAL HELP

The best time to refer a bereaved person for counseling is after the shock of the death has worn off and the griever is being seen as an outpatient about 3 to 4 weeks after the death. At that time, the pain is felt intensely, the sense of loss is becoming real, and fear and disorganization are growing. Some people may require referral to a professional, such as a grief counselor, or a mental health professional, such as a psychiatrist, a psychologist, a social worker, or a clinical nurse specialist.

The method of treatment used by the various professionals who do grief counseling may vary according to their training and theoretical orientation (see Chapter 2). But generally speaking, they share certain characteristics, namely, a nonjudgmental supportive attitude, compassion, and a genuine wish to help the bereaved person and family resume adequate social functioning and a sense of well-being (Osterweis, 1984). The approaches used by most professionals consist of helping the bereaved develop new coping skills, modify existing ones, work through the grief process, and prevent the development of pathologic grief. If the bereaved individual presents evidence of a clinical depression or any other associated psychiatric entity (see Chapter 4 on Pathologic Grief), treatment with a psychiatrist should not be delayed. Generally speaking, if the griever develops severe difficulty in functioning and has a past history of "maladaptive attitudes and beliefs" and a history of poor social adjustment prior to the bereavement, he should be referred for psychotherapy (Krupnick & Horowitz, 1981).

For the majority of individuals, a one-to-one approach is more beneficial in the early phases of acute grief and in cases of pathologic grief. In the early phase, even before considering a referral, some bereaved individuals either ask for or welcome suggestions about books or other written material to help them understand and cope with the death. It is important for health professionals to have a reading list available in order to make appropriate recommendations. Later, the mutual help programs appear to be more helpful to a substantial number of bereaved individuals (see Suggested Readings).

SELF-HELP SUPPORT GROUPS

Referring to mutual support groups, Parkes, the British authority on bereavement, commented that "the person best qualified to understand and help with the problems of a bereaved person is another bereaved person" (Parkes, 1980). Mutual support groups basically are associations of people who share similar problems, plights, and concerns, and who expect to get support from each other. These groups rest on the fact that people have a need to share, to give, and to feel that they are not alone in their plights. Some of them even encourage their members to pursue an activist role and fight for a cause (Killilea, 1976; Spiegel, 1980). Certain groups are organized around a mutual concern with acute and chronic life-threatening illnesses.

Many of the support groups are organized by specific categories of persons, such as parents of premature babies, families of patients with Huntington's disease, parents of children with cystic fibrosis, or individuals and families facing cancer deaths. Such groups as "Make Today Count" or "Candlelighters" offer to adults and children faced with terminal cancer the kind of support, education, and practical advice that is helpful during the last few months of their lives. A few of these groups invite family members to join during the illness, but the follow-up after bereavement is more uncertain and variable.

Groups that specifically focus on post-bereavement support have two distinct goals: (1) to help people deal with the aftermath of bereavement, the problem of adjusting during the grief process, and the reorganization of life as a single person; examples would be groups like THEOS (They Help Each Other Spiritually) or the Widow-to-Widow program (Silverman, 1970; Silverman et al., 1974); and (2) to help specific groups of survivors cope with a special kind of death, such as suicide, homicide, or death of a child; examples of such groups would be The Compassionate Friends for bereaved parents (Burnell & Burnell, 1986; Videka-Sherman, 1982), Seasons for Survivors of Suicide, Parents of Murdered Children (P.O.M.C.), Military Widows, Mothers Against Drunk Driving (MADD) and Sudden Infant Death Syndrome (SIDS). A few of these groups, in addition to giving support, are committed to advocacy and political action to correct the circumstances that caused the death. It has been shown that for some members, the activism as well as the support can be an effective help to the survivors in their grief process (Killilea, 1976; Spiegel, 1980).

One might raise the question of how effective these support groups are. The research at this point is not conclusive because of many problems in methodology. But it appears that such groups do have a real value in reassuring the bereaved that they are not "going crazy" and in offering them a forum where they can talk openly about their feelings with others who are able to listen without feeling uncomfortable (Osterweis, 1984). The groups are run by lay persons who do not profess to compete with or substitute for professionals. The amount of involvement is left entirely to the individual, and there is no attempt to coerce, pressure, or proselytize. Individuals are free to come for as long as they wish or to quit at any time.

In the U.S. the popularity of self-help groups is still growing, now numbering in the thousands (Abraham, 1976). Anyone interested in locating a special support group can write to The National Self Help Clearinghouse, 33 West 42nd Street, Room 1206-A, New York, N.Y., 10036. The Clearinghouse has a referral service to help locate appropriate self help groups.

Another source of information in this area can be found in *The Self-Help Source Book: Finding and Forming Mutual Aid Self-Help Groups* (Madara & Meese, 1986), New Jersey Self Help Clearinghouse, Saint Clares, Riverside Medical Center, Denville, N.J., 07834.

We recommend that hospitals and practitioners compile a resource file of local listings of community support groups and agencies with specific names of contact persons and telephone numbers. This would enable the staff to make direct referrals. Our experience is that the more specific the referral, the more likely the bereaved person or family is likely to follow through, just as it would with a referral to a colleague.

Here we will provide a partial list of the National Headquarters of a few selected groups. Information about local chapters can be obtained by calling or writing to these headquarters.

For Widows

> NRTA (National Retired Teachers Association)
> AARP (American Association of Retired Persons)
> Widowed Persons Service
> 1909 K Street NW
> Washington, D.C. 20049

> THEOS (They Help Each Other Spiritually)
> Office Building
> Penn Hills Mall, Suite 306
> Pittsburgh, PA 15235

> Parents Without Partners (check local chapters)
> 7910 Woodmont Ave.
> Washington, D.C. 20014

For Bereaved Parents

> The Compassionate Friends, Inc.
> P.O. Box 1347
> Oak Brook, IL 60521
> Tel: (312) 323-5010

> SHARE
> St. John's Hospital
> 800 East Carpenter
> Springfield, IL 62769
> Tel: (217) 544-6464

> HAND (Helping After Neonatal Death)
> P.O. Box 3805
> San Francisco, CA 94119
> Tel: (415) 538-7061

National Tay-Sachs and Allied Diseases Assn., Inc.
122 East Forty Second Street
New York, N.Y. 10017

MADD (Mothers Against Drunk Drivers)
669 Airport Freeway, Suite 310
Hearst, Texas 76053
(817) 268-6233

The Foundation for Sudden Infant Death Syndrome
310 S. Michigan Ave.
Chicago, IL 60604

National SIDS Foundation
8240 Professional Place
Landover, MD 20785

Candlelighters
2025 Eye Street N.W., Suite 1011
Washington, D.C. 20006
Tel: (202) 659-5136

Center for Attitudinal Healing
19 Main Street
Tiburon, CA 94920

P.O.M.C. (Parents of Murdered Children)
Tel: (513) 721-LOVE

For Cancer Patients and Their Families

Make Today Count
Box 222
Osage Beach, MO 65065
Tel: (314) 348-1619

National Hospice Organization
1901 Fort Myer Drive
Arlington, VA 22101

For Survivors of Suicide

Suicide Prevention Centers, Inc.
P.O. Box 1393
Dayton, Ohio 45401
Tel: (513) 223-9096

REFERENCES

Aaron, H. J., & Schwartz, W. B. (1984). *The painful prescription: Rationing hospital care.* Washington, DC: Brookings Institute.

Abraham, R. B. (1976). Mutual helping styles of caregiving in a mutual aid program—The widowed service line. In G. Caplan & M. Killilea (Eds.), *Support systems and mutual help.* New York: Grune & Stratton.

Abrams, N., & Brucker, M. (1983). *Medical ethics: A clinical textbook and reference for health care professionals.* Cambridge: MIT Press.

Abrams, R. (1972). The responsibility of social work in terminal cancer. In B. Schoenberg, A. C. Carr, D. Peretz, & A. H. Kutscher (Eds.), *Psychosocial aspects of terminal care* (pp. 173–82). New York: Columbia University Press.

Abrams, R. (1974). *Not alone with cancer.* Illinois: Charles C. Thomas.

Adams, C. L., & Proulx, J. R. (1975). The role of the nurse in the maintenance and restoration of hope. In B. Schoenberg, I. Gerber, A. Wiener, A. H. Kutscher, D. Peretz & A. C. Carr (Eds.), *Bereavement: Its psychosocial aspects.* New York: Columbia University Press.

Aldrich, C. K. (1963). The dying patient's grief. *JAMA, 184,* 109–111.

Aldrich, C. K. (1974). Some dynamics of anticipatory grief. In B. Schoenberg, A. Carr, A. Kutscher, D. Peretz, & I. Goldberg (Eds.), *Anticipatory grief.* New York: Columbia University Press.

American Psychiatric Association (1987). *Diagnostic and statistical manual of mental disorders* (3rd ed. rev.). Washington DC: Author.

Anderson, C. (1949). Aspects of pathological grief and mourning. *International Journal of Psycho-Analysis, 30,* 48–55.

Annas, G. J., Glantz, L. H., & Katz, B. F. (1981). *The rights of doctors, nurses, and allied health professionals.* New York: Avon.

Aries, P. (1974). *Western attitudes toward death: From the middle ages to present* (Symposia in Comparative History Series). Baltimore: Johns Hopkins University Press.

Aronson, G. (1959). Treatment of the dying person. In *The meaning of death* (pp. 255–256). New York: McGraw-Hill.

Artiss, K. L., & Levine, A. S. (1973). Doctor-patient relationship in severe illness. *The New England Journal of Medicine, 288* (23), 1210–1214.

Averill, J. R. (1968). Grief: Its nature and significance. *Psychological Bulletin, 70,* 721–748.

Baker, B., & Lynne M. (1979). Psychiatric nursing consultation: The use of an inservice model to assist nurses in the grief process. *Journal of Psychiatric Nursing, 17* (5), 15.

Barnard, C. (1980). *Good life good health: A doctor's case for euthanasia and suicide.* Englewood Cliffs: Prentice-Hall.

Barton, D. (1977). *Dying and death: A clinical guide for caregivers.* Baltimore: Williams & Wilkins.

Barton, D., & Crowder, M. (1975). The use of role playing techniques as an instructional aid in teaching about death, dying and bereavement. *Omega, 6,* 243–250.

Beauchamp, T. L., & Perlin, S. (Eds.) (1978). *Ethical issues in death and dying.* Englewood Cliffs: Prentice Hall.

Beck, A., Rush, J., Shaw, B., & Emergy, G. (1979). *Cognitive therapy of depression.* New York: Guilford Press.

Beckey, R. D., Price, R. A., Okerson, M., & Walker, K. R. (1985). Development of a perinatal grief checklist. *Journal of Obstetrics, Gynecology and Neonatal Nursing,* May/June, 197–199.

Belitsky, R., & Jacobs, S. (1986). Bereavement, attachment theory, and mental disorders. *Psychiatric Annals, 16* (5), 277–280.

Benfield, G., Leib, S., & Volman, J. (1978). Grief response of parents to neonatal death and parent participation in deciding care. *Pediatrics, 62,* 171–177.

Benoliel, J. Q. (1974). Anticipatory grief in physicians and nurses. In B. Schoenberg, A. Carr, A. Kutscher, D. Peretz, & I. Goldberg (Eds.), *Anticipatory grief* (pp. 218–228). New York: Columbia University Press.

Benoliel, J. Q. (1976). Overview: Care, cure and the challenge of choice. In A. Earle, N. T. Argondizzo, & A. H. Kutscher (Eds.) *The nurse as caregiver for the terminal patient and his family* (pp. 9–30). New York: Columbia University Press.

Benoliel, J. Q. (1985). Loss and terminal illness. *Nursing Clinics of North America, 20* (2), 439–48.

Berardo, F. M. (1970). Survivorship and social isolation: The case of the aged widower. *Family Coordinator, 19,* 11–25.

Berezin, N. (1982). *After a loss in pregnancy: Help for families affected by a miscarriage, stillbirth, or loss of a newborn.* New York: Simon & Schuster.

Berger, L. R. (1978). Requesting the autopsy: A pediatric perspective. *Clinical Pediatrics, 17,* 445–452.

Bergman, A. (1974). Psychological aspects of sudden unexpected death in infants and children. *Pediatric Clinics of North America, 21,* 115–121.

Bergman, A. B., Pomeroy, M. A., & Beckwith, J. B. (1969). The psychiatric toll of the sudden infant death syndrome. *General Practice, 40,* 99–105.

Bertman, S. L., Greene, H., & Wyatt, C. A. (1982). Humanistic health care education in a hospice/palliative care setting. *Death Education, 5,* 391–407.

Beszterczey, A. (1977). Staff stress on a newly developed palliative care service: The psychiatrist's role. *Canadian Psychiatric Association Journal, 22,* 347–353.

Binger, C. M., Ablin, A. R., Feuerstein, R. C., Kushner, J. H., Zoger, S., & Mikkelsey, C. (1969). Childhood leukemia: Emotional impact on patient and family. *New England Journal of Medicine, 280,* 414–418.

Blachly, P., Disher, B., & Rodnner, G. (1968). Suicide by physicians. *Bulletin of Suicidology, 4,* 1–18.

Bock, E. W., & Webber, J. L. (1972). Suicide among the elderly: Isolating widowhood and mitigating alternatives. *Journal of Marriage and the Family, 34,* 24–31.

Borg, S., & Lasker, J. (1982). *When pregnancy fails: Families coping with miscarriage, stillbirth and infant death.* Boston: Beacon Press.

Bornstein, P. E., Clayton, P. J., Halikas, J. A., Maurice, W., & Robbins, E. (1973). The depression of widowhood at 13 months. *British Journal of Psychiatry, 122,* 561–566.

Bowlby, J. (1970). Separation and loss within the family. In E. J. Anthony & C. Koupernick (Eds.), *The child and his family: Vol. 1.* New York: John Wiley.

Bowlby, J. (1973). *Separation, anxiety and anger: Vol. 2. Attachment and loss.* New York: Basic Books.

Bowlby, J. (1980). *Loss: Sadness and depression: Vol. 3. Attachment and loss.* New York: Basic Books.

Bowlby, J., & Parkes, C. M. (1970). Separation and loss. In E. J. Anthony &

C. Koupernick (Eds.), *The child in his family: Vol. 1. International Yearbook of Child Psychiatry & Allied Professions*. New York: John Wiley.

Bridge, M. (1987). *Personal communication*. Honolulu: Life Foundation.

Bright, P. D. (1987). Adolescent pregnancy and loss. *Maternal-Child Nursing Journal, 16* (1), 1–12.

Brown, G. (1982). Early loss and depression. In C. M. Parkes & J. Stevenson-Hine (Eds.), *The place of attachment in human behavior*. New York: Basic Books.

Brown, J. T. & Stoudemire, G. A. (1983). Normal and pathological grief. *JAMA, 250*, 378–382.

Bugen, L. A. (1977). Human grief: A model for prediction and intervention. *American Journal of Orthopsychiatry, 42*, 196–206.

Bunch, J., Barraclough, B., Nelson, B., & Sanisbury, P. (1971). Suicide following death of parents. *Social Psychiatry, 6*, 193–199.

Burnell, A. (1984). *Picking up the pieces: Coping with grief*. Unpublished doctoral dissertation, Columbia Pacific University, San Rafael, CA.

Burnell, A. L. (in press). Special problems of parents who experience the death of a child. *First International Symposium on Grief and Bereavement: Vol. 1. Psychodynamics*. London: Freund Publishing House.

Burnell, G. M. (1977). Maternal reaction to the loss of multiple births. In R. H. Moos (Ed.), *Coping with physical illness*. New York: Plenum.

Burnell, G. M., & Burnell, A. L. (1986). The Compassionate Friends: A support group for bereaved parents. *The Journal of Family Practice, 22* (3), 295–296.

Burnell, G. M., & Norfleet, M. A. (1987). Women's self-reported responses to abortion. *The Journal of Psychology, 12* (1), 71–76.

Burnell, G. M., Dworsky, W. A., & Harrington, R. L. (1972). Postabortion group therapy. *American Journal of Psychiatry, 129*, 220–223.

Bywater, E. M. (1981). Adolescents with cystic fibrosis: Psychological adjustment. *Archives of Diseases of Children, 56*, 538–543.

Cain, A. C. (Ed.). (1972). *Survivors of suicide*. Springfield: Charles C. Thomas.

Cain, A., & Cain, B. (1964). On replacing a child. *Journal of the American Academy of Child Psychiatry, 3*, 443–456.

Cain, A., Fast, I., & Erikson, M. (1964). Children's disturbed reactions to the death of a sibling. *American Journal of Orthopsychiatry, 34*, 741–752.

Campbell, D. W. (1980). Death anxiety on a coronary care unit. *Psychosomatics, 21* (2), 127.

Caplan, G. (1963). Emotional crisis. In A. Deutsch & H. Fishman (Eds.), *Encyclopedia of Mental Health: Vol. 2*. New York: Franklin Watts.

Caroff, P., & Dobrof, R. (1974). Social work: Its institutional role. In B.

Schoenberg, A. Carr, A. Kutscher, D. Peretz, & I. Goldberg (Eds.), *Anticipatory Grief*. New York: Columbia University.

Carr, D., & Knupp, S. F. (1985). Grief and perinatal loss: A community hospital approach to support. *Journal of Obstetrics, Gynecology and Neonatal Nursing*, March/April, 130–136.

Chaloner, L. (1962, November). How to answer questions children ask about death. *Parents Magazine*, pp. 99–102.

Check, W. A. (1985). Homicide, suicide and other violence gain increasing medical attention. *JAMA, 254,* 721–730.

Chigier, E. (in press). *First International Symposium on Grief and Bereavement*. London: Freund Publishing House.

Christopherson, L. K., & Gonda, T. A. (1974). Organ transplantation. In B. Schoenberg, A. Carr, A. Kutscher, D. Peretz, & I. Goldberg (Eds.), *Anticipatory Grief,* (pp. 107–114). New York: Columbia University Press.

Clark, R. E., & LaBeff, E. E. (1982). Death-telling: Managing the delivery of bad news. *Journal of Health and Social Behavior, 23* (4), 366–380.

Clayton, P. (1971). The bereavement of the widowed. *Diseases of the Nervous System, 32,* 597–603.

Clayton, P. (1974). Mortality and morbidity in the first year of widowhood. *Archives of General Psychiatry, 125,* 747–750.

Clayton, P. J. (1975). The effect of living alone on bereavement symptoms. *American Journal of Psychiatry, 132,* 133–137.

Clayton, P. J. (1980). Bereavement and its management. In E. S. Paykel (Ed.), *Handbook of Affective Disorders*. Edinburgh: Churchill Livingstone.

Clayton, P. J., Halikas, J. A., Maurice, W. L. (1972). The depression of widowhood. *British Journal of Psychiatry, 120,* 71–77.

Clayton, P. J., & Darvish, H. S. (1979). Course of depressive symptoms following the stress of bereavement. In J. E. Barrett (Ed.), *Stress and Mental Disorder*. New York: Raven Press.

Cohen, G. (1979). DOA: Preliminary report on an emergency room protocol. *Clinical Proceedings of the Children's Hospital National Medical Center, 35,* 159–165.

Cohen, G. J. (in press). Bereavement: Responsibilities of health professionals. *First International Symposium on Grief and Bereavement: Vol. 2. Counseling and Therapy*. London: Freund Publishing House.

Cohen, L., Zilkha, S., Middleton, J., & O'Donohue, N. (1978). Perinatal mortality: Assisting parental affirmation. *American Journal of Orthopsychiatry,. 48,* 727–731.

Committee on the Health Consequences of the Stress of Bereavement. (1984). *Site visit case studies*. Institute of Medicine, National Academy of Sciences.

Staff. (1982). *Compassionate Friends Newsletter*, 5 (2), pp. 2–5.

Condon, J. T. (1986). Management of established pathological grief reaction after stillbirth. *American Journal of Psychiatry 143* (8) pp. 987–992.

Connerford, B. (1974). Parental anticipatory grief and guidelines for caregivers. In B. Schoenberg, A. Carr, A. Kutscher, D. Peretz, & I. Goldberg (Eds.), *Anticipatory Grief*. New York: Columbia University Press.

Consensus Panel. (1984). Drugs and insomnia: The use of medications to promote sleep. *JAMA, 251* (18), 2410–2414.

Cox, P. R., & Ford, J. R. (1964). The mortality of widows shortly after widowhood. *Lancet, 1*, 163–164.

Craig, Y. (1977). The bereavement of parents and their search for meaning. *British Journal of Social Work, 7*, 41–54.

Daniels, M., & Manning, D. (1983). A clinic for pregnant teens. *American Journal of Nursing, 83*, 68–71.

Davidson, G. W. (1975). The "Waiting Vulture Syndrome." Chapter 30. In B. Schoenberg, I. Gerber, A. Wiener, A. H. Kutscher, D. Peretz, & A. C. Carr (Eds.), *Bereavement: Its psychosocial aspects*, pp. 357–361. New York: Columbia University Press.

Davidson, G. W. (1977). Death of a wished for child. *Death Education, 1*, 265–275.

Davis, A. J. (1984). *Listening and responding*. St. Louis: Mosby.

Davis, A., & Aroskar, M. A. (1983). *Ethical dilemmas and nursing practice* (2nd ed.). Norwalk: Appleton Century Crofts.

Davis, F. (1966). Uncertainty in medical prognosis, clinical and functional. In W. R. Scott & E. H. Volkart (Eds.), *Medical Care*. New York: John Wiley.

DeFrain, J., Taylor, J., & Ernst, L. (1982). *Coping with sudden infant death*. Lexington: Lexington Books.

Deutsch, H. (1937). Absence of grief. *Psychoanalytic Quarterly, 6*, 12–22.

DeVaul, R. A., Zisook, S., & Faschingbauer, T. R. (1979). Clinical aspects of grief and bereavement. *Primary Care, 6* (2), 391–402.

Donnelly, K. (1982). *Recovering from the loss of a child*. New York: Macmillan.

Doyle, D. (1982). Nursing education in terminal care. *Nurse Education Today, 2* (4), 4–6.

Dubin, W. R. & Sarnoff, J. R. (1986). Sudden unexpected death: Intervention with the survivors. *Annals of Emergency Medicine, 15* (1), 54–57.

Easson, W. M. (1970). *The dying child: The management of the child or adolescent who is dying*. Springfield: Charles C. Thomas.

Easson, W. M. (1980). A child's death and the family. *International Journal of Family Psychiatry, 1*, 401–412.

Eisendrath, S. J., & Jonsen, A. R. (1983). The living will: Help or hindrance? *JAMA, 249* (15), 2054–2058.

Elliott, G. R., & Eisdorfer, C. (Eds.). (1982). *Stress and human health: A study by the Institute of Medicine, National Academy of Sciences.* New York: Springer.

Engel, G. L. (1961). Is grief a disease? A challenge for medical research. *Psychosomatic Medicine, 23,* 18–22.

Engel, G. L. (1964). Grief and grieving. *American Journal of Nursing 64,* 93–98.

Engel, G. L. (1968). A life setting conducive to illness; The Giving-Up-Given-Up Complex. *Annals of Internal Medicine, 69* (2), 294–300.

Engel, G. (1971). Sudden and rapid death during psychological stress. *Annals of Internal Medicine, 74,* 771–782.

Evans, A. E. (1968). "If a child must die. . . ." *New England Journal of Medicine, 278,* 138–142.

Faulstich, M. E. (1987). Psychiatric aspects of AIDS. *American Journal of Psychiatry, 144* (5), 551–556.

Fawzy, F. I., Wellisch, D. K., Pasnau, R. O., & Leibowitz, B. (1983). Preventing nursing burnout: A challenge for liaison psychiatry. *General Hospital Psychiatry, 5* (2), 141–149.

Feifel, H. (1965). The function of attitudes towards death. In *Death and dying: Attitudes of patients and physicians: Vol. 5. Symposium 11.* New York: Group for the Advancement of Psychiatry.

Feifel, H. (1971). The meaning of death in American society: Implications for education. In B. Green & D. Irish (Eds.), *Death education: Preparation for living.* Cambridge: Schenkman.

Feifel, H. (Ed.). (1977). *New meaning of death.* New York: McGraw-Hill.

Fletcher, A. (1984). Site visit. *Site visit case studies* (Committee on the Health Consequences of the Stress of Bereavement). Washington, DC: Institute of Medicine, National Academy of Sciences.

Forrest, G. C., Standish, E., & Baum, J. D. (1982). Support after perinatal death: A study of support and counseling after perinatal bereavement. *British Medical Journal, 285,* 1475–1479.

Foster, D. J., O'Malley, J. E., & Koocher, G. P. (1981). The parent interviews. In G. P. Koocher & J. E. O'Malley (Eds.). *The Damocles Syndrome: Psychosocial consequences of surviving childhood cancer.* New York: McGraw-Hill.

Fox, R. C. (1957). Training for uncertainty. In R. K. Merton, G. Reader, & P. Kendall (Eds.). *The student physician.* Cambridge: Harvard University Press.

Frankl, V. E. (1959). *Man's search for meaning.* New York: Pocket Book.

Freihofer, P., & Felton, G. (1976). Nursing behaviors in bereavement: An exploratory study. *Nursing Research, 5,* 332–337.

Freud, S. (1917). Mourning and melancholies. In J. Strachey (Ed. and Trans.).

The standard edition of the complete psychological works of Sigmund Freud (Vol. 14). London: Hogarth Press. (Original work published in 1917.)

Friedman, S. B. et al. (1963). Behavioral observations on parents anticipating the death of a child. *Pediatrics, 32,* 610–625.

Frierson, R. L., Lippmann, S. B., & Johnson, J. (1987). AIDS: Psychological stresses on the family. *Psychosomatics, 28* (2), 65–68.

Fuller, R. L., & Geis, S. (1985). Communicating with the grieving family. *Journal of Family Practice, 21* (2), 139–144.

Fulton, R., & Fulton, J. A. (1971). A psychosocial aspect of terminal care: Anticipatory grief. *Omega, 2,* 91–99.

Fulton, R. L., & Langton, P. A. (1964). Attitudes towards death: An emerging mental health problem. *Nursing Forum, 3* (1), 104–112.

Funk, W. (1978). *Word origins and their romantic stories.* New York: Bell.

Furman, E. (1974). *A child's parent dies.* New Haven: Yale University Press.

Futterman, E. H., Hoffman, I., & Sabshin, M. (1972). Parental anticipatory mourning. In B. Schoenberg, A. C. Carr, D. Peretz, & A. H. Kutscher (Eds.), *Psychosocial aspects of terminal care.* New York: Columbia University Press.

Gallagher, D. E., Breckenridge, J. N., Thompson, L. W., & Peterson, J. A. (1983). Effects of bereavement on indicators of mental health in elderly widows and widowers. *Journal of Gerontology, 38,* 565–571.

Gartley, W., & Bernasconi, M. (1967). The concept of death in children. *Journal of Genetic Psychology, 110,* 71–85.

Gauthier, Y., & Marshall, W. (1977). Grief: A cognitive behavioral analysis. *Cognitive Therapy and Research, 1,* 39–44.

Geertz, C. (1973). *The interpretation of culture.* New York: Basic Books.

Gentry, W. D., & Parkes, K. R. (1982). Psychological stress in intensive care unit and non-intensive care unit nursing: A review of the past decade. *Heart and Lung, 11* (1), 43–47.

Gerber, I., Rusalem, R., Hannon, N., Battin, D., & Arkin, A. (1975). Anticipatory grief and aged widows and widowers. *Journal of Gerontology, 30,* 225–229.

Giaquinta, B. (1977). Helping families face the crisis of cancer. *American Journal of Nursing, 77,* 1585–1588.

Gilson, G. (1976). Care of the family who has lost a newborn. *Postgraduate Medicine, 60,* 67–70.

Giulian, G. G., Gilbert, E. F., & Moss, R. L. (1987). Elevated fetal hemoglobin levels in Sudden Infant Death Syndrome. *The New England Journal of Medicine, 316,* 1122–1126.

Glaser, B. G., & Strauss, A. L. (1965). *Awareness of dying.* Chicago: Aldine.

Glaser, B. G., & Strauss, A. L. (1968). *Time for dying.* Chicago: Aldine.

Glick, I. O., Weiss, R. S., & Parkes, C. M. (1974). *The first year of bereavement.* New York: Wiley.

Goin, M. K., Burgoyne, R. W., & Goin, J. M. (1979). Timeless attachment to a dead relative. *American Journal of Psychiatry, 136,* 988–989.

Goldberg, I. K., Kutscher, A. H., & Malitz, S. (Eds.). (1986). *Pain, anxiety and grief: Pharmaco-therapeutic care of the dying patient and the bereaved.* New York: Columbia University Press.

Goldreich, G. (1977). What is death? The answers in children's books. *Hasting Center Report, 7,* 10–15.

Gonda, T. A. (1972). Organ transplantation and the psychosocial aspects of terminal care. In B. Schoenberg, A. C. Carr, D. Peretz, & A. H. Kutscher (Eds.), *Psychosocial aspects of terminal care.* New York: Columbia University Press.

Gonsiorek, J. C. (1982). The use of diagnostic concepts in working with gay and lesbian populations. *Journal of Homosexuality, 6* (3), 9–20.

Goodell, A. (1980). Responses of nurses to the stresses of caring for pediatric oncology patients. *Issues in Comprehensive Pediatric Nursing, 4,* 2–6.

Gorer, G. (1965). *Death, grief and mourning.* New York: Doubleday.

Grant, I., Kyle, G. C., Teichman, A., & Mendels, J. (1974). Recent life events and diabetes in adults. *Psychosomatic Medicine, 37,* 121–128.

Green, M., & Solnit, A. J. (1959). Psychologic considerations in the management of deaths on pediatric hospital services, Part I; The doctor and the child's family. *Pediatrics, 24,* 106–112.

Green, S. A., & Goldberg, R. L. (1986). Management of acute grief. *American Family Physician, 33* (2), 185–190.

Greene, W. A. (1954). Psychological factors and reticulo-endothelial disease. *Psychosomatic Medicine, 16,* 220–230.

Greene, W. A. (1965). Disease response to life stress. *Journal of the American Womens' Association, 20,* 133–140.

Greene, W. A., Young, L. E., & Swisher, S. N. (1956). Psychological factors and reticulo-endothelial diseases. *Psychosomatic Medicine, 18,* 284–303.

Gribbons, P. E., & Marshall, R. E. (1982). Nurse burnout in an NICU. In Marshall, R. E., Kasman, C. & L. S. Cape (Eds.), *Caring for Sick Newborns.* Philadelphia: Saunders.

Grollman, E. (1967). *Explaining death to children.* Boston: Beacon Press.

Hackett, T. P. (1974). Reorganizing and treating abnormal grief. *Hospital Physician, 1,* 49–56.

Hagen, J. M. (1974). Infant death: Nursing interaction and intervention with grieving families. *Nursing Forum, 13* (4), 371–385.

Hampe, S. O. (1975). Needs of the grieving spouse in a hospital setting. *Nursing Research, 24,* 113–120.

Hamric, A. B. (1977). Deterrents to therapeutic care of the dying person: A nurse's perspective. In D. Barton (Ed.), *Dying and death: A clinical guide for caregivers.* Baltimore: Williams & Wilkins.

Hansen, J. C., & Frantz, T. T. (Eds.). (1984). *Death and grief in the family.* Rockville: Aspen Systems Corporation.

Harper, B. C. (1977). *Death: The coping mechanism of the health professional.* Greenville: Southeastern University Press.

Hart, J. T. (1971). The inverse care law. *Lancet, 1,* 405–412.

Hauser, E., & Feinberg, F. (1976). Operational approach to delayed grief and mourning process. *Journal of Psychiatric Nursing, 2,* 26–29.

Hay, D., & Oken, D. (1977). The psychological stresses of Intensive Care Unit nursing. In R. H. Moos (Ed.), *Coping with physical illness.* New York: Plenum.

Heller, D. B., & Schneider, C. D. (1977–78). Interpersonal methods for coping with stress: Helping families of dying children. *Omega, 8,* 319–331.

Helsing, K. J., & Szklo, M. (1981). Mortality after bereavement. *American Journal of Epidemiology, 114,* 41–52.

Helsing, K. J., Comstock, G. W., & Szklo, M. (1982). Causes of death in a widowed population. *American Journal of Epidemiology, 116,* 524–532.

Hildebrand, W. L., & Schreiner, R. L. (1980). Helping parents cope with perinatal death. *American Family Physician, 22,* 121–125.

Holland, J. C., & Tross, C. (1985). The psychosocial and neuropsychiatric sequelae of the Acquired Immune Deficiency Syndrome and related disorders. *Annals of Internal Medicines, 103* (3), 760–764.

Hollingsworth, C., & Pasnau, R. O. (Eds.). (1977). *The family in mourning: A guide for health professionals.* New York: Grune & Stratton.

Hollingsworth, C. E., Hoffman, R., Scalzi, C., & Sokol, B. (1977). Patient progress rounds on a university hospital cardiology service. *American Journal of Psychiatry, 134* (1), 42–44.

Hollister, L. (1972). Psychotherapeutic drugs in the dying and bereaved. *Journal of Thanatology, 2,* 623–629.

Holmes, T. H., & Rahe, R. H. (1967). The social readjustment rating scale. *Journal of Psychosomatic Research, 11,* 213–218.

Holroyd, J., & Guthrie, D. (1979). Stress in families of children with neuromuscular disease. *Journal of Clinical Psychology, 35,* 734–739.

Honolulu Advertiser, The. (March 15, 1987). Hope amid sorrow. Editorial, p. 2.

Horowitz, M. H. (1978). Adolescent mourning reactions to infant and fetal loss. *Social Casework, 59,* 551–559.

Horowitz, M. J., Krupnick, J., Kaltreider, N., Wilner, N., Leong, A., & Marmar, C. (1981). Initial psychological response to parental death. *Archives of General Psychiatry, 38,* 316–323.

Horowitz, M. J., Weiss, D., Koltreider, N., Krupnick, J., Wilner, N., Marmar, C., & DeWitt, K. (1984). Response to death of a parent: A follow-up study. *Journal of Nervous and Mental Diseases, 172* (7), 383–392.

Horowitz, M., Wilner, N., Marmar, C., & Krupnick, J. (1980). Pathological grief and the activation of latent-images. *American Journal of Psychiatry, 137,* 1157–1162.

Humphry, D., & Wickett, A. (1986). *The right to die.* New York: Harper & Row.

Jackson, E. N. (1957). *Understanding grief: Its roots, dynamics, and treatment.* Nashville: Abingdon Press.

Jacobs, S. (1982). Antidepressants and bereaved patients. *Hospital and Community Psychiatry, 33* (7), 532.

Jacobs, S., & Ostfeld, A. (1977). An epidemiological review of the mortality of bereavement. *Psychosomatic Medicine, 39,* 344–357.

Jacobs, S. C., & Douglas, L. (1979). Grief: A mediating process between a loss and illness. *Comparative Psychiatry, 20,* 165–175.

Jacobsen, G. A. (1984). Hospice: Art of caring. *Ca-A Cancer Journal for Clinicians, 34* (4), 202–203.

Janis, I. L. (1958). *Psychological stress.* New York: Wiley.

Kaffman, M., & Elizur, E. (1983). Bereavement responses of kibbutz and non-kibbutz children following the death of a father. *Journal of Child Psychology and Psychiatry, 24,* 435–442.

Kalish, R. A. (1985). *Death, grief and caring relationships.* Monterey: Brooks/Cole.

Kalish, R. A., & Reynolds, D. K. (1981). *Death and ethnicity: A psycho-cultural study.* Farmingdale: Baywood. (originally published by University of Southern California Press, 1976).

Kaplan, D. M., Grobstein, R., & Smith, A. (1976). Predicting the impact of severe illness in families: A study of the variety of responses to fatal illness. *Health and Social Work, 1,* 71–82.

Kapp, M. B. (1982). Response to the Living Will furor: Directives for maximum care. *The American Journal of Medicine, 72,* 855–859.

Kasper, S. (1959). The doctor and death. In H. Feifel (Ed.), *The meaning of death.* New York: McGraw-Hill.

Kastenbaum, R. J. (1969). Death and bereavement in later life. In A. H. Kutscher (Ed.), *Death and bereavement.* Springfield: Charles C. Thomas.

Katon, W., Kleinman, A., & Rosen, G. (1982). Depression and somatization. *American Journal of Medicine, 71,* 127–135, 241–246.

Katz, J., & Gardner, R. (1972). The intern's dilemma: The request for autopsy consent. *Psychiatry in Medicine, 3,* 197–203.

Kavanaugh, R. (1974). *Facing death.* Baltimore: Penguin Books.

Kelly, G. (1958). *Medico-moral problems.* St. Louis: Catholic Hospital Association.

Kemler, B. (1981). Anticipatory grief and survival. In G. P. Koocher & J. E. O'Malley (Eds.), *The Damocles Syndrome: Psychosocial consequences of surviving childhood cancer.* New York: McGraw-Hill.

Kerner, J., Harvey, B., & Lewiston, N. (1979). The impact of grief: A retrospective study of family function following the loss of a child with cystic fibrosis. *Journal of Chronic Diseases, 32,* 221–225.

Killilea, M. (1976). Mutual help organizations: Interpretations in the literature. In G. Caplan & M. Killilea (Eds.), *Systems and mutual help.* New York: Grune & Stratton.

Kirkley-Best, E., & Kellner, K. R. (1982). The forgotten grief: A review of the psychology of stillbirth. *American Journal of Orthopsychiatry, 52,* 420–429.

Klaus, M., & Kennell, J. (1982). *Parent-infant bonding* (2nd ed.). St. Louis: Mosby.

Kleinman, A. (1982). Neurasthenia and depression. *Culture, Medicine and Psychiatry, 6,* 117–190.

Kleinschmidt, H. J., Waxenberg, S. E., & Cuker, R. (1965). Psychophysiologic and psychiatric management of thyrotoxicosis: A two year follow-up study. *Journal of the Mount Sinai Hospital, 23,* 131–153.

Klerman, G. L., & Izen, J. (1977). The effects of bereavement and grief on physical health and general well being. *Advances in Psychosomatic Medicine, 9,* 63–68.

Kliman, G. (1980). Death: Some implications in child development and child analysis. *Advances in Thanatology, 4,* 43–50.

Koocher, G. P. (1979). Adjustment and coping strategies among the caretakers of cancer patients. *Social Work in Health Care, 5,* 145–150.

Kornfeld, D. S. (1969). Psychiatric view of the intensive care unit. *British Medical Journal, 1,* 108–110.

Kosten, T. R., Jacobs, S. C., & Kasl, S. V. (1985). Terminal illness, bereavement, and the family. In D. C. Turk, & R. D. Kerns, *Health, illness and families: A life span perspective.* New York: Wiley.

Krant, M. J. (1975). The health professional. In B. Schoenberg, I. Gerber, A. Wiener, A. H. Kutscher, D. Peretz, & A. C. Carr (Eds.), *Bereavement: Its psychosocial aspects.* New York: Columbia University Press.

Kraus, A. S., & Lilienfeld, A. M. (1959). Some epidemiological aspects of high mortality rate in the young widowed group. *Journal of Chronic Diseases, 10,* 207–217.

Kreuger, A., Gyllenskold, K., Pehrsson, G., & Sjolin, S. (1981). Parent reactions to childhood malignant diseases. *The American Journal of Pediatric Hematology/Oncology, 3,* 233–238.

Krupnick, J., & Horowitz, M. (1981). Stress response syndromes: Recurrent themes. *Archives of General Psychiatry, 38,* 428–435.

Kubler-Ross, E. (1969). *On death and dying.* New York: Macmillan.

Kubler-Ross, E. (1981). *Living with death and dying.* New York: Macmillan.

Kupst, M. J., Schulman, J. L., Honig, G., Maurer, H., Morgan, E., & Fochtman, D. (1982). Family coping with childhood leukemia: One year after diagnosis. *Journal of Pediatric Psychology, 7,* 157–174.

Kutscher, A. H., & Kutscher, A. H., Jr. (1974). Medical school curriculum and anticipatory grief: Faculty attitudes. Chap. 24, pp. 213–217. In B. Schoenberg, A. Carr, A. Kutscher, D. Peretz, & I. Goldberg (Eds.), *Anticipatory grief.* New York: Columbia University Press.

LaGrand, L. E. (1980). Reducing burnout in the hospice and death education movement. *Death Education, 2,* 113–122.

LaGrand, L. E. (1981). Loss reactions of college students: A descriptive analysis. *Death Education, 5,* 235–248.

Lamm, M. (1969). *The Jewish way in death and mourning.* London: Jonathan David.

Lansky, S. B., Cairns, N. V., Hassanein, R., Wehr, J., & Lowman, J. T. (1978). Childhood cancer: Parental discord and divorce. *Pediatrics, 62,* 184–188.

Law Reform Commission of Canada. (1983). *Report on euthanasia, aiding suicide and cessation of treatment.* (Working paper no. 28). Ottawa: Ministry of Supply and Services Canada.

Lazare, A. (1979). Unresolved grief. In A. Lazare (Ed.), *Outpatient psychiatry: Diagnosis and treatment.* Baltimore: Williams & Wilkins.

Leaverton, D. R., White, C. A., McCormick, C. R., Smith, P., & Sheikholislam, B. (1980). Parental loss antecedent to childhood diabetes mellitus. *Journal of the American Academy of Child Psychiatry, 19,* 678–689.

Lebow, G. H. (1976). Facilitating adaptation in anticipatory mourning. *Social Casework, 57,* 458–465.

Legg, C., & Sherick, I. (1976). The replacement child—a developmental tragedy: Some preliminary comments. *Child Psychiatry and Human Development, 7,* 113–126.

Lerner, M. (1970). When, why and where people die. In O. G. Brim & H. E. Freeman (Eds.), *The dying patient.* New York: Russell Sage Foundation.

Levau, I. (1982). Mortality and psychopathology following the death of an adult child: An epidemiological review. *Israel Journal of Psychiatry and Related Sciences, 19,* 23–38.

Levintan, H. (1985). Onset of asthma during intense mourning. *Psychosomatics, 26* (12), 939–941.

Lewis, E. (1976). The management of stillbirth—coping with an unreality. *Lancet, 2,* 619–620.

Lewis, E. (1979). Mourning by the family after a stillbirth or neonatal death. *Archives of Diseases in Childhood, 54,* 303–306.

Lewis, E., & Page, A. (1978). Failure to mourn a stillbirth: An overlooked catastrophe. *British Journal of Medical Psychology, 51,* 237–241.

Lewis, S., & Armstrong, S. H. (1977–78). Children with terminal illness: A selected review. *International Journal of Psychiatry in Medicine, 8,* 73–82.

Lieberman, P. B., & Jacobs, S. C. (1987). Bereavement and its complications in medical patients: A guide for consultation—liaison psychiatrists. *International Journal of Psychiatry in Medicine, 17* (1), 23–29.

Lieberman, S. (1978). Nineteen cases of morbid grief. *British Journal of Psychiatry, 132,* 159–163.

Lifton, R. J. (1977). The sense of immortality. In H. Feifel (Ed.), *New meanings of death.* New York: McGraw-Hill.

Lindemann, E. (1944). Symptomatology and management of acute grief. *American Journal of Psychiatry, 101,* 141–148.

Lindemann, E., & Greer, I. M. (1972). A study of grief: Emotional responses to suicide. In A. Cain (Ed.), *Survivors of suicide* (pp. 63–69). Springfield: Charles C. Thomas.

Lippman, C. A., & Carlson, K. (1977). A model liaison program for the obstetric staff: Workshop on the tragic birth. In C. E. Hollingsworth & R. O. Pasnau (Eds.), *The family in mourning: A guide for health professionals.* New York: Grune & Stratton.

Lo, B. (1987). Behind closed doors: Promises and pitfalls of ethics committees. *New England Journal of Medicine, 317* (1), 46–50.

Lopata, H. (1973). Self-identity in marriage and widowhood. *The Sociological Quarterly, 14,* 407–418.

MacMahon, B., & Pugh, T. F. (1965). Suicide in the widowed. *American Journal of Epidemiology, 81,* 23–31.

Macon, L. B. (1979). Help for bereaved parents. *Social Casework, 60,* 558–565.

Madara, E. J., & Meese, A. (1986). *The self help source book: Finding and forming mutual aid self help groups.* Denville: Self Help Clearinghouse.

Maddison, D., & Viola, A. (1968). The health of widows in the year following bereavement. *Journal of Psychosomatic Research, 12,* 297–306.

Mandell, F., & Wolfe, L. C. (1975). Sudden infant death syndrome and subsequent pregnancy. *Pediatrics, 56,* 774–776.

Marks, M. J. B. (1976). The grieving patient and his family. *American Journal of Nursing, 76* (9), 1488–1490.

Marks, F. (in press). Seminars for medical students in the management of stillbirth. *First International Symposium on Grief and Bereavement: Vol. 2. Counseling and Therapy.* London: Freund Publishing House.

Markusen, E., Owen, G., Fulton, R., & Bendiksen, R. (1977–78). SIDS: The survivor as victim. *Omega, 8,* 277–284.

Martelli, L. J. (1987). *When someone you know has AIDS*. New York: Crown Publishers.

Martinson, I., Moldow, D., & Henry, W. (1980). *Home care for the child with cancer.* (DHHS Final Report, Grant No. CA 19490). Washington, DC: National Cancer Institute.

Martocchio, B. C. (1985). Grief and bereavement: Healing through hurt. *Nursing Clinics of North America, 20* (2), 327–341.

Mawson, D., Marks, I., Ramm, L., & Stern, R. (1981). Guided mourning for morbid grief: A controlled study. *British Journal of Psychiatry, 138,* 185–193.

May, H. J., & Breme, F. J. (1982–83). SIDS family adjustment scale: A method of assessing family adjustment to sudden infant death syndrome. *Omega, 13,* 59–74.

McCollum, A. T., & Schwartz, A. H. (1972). Social work and the mourning parent. *Social Work, 17,* 25–36.

McCue, J. D. (1982). The effects of stress on physicians and their medical practice. *The New England Journal of Medicine, 306,* 458–463.

Medical Ethics Advisor (1987). New Jersey: Medical Facilities must honor patient wishes. *3* (8), 93–98.

Mellins, R. B., & Haddad, G. G. (1983). Sudden infant death syndrome. In R. E. Behrman & V. C. Vaughn (Eds.), *Textbook of Pediatrics: Vol. 3* (12th ed.). Philadelphia: Saunders.

Melson, S. J., & Rynearson, E. K. (1982). Unresolved bereavement: Medical reenactment of a loved one's terminal illness. *Postgraduate Medicine, 72* (1), 172–179.

Miles, M. S. (1980). The effects of a course on death and grief on nurses' attitudes toward dying patients and death. *Death Education, 4* (1), 245–260.

Miles, M. S. (1985). Emotional symptoms and physical health in bereaved parents. *Nursing Research, 34* (2), 76–81.

Miles, S., & Demi, A. S. (1986). Guilt in bereaved parents. In T. A. Rando (Ed.), *Parental loss of a child: Clinical and research considerations.* Champaign: Research Press.

Moffatt, B. C. (1986). *When someone you love has AIDS*. New York: Penguin.

Morgan, D. (1980). Not all sadness can be treated with antidepressants. *West Virginia Medical Journal, 76,* 136–137.

Morgan, J. H., & Goering, R. (1978). Caring for parents who have lost an infant. *Journal of Religion and Health, 17,* 290–298.

Morillo, E., & Gardner, L. I. (1979). Bereavement as an antecedent factor in thryotoxicosis of childhood: Four case studies with survey of possible metabolic pathways. *Psychosomatic Medicine, 41,* 545–555.

Morin, S. F., & Batchelor, W. F. (1984). Responding to the psychological crisis of AIDS. *Public Health Reports, 99* (1), 4–10.

Mount, B. M. (1986). Dealing with our losses. *Journal of Clinical Oncology, 4* (7), 1127–1134.

Mount, B., & Voyer, J. (1980). Staff stress in palliative/hospice care. In Ajemian & B. Mount (Eds.), *The R.V.H. Manual on Palliative/Hospice Care.* New York: ARNO Press.

Mulhern, R., Laurer, M., & Hoffmann, R. (1983). Death of a child at home or in the hospital: Subsequent psychological adjustment of the family. *Pediatrics, 71,* 743–747.

Mullaney, J., & Fox, Z. (1981). Clinical nurse specialist and social worker. In J. Browne, B. Kirhn, & F. Watt (Eds.), *Rehabilitation services and the social work role: Challenge for change.* Baltimore: Williams & Wilkins.

Murphy, G. E., & Robins, E. (1967). Social factors in suicide. *JAMA, 199,* 303–308.

Musaph, H. (1973). Anniversary disease. *Psychotherapic Psychosomatique (Basel), 22* (2–6), 325–333.

Nagy, N. H. (1948). The child's theories concerning death. *Journal of Genetic Psychology, 73,* 3–27.

National Institute of Mental Health. (1986). Coping with AIDS: Psychological and social considerations in helping people with HTLV-VIII Infection. (DHHS Publication No. 85-1432) Washington, DC: U.S. Government Printing Office.

Nichols, S. E. (1986). Psychotherapy and AIDS. In T. S. Stein & C. S. Cohen (Eds.), *Contemporary perspectives on psychotherapy with lesbians and gay men.* New York: Plenum.

Nichols, S. E., & Ostrow, D. G. (Eds.). (1984). *Psychiatric implications of Acquired Immune Deficiency Syndrome.* Washington, DC: American Psychiatric Press.

Ochoa, M., Prichard, E. R., & Schwartzer, E. L. (1975). Social work and the bereaved. In B. Schoenberg, I. Gerber, A. Weiner, A. H. Kutscher, D. Peretz & A. C. Carr (Eds.), *Bereavement: Its psychosocial aspects* (pp. 243–255). New York: Columbia University Press.

Osterweis, M., Solomon, F., & Green, M. (Eds.). (1984). *Bereavement: Reactions, consequences and care.* Washington, DC: National Academy Press.

Owen, G., Fulton, R., & Markusen, E. (1982–83). Death at a distance: A study of family survivors. *Omega, 13,* 191–225.

Pakes, E. H. (1979). *Physicians' response to the diagnosis of cancer in his child patient.* Unpublished manuscript.

Parkes, C. M. (1970). The first year of bereavement: A longitudinal study of the reaction of London widows to the death of their husbands. *Psychiatry, 33,* 444–467.

Parkes, C. M. (1970). "Seeking" and "finding" a lost object: Evidence from recent studies of the reaction to bereavement. *Social Science and Medicine*, 4, 187–201.

Parkes, C. M. (1975). Determinants of outcome following bereavement. *Omega*, 6, 303–323.

Parkes, C. M. (1980). Bereavement counseling: Does it work? *British Medical Journal, 281*, 3–6.

Parkes, C. M. (1986). *Bereavement studies of grief in adult life.* (3rd ed.). New York: International Universities Press.

Parkes, C. M., & Brown, R. J. (1972). Health after bereavement: A controlled study of young Boston widows and widowers. *Psychosomatic Medicine, 34*, 449–461.

Parkes, C. M., & Weiss, R. S. (1983). *Recovery from bereavement.* New York: Basic Books.

Parkes, C. M., Benjamin, B., & Fitzgerald, R. G. (1969). Broken heart: A statistical study of increased mortality among widowers. *British Medical Journal, 1*, 740–743.

Phillips, D. F. (1972). The hospital and the dying patient. *Journal of the American Hospital Association, 46*, 4.

Plank, E. N. (1971). *Working with children in hospitals.* Chicago: Year Book Medical Publishers.

Poppoff, D. (1975). About death and dying: Part 2. *Nursing, 5* (8), 16–22.

Poppoff, D. (1975). What are your feelings about death and dying? *Nursing, 5* (9), 53–62.

Poznanski, E. (1972). The "replacement child": A saga of unresolved parental grief. *Journal of Pediatrics, 81*, 1190–1193.

President's Commission for the Study of Ethical Problems in Medicine and Biomedical and Behavioral Research (1983). *Deciding to forego life-sustaining treatment.* Washington, D.C.: U.S. Government Printing Office.

Prichard, E. R. (1974). The social worker's responsibility. In B. Schoenberg, A. Carr, A. Kutscher, D. Peretz, & I. Goldberg (Eds.), *Anticipatory Grief* (pp. 237–245). New York: Columbia University Press.

Quint, J. (1967). *The nurse and the dying patient.* New York: Macmillan.

Rabin, D. L., & Rabin, L. H. (1970). Consequences of death for physicians, nurses and hospitals. In O. G. Brim & H. E. Freeman (Eds.), *The dying patient.* New York: Russell Sage Foundation.

Raether, H. C., & Slater, R. C. (1977). Immediate post-death activities in the United States. In H. Feifel (Ed.), *New meanings of death.* New York: McGraw-Hill.

Rahe, R. (1975). A liaison psychiatrist on the coronary care unit. In R. O. Pasnau, *Consultation-liaison psychiatry.* New York: Grune & Stratton.

Rainey, L. C., Wellisch, D. K., Fawzy, F. I., Wolcott, D., & Pasnau, R. O. (1983). Training health professionals in psychosocial aspects of cancer: A continuing education model. *Journal of Psychosocial Oncology, 1* (2), 41–60.

Ramsay, R. W. (1979). Bereavement: A behavioral treatment of pathological grief. In P. O. Sioden, S. Bates, & W. S. Dorkens, III (Eds.), *Trends in behavior therapy.* New York: Academic Press.

Rando, T. A. (1981). Concepts of death, dying, grief and loss. In *Hospice Education Program for Nurses* (DHHS-HRA 81–27). Washington, DC: U.S. Government Printing Office.

Rando, T. A. (1983). An investigation of grief and adaptation in parents whose children have died from cancer. *Journal of Pediatric Psychology, 8,* 3–20.

Rando, T. A. (1984). *Grief, dying and death.* Champaign: Research Press.

Rando, T. A. (1987). *Parental loss of a child.* Champaign: Research Press.

Raphael, B. (1983). *The anatomy of bereavement.* New York: Basic Books.

Raphael, B., & Maddison, D. (1976). The care of bereaved adults. In O. W. Hill (Ed.), *Modern trends in psychosomatic medicine.* London: Butterworth.

Reed, E. (1972). *Helping children with the mystery of death.* New York: Abingdon Press.

Rees, D. W. (1975). The bereaved and their hallucinations. Chapter 7 in B. Schoenberg, I. Gerber, A. Wiener, A. H. Kutscher, D. Peretz, & A. Carr (Eds.), *Bereavement: Its Psychosocial Aspects.* New York: Columbia University Press.

Rees, W. D., & Lutkins, S. G. (1967). Mortality of bereavement. *British Medical Journal, 4,* 13–16.

Reilly, M. E., & Cohen, G. J. (1983). Follow-up study of the effectiveness of an emergency room DOA protocol. *Clinical Proceedings of Children's Hospital National Medical Center, 39,* 92–99.

Resnik, H. L. P. (1969). Psychological resynthesis: Clinical approach to the survivors of a death by suicide. In E. S. Shneidman & M. Ortega (Eds.), *Aspects of depression.* Boston: Little Brown.

Reynolds, R. (1978). Autopsies—benefit to the family. *American Journal of Clinical Pathology, 69,* 220–222.

Richmond, J. B., & Waisman, H. A. (1955). Psychological aspects of management of children with malignant diseases. *American Journal of Diseases of Children, 89,* 42–47.

Rinear, E. E. (1975). Helping the survivors of expected death. *Nursing, 5* (3), 60–65.

Rinear, E. E. (1975). The nurse's role when death is unexpected. *R.N., 38* (12), 50–55.

Rogers, J., Sheldon, A., Barwick, C., Letorfsky, K., & Lancee, W. (1982). Help for families of suicide survivors support program. *Canadian Journal of Psychiatry, 27,* 444–448.

Rosenblatt, P. C., Walsh, R. P., & Jackson, D. A. (1977). *Grief and mourning in cross-cultural perspective.* Washington, DC: HRAF Press.

Roskin, M. (1980). Integrating primary prevention into social work practice. *Social Work, 25,* 192–197.

Rothenberg, M. (1967). Reactions of those who treat children with cancer. *Pediatrics, 40,* 507–510.

Rutter, M. (1966). *Children of sick parents.* London: Oxford University Press.

Sahler, O. J. (Ed.). (1978). *The child and death.* St. Louis: Mosby.

Sanders, C. (1979–80). A comparison of adult bereavement in the death of a spouse, child, and parent. *Omega, 10,* 303–322.

Sargent, et al. (1977). Preventing physician suicide. *JAMA 237,* 143–145.

Schmale, A. H., & Iker, H. P. (1966). The affect of hopelessness and the development of cancer: I, Identification of uterine cervical cancer in women with atypical cytology. *Psychosomatic Medicine, 28,* 714–721.

Schmidt, D. D., & Messner, E. (1975). The management of ordinary grief. *Journal of Family Practice, 2* (4), 259–262.

Schoenberg, B., Carr, A., Kutscher, A., Peretz, D., Goldberg, I. (Eds.). (1974). *Anticipatory Grief.* New York: Columbia University Press.

Schreiner, R. L. (1984). The death of a newborn. In M. Green & R. J. Haggerty (Eds.), *Ambulatory Pediatrics: Vol. 3.* Philadelphia: Saunders.

Schreiner, R. L., Gresham, E. L., & Green, M. (1979). Physician's responsibility to parents after death of an infant. *American Journal of Diseases of Children, 133,* 723–726.

Schultz, R., & Alderman, D. (1978). Physicians' death anxiety and patient outcomes. *Omega, 9,* 327–332.

Schuyler, D. (1973). Counseling suicide survivors: Issues and answers. *Omega, 4,* 313–321.

Scottolini, A. G., & Weinstein, S. R. (1983). The autopsy in clinical quality control. *JAMA, 250* (9), 1192–1194.

Segal, S., Fletcher, M., & Meekison, W. G. (1986). Survey of bereaved parents. *Canadian Medical Association Journal, 134* (1), 38–42.

Seitz, P. M., & Wattick, L. H. (1974). Perinatal death and the grieving mother. *American Journal of Nursing, 11,* 2028–33.

Shanfield, S. B. (1983). Predicting bereavement outcome: Marital factors. *Family Systems Medicine, 1* (1), 42–46.

Shepherd, D., & Barraclough, B. M. (1974). The aftermath of suicide. *British Medical Journal, 2,* 600–603.

Shneidman, E. S. (1973). *Deaths of Man.* New York: Quadrangle.

Short, M. J., & Wilson, W. P. (1969). Roles of denial in chronic dialysis. *Archives of General Psychiatry, 20,* 433–437.

Shubin, S. (1978). Burnout: The professional hazard you face in nursing. *Nursing, 78* (8), 22–27.

Shuchter, S. R. (1982). Antidepressant treatment of grief reaction. *Scientific Proceedings of the 135th Annual Meeting of the American Psychiatric Association,* Torönto, Canada, May 15–21.

Shuchter, S. R. (1984). How the family physician can help patients adjust to the death of a spouse. *Medical Aspects of Human Sexuality, 18,* 30–32, 36, 41–44, 49–54.

Shuchter, S. R., & Zisook, S. (1987). A multidimensional model of spousal bereavement. In S. Zisook (Ed.), *Biopsychosocial aspects of bereavement.* Washington, DC: American Psychiatric Press.

Shuchter, S. R., & Zisook, S. (1987). The therapeutic tasks of grief. In S. Zisook (Ed.), *Biopsychosocial aspects of bereavement.* Washington, DC: American Psychiatric Press.

Siegel, R. L., & Hoefer, D. D. (1981). Bereavement counseling for gay individuals. *American Journal of Psychotherapy, 35* (4), 517–525.

Silverman, P. R. (1970). The widow as a caregiver in a program of preventive intervention with other widows. *Mental Hygiene, 54* (4), 540–547.

Silverman, P. R., MacKenzie, D., Pettipas, M., & Wilson, E. W. (Eds.). (1974). *Helping each other in widowhood.* New York: Health Sciences Publishing.

Solomon, F., White, C., Patton, D. L., & Mendelson, W. (1979). Sleeping pills, insomnia and medical practice. *New England Journal of Medicine, 300,* 803–809.

Spiegel, D. (1980). The recent literature: Self-help and mutual support groups. *Community Mental Health Review, 5,* 15–25.

Spikes, J. (1979). Physician's reactions to death. *Continuing Education, 10,* 54–64.

Spikes, J., & Holland, J. C. (1975). The physician's response to the dying patient. In J. Strain & S. Grossman (Eds.), *Psychological care of the mentally ill: A primer in liaison psychiatry.* New York: Appleton-Century-Crofts.

Spinetta, J., Swarner, J., & Sheposh, J. (1981). Effective parental coping following the death of a child from cancer. *Journal of Pediatric Psychology, 6,* 251–263.

Start, C. (1973). *On becoming a widow.* New York: Family Library.

Stedeford, A. (1983). *Facing death: Patients, families and professionals.* London: Heinemann.

Stone, H. W. (1972). *Suicide and grief.* Philadelphia: Fortress Press.

Storch, J. (1982). *Patients' rights: Ethical and legal issues in health care and nursing.* Toronto: McGraw-Hill Ryerson.

Strain, J. J., & Grossman, S. (1975). *Psychological care of the medically ill: A primer in liaison psychiatry.* New York: Appleton Century Crofts.

Stringham, J. G., Riley, J. H., & Ross, A. (1982). Silent birth: Mourning a stillborn baby. *Social Work, 27,* 322–327.

Stroebe, M. S., & Stroebe, W. (1983). Who suffers more? Sex differences in health risks of the widowed. *Psychological Bulletin, 93,* 279–301.

Stroebe, M. S., Stroebe, W., Gergen, K. J., & Gergen, M. (1981–82). The broken heart: Reality or myth? *Omega, 12,* 87–106.

Stromberg, E. D. (1987). Crisis intervention by the hospital social worker with families of shock trauma patients. *First International Symposium on Grief and Bereavement: Vol. 2. Counseling and Therapy.* London: Freund Publishing House.

Stuart, G. W., Sundeen, S. J. (1987). *Principles and practice of psychiatric nursing.* St. Louis: Mosby.

Stubblefield, K. (1977). A preventive program for bereaved families. *Social Work in Health Care, 2,* 379–389.

Sudnow, D. (1967). *Passing on.* Englewood Cliffs: Prentice Hall.

Thompson, L., Breckenridge, J., Gallagher, D., & Peterson, J. (1984). Effects of bereavement on self-perceptions of physical health in elderly widows and widowers. *Journal of Gerontology, 39,* 309–314.

Tietz, W., McSherry, L., & Britt, B. (1977). Family sequelae after a child's death due to cancer. *American Journal of Psychotherapy, 31* (3), 417–425.

Todres, I. D., Howell, M. C., & Shannon, D. C. (1974). Physicians' reactions to training in pediatric intensive care unit. *Pediatrics, 53* (3), 375–383.

Treuting, T. F. (1962). The role of emotional factors in the etiology and course of diabetes mellitus: A review of the recent literature. *American Journal of Medical Sciences, 244,* 93–109.

Turco, R. (1981). The treatment of unresolved grief following the loss of an infant. *American Journal of Obstetrics and Gynecology, 141,* 503–507.

Turnbull, Richard (Ed.). (1986). *Terminal care.* Washington, DC: Hemisphere.

United States Department of Health, Education and Welfare (1978). *Facts of life and death.* Washington, D.C., U.S. Government Printing Office.

University of Oregon Health Sciences Center, Dept. of OBGYN. (1987). *When hello means goodbye.* (Booklet) Eugene: University of Oregon Press.

Vachon, M. L. S. (1983). Bereavement programmes and intervention in palliative care. In E. A. Mirand, W. B. Hutchinson, & E. Mihich (Eds.), *Thirteenth International Cancer Congress, Part E Cancer Management* (pp. 451–461). New York: Liss.

Vachon, M. L. S. (1983). On the suffering of caregivers in the care of the critically ill and dying. In C. Levine (Ed.), *Death, suffering and well-being.* New York: Plenum.

Vachon, M. L. S. (1987). *Occupational stress in the care of the critically ill, the dying, and the bereaved.* Washington, DC: Hemisphere.

Vachon, M. L. S., Lyall, W. A. L., & Freeman, S. J. J. (1978). Measurement and management of stress in health professionals working with advanced cancer patients. *Death Education, 1,* 365–375.

Vachon, M. L. S., Sheldon, A. R., Lance, W. J., Lyall, W. A., Rogers, J., & Freeman, S. (1982). Correlates of enduring stress patterns following bereavement: Social network, life situation, and personality. *Psychological Medicine, 12,* 783–788.

Vaughn, V. C. (1983). Critical life events: Sibling births, separations, and deaths in the family. In M. Levine, W. Carey, A. Crocker, & R. Gross (Eds.), *Developmental-behavioral Pediatrics.* Philadelphia: Saunders.

Veatch, R. M. (1977). Caring for the dying person: Ethical issues at stake. In D. Barton (Ed.), *Dying and death: A clinical guide for caregivers.* Baltimore: Williams & Wilkins.

Veatch, R. M. (1981). *A theory of medical ethics.* New York: Basic Books.

Videka-Sherman, L. (1982). Effects of participation in a self-help group for bereaved parents: Compassionate Friends. *Prevention in the Human Services, 1,* 69–77.

Volkan, V. (1966). Normal and pathological grief reactions: A guide for the family physician. *Virginia Medical Monthly, 93,* 651–656.

Volkan, V. (1975). More on "Re-grief" therapy. *Journal of Thanatology, 3,* 77.

Vollman, R. R., Gonzert, A., Richer, L., & Williams, W. V. (1971). The reactions of family systems to sudden and unexpected death. *Omega, 2,* 101–106.

Wahl, C. (1973). Psychological treatment of the dying patient. In University of Southern California, Ethel Percy Andrus Gerontology Center. *Dealing With Death* (pp. 18–23). Los Angeles: Author.

Waller, D. A., Todres, I. D., & Cassem, N. H. (1979). Coping with post prognosis in the Pediatric Intensive Care Unit. *American Journal of Diseases of Children, 133,* 1121–1125.

Wanzer, S. H., Adelstein, S. J., Crawford, R. E., Federman, D. D., Hook, E. D., Moertel, C. G., Safar, P., Stone, A., Taussig, H. B., & Zan-Eys, J. (1984). The physician's responsibility toward hopelessly ill patients. *New England Journal of Medicine, 310* (15), 959.

Wass, H., & Corr, C. A. (Eds.). (1984). *Childhood and death.* Washington, DC: Hemisphere.

Wass, H., Corr, C. A., Tacholski, R. A., & Sanders, C. M. (1985). *Death education I & II: An annotated resource guide.* Washington DC: Hemisphere.

Watson, S., & Hickey, P. A. (1984). Cancer surgery: Help for the family in waiting. *American Journal of Nursing, 84* (5), 604–607.

Weiner, M. F., & Caldwell, T. (1981). Stresses and coping in ICU nursing II: Nurse support groups on intensive care units. *General Hospital Psychiatry, 3* (2), 129–134.

Weinman-Lear, M. (1980). *Heartsounds.* New York: Pocket Books.

Weisman, A. D. (1972). *On dying and denying.* New York: Behavioral Publications.

Weisman, A. D. (1977). The psychiatrist and the inexorable. In H. Feifel (Ed.), *New meaning of death.* New York: McGraw-Hill.

Weisman, A. D., & Hackett, T. P. (1961). Predilection to death. *Psychosomatic Medicine, 23,* 232–255.

Weisman, A. D., & Kastenbaum, R. (1968). The psychological autopsy: A study of the terminal phase of life. *Community Mental Health Journal Monographs, 4.*

Welu, T. C. (1975). Pathological bereavement: A plan for its prevention. In B. Schoenberg, I. Gerber, A. Wiener, A. H. Kutscher, D. Peretz, & A. C. Carr (Eds.), *Bereavement: Its psychosocial aspects* (pp. 139–149). New York: Columbia University Press.

Winder, A., & Elam, J. (1978). Therapist for the cancer patient's family: A new role for the nurse. *Journal of Psychiatric Nursing, 16* (10), 22–27.

White, L. P. (1977). Death and the physician: Mortui vivos docent. In H. Feifel (Ed.), *New meaning of death.* New York: McGraw-Hill.

Whitis, P. R. (1972). The legacy of a child's suicide. In A. C. Cain (Ed.), *Survivors of suicide* (pp. 155–166). Springfield: Charles C. Thomas.

Wiener, J. M. (1970). Reaction of the family to the fatal illness of a child. In B. Schoenberg, A. C. Carr, D. Peretz, & A. H. Kutscher (Eds.) *Loss and grief.* New York: Columbia University Press.

Wiener, A., Gerber, I., Battin, D., & Arkin, A. M. (1975). The process and phenomenology of bereavement. In B. Schoenberg, I. Gerber, A. Wiener, A. H. Kutschner, D. Peretz, and A. C. Carr (Eds.), *Bereavement: Its psychosocial aspects.* New York: Columbia University Press.

Willis, W. (1977). Bereavement management in the Emergency Department. *Journal of Emergency Nursing, 2,* 35–39.

Wolff, J. R., Nielson, P. E., & Schiller, P. (1970). The emotional reaction to a stillbirth. *American Journal of Obstetrics and Gynecology, 108,* 73–77.

Woodward, S., Pope, A., Robson, W. J., & Hogan, O. (1985). Bereavement counselling after sudden infant death. *British Medical Journal, 290* (6465), 363–365.

Worden, J. W. (1982). *Grief counseling and grief therapy.* New York: Springer.

Worlow, D. (1978). What do you say when the baby is stillborn? *R.N., 41* (7), 74.

Young, M., Benjamin, B., & Wallis, C. (1963). The mortality of widowers. *Lancet, 2,* 454–456.

Zelman, A. (1984) cited in Committee on the Health Consequences of the Stress of Bereavement. Site Visit Case Studies, Institute of Medicine, National Academy of Sciences.

Zisook, S. (Ed.). (1987). *Biopsychosocial aspects of bereavement.* Washington, DC: American Psychiatric Press.

Zisook, S. (1987). Unresolved grief. In S. Zisook (Ed.), *Biopsychosocial aspects of bereavement.* Washington, DC: American Psychiatric Press.

Zisook, S. (1987). Differentiating normal grief from major depression. *Clinical Advances in the Treatment of Depression, 1* (1), 4–5.

Zisook, S., & DeVaul, R. A. (1976–77). Grief-related facsimile illness. *International Journal of Psychiatry in Medicine, 7* (4), 329–336.

Zisook, S., & DeVaul, R. A. (1983). Grief, unresolved grief, and depression. *Psychosomatics, 24,* 247–256.

Zisook, S., & Shuchter, S. R. (1986). The first four years of widowhood. *Psychiatric Annals, 16,* 288–298.

Zisook, S., DeVaul, R. A., & Click, M. A., Jr. (1982). Measuring symptoms of grief and bereavement. *American Journal of Psychiatry, 139* (2), 1590–1593.

Zisook, S., Shuchter, S. R., & Lyons, L. E. (1987). Adjustment to widowhood. In Zisook, S. (Ed.), *Biopsychosocial aspects of bereavement.* Washington, DC: American Psychiatric Press.

Zisook, S., Shuchter, S., & Schuckit, M. (1985). Factors in the persistence of unresolved grief among psychiatric outpatients. *Psychosomatics, 26* (6), 497–503.

SUGGESTED READINGS

WIDOWS

Brooks, A. M. (1985). *The grieving time: A year's account of recovery from loss.* New York: Dial Press.

Caine, L. (1974). *Widow.* New York: Bantam Books, Inc.

Gatov, E. (1985). *Widows in the dark: Rescuing your financial position.* An Income-Saving and Survival Guide. Bolinas: Common Knowledge Press. Available from E. Gatov, P.O. Box 236, Kentfield, CA 94914.

Klopfenstein, J. (1976). *My walk through grief.* Scottsdale: Herald Press.

Lewis, C. S. (1976). *A grief observed.* New York: Bantam Books, Inc.

Loewinsohn, R. J. (1979). *Survival handbook for widows (and for relatives and friends who want to understand).* Chicago: Follett Publishing Co.

Manning, D. (1984). *Don't take my grief away.* New York: Harper and Row.

Start, C. (1973). *On becoming a widow.* New York: Family Library.

Wylie, B. J. (1986). *The survival guide for widows.* New York: Ballantine Books, Inc.

FOR BEREAVED PARENTS

Bardow, J. (1982). *The ultimate loss; Coping with the death of a child.* Beaufort: Beaufort Book Co.

Donnelly, K. F. (1982). *Recovering from the loss of a child*. New York: MacMillan.
Knapp, R. J. (1986). *Beyond endurance: When a child dies*. New York: Schocken Books, Inc.
Schatz, W. H. (1984). *Healing a father's grief*. Redmond: Medic Publishing Co.
Schiff, H. S. (1977). *The bereaved parent*. New York: Penguin Books.

For Children Ages 4 to 8

Clardy, A. F. (1984). *Dusty was my friend*. New York: Human Sciences Press.
Fassler, J. (1971). *My grandpa died today*. New York: Human Sciences Press.
Green, P. (1978). *A new mother for Martha*. New York: Human Sciences Press.
Hickman, M. W. (1984). *Last week my brother Anthony died*. Knoxville: Abingdon Press.
Ross, E. K. (1982). *Remember the secret*. New York: MacMillan.
Viorst, J. (1975). *The tenth good thing about Barney*. New York: Atheneum.

For Children Ages 9 to 14

Bernstein, J. & Gallo, S. (1977). *When people die*. New York: Dutton.
Jampolsky, G. (1978). *There's a rainbow behind every dark cloud*. Milbrae: Celestial Arts.
Krementz, J. (1981). *How it feels when a parent dies*. New York: Knopf.
Levy, E. L. (1982). *Children are not paper dolls*. Greeley: Harvest Printing.
Smith, D. (1973). *A taste of blackberries*. New York: T. Y. Crowell.
Watts, R. G. (1975). *Strangest talk about death with young people*. Philadelphia: Westminster Press.

For Children Over 14

Gunther, J. (1949). *Death be not proud*. New York: Harper and Row.
LeShan, E. (1976). *Learning to say good-bye: When a parent dies*. New York: Avon Books.
Lunk, D. L. (1976). *Eric*. New York: Dell.

For Grieving Families and Friends

Carroll, D. (1985). *Living with dying: A loving guide for family and close friends*. New York: McGraw Hill.

Grollman, E. A. (Ed.) (1980). *When your loved one is dying.* Boston: Beacon Press.

Grollman, E. A. (1981). *What helped me when my loved one died.* Boston: Beacon Press.

Kubler-Ross, E. (1981). *Living with death and dying.* New York: MacMillan.

Kushner, H. S. (1978). *To live until we say goodbye.* Englewood Cliffs: Prentice-Hall.

Kushner, H. S. (1983). *When bad things happen to good people.* New York: Avon Books.

Staudacher, C. (1987). *Beyond grief: A guide for recovering from the death of a loved one.* Oakland: New Harbinger Publications.

Stedeford, A. (1984). *Facing death: Patients, families and professionals.* London: William Heinemann Medical Books.

Weizman, S. G. & Kamm, P. (1984). *About mourning.* New York: Human Sciences Press.

TELLING CHILDREN ABOUT DEATH

Gordon, A. & Klass, D. (1979). *They need to know: How to teach children about death.* Englewood Cliffs: Prentice-Hall.

Grollman, E. A. (1967). *Explaining death to children.* Boston: Beacon Press.

Grollman, E. A. (1976). *Talking about death: A dialogue between parent and child with parent's guide and recommended resources.* Boston: Beacon Press.

Jackson, E. N. (1965). *Telling a child about death.* New York: Hawthorn Books.

Klopfenstein, J. (1977). *Tell me about death, mommy.* Scottdale: Herald Press.

Schaefer, D. & Lyons, C. (1986). *How do we tell the children?* A parents' guide to helping children understand and cope when someone dies. New York: Newmarkt Press.

PERINATAL LOSS

Berezin, N. (1982). *After a loss in pregnancy; Help for families affected by a miscarriage, a stillbirth or a newborn's death.* New York: Simon and Schuster.

Borg, S. O. & Lasker, J. (1981). *When pregnancy fails; Families coping with miscarriages, stillbirth and infant death.* Boston: Beacon Press.

Covington, S. N. (1986). *Silent birth . . . If your baby dies.* Available from S. N. Covington, 9715 Medical Center Dr., Suite 503, Rockville, MD, 20850.

Limbo, R. K. & Wheeler, S. R. (1987). *When a baby dies: A handbook for healing and helping.* Holmen: Harsand Press.

SIDS

DeFrain, J. D. (1982). *Coping with sudden infant death.* Newbury Park: Lexington Books.

STILLBIRTH

University of Oregon Health Sciences Center, Department of OBGYN. (1987). *When hello means goodbye.* Portland: University of Oregon.

MISCARRIAGE

Friedmann, R. & Gradstein, B. (1982). *Surviving pregnancy loss.* Boston: Little Brown.
Ilse, S. & Burns, L. H. (1985). *Miscarriage: A shattered dream.* Long Lake: Wintergreen Press.
Panuthos, C. & Romeo, C. (1984). *Ended beginnings.* South Hadley: Bergin and Garvey Publishers.

SUICIDE

Berent, I. (1981). *The algebra of suicide.* New York: Human Sciences Press.
Cain, A. (Ed.) (1972). *Survivors of suicide.* Springfield: Charles C. Thomas.
Hendin, H. (1982). *Suicide in America.* New York: W. W. Norton.
Hewett, J. H. (1980). *After suicide.* Philadelphia: Westminster Press.

TEENAGE SUICIDE

Klagsbrun, F. (1981). *Too young to die.* New York: Pocket Books.

TERMINAL ILLNESS

van Bommel, H. (1987). *Choices for people who have a terminal illness, Their families and their caregivers.* Toronto: NC Press Limited.

Euthanasia

Humphry, D. (1986). *Let me die before I wake.* Published by the Hemlock Society, L.A. Distributed by Grove Press, New York.

Humphry, D. & Wickett, A. (1986). *The right to die.* New York: Harper and Row.

Rollin, B. (1985). *Last wish.* New York: Signet.

MADD

Lord, J. H. (1987). *No time for good byes: Coping with sorrow, anger and injustice after a tragic death.* Ventura: Pathfinder Publishing.

APPENDIXES

Age-Related Concepts of Death for Children

Children ages 2–3.
> No idea of what death means. They can confuse it with sleep and experience some anxiety at age 3; however, this is more usual at ages 5–6.

Children ages 3–6.
> a. Does not know death as such. The child attributes life and consciousness to the dead. Death is seen as departure and sleep—alive but in a limited way, only somewhat changed. Does not fully separate death from life; i.e., idea that the individual continues to live in the ground still eating, going to the toilet, breathing and playing.
>
> b. Physical death can be acknowledged but considered as a temporary or gradual event. It seems reversible and not final; i.e., peek-a-boo or leaving and coming back.
>
> c. May consider it an unnatural event or an event outside of themselves; i.e., caused by violence or accident or attack. They may suspect that angry feelings can cause death but they may live if lucky and careful. The most frightening awareness is that they may die someday.

Children ages 6–9.
  a. Death is personified as a separate person or spirit; i.e., a skeleton, ghost, angel of death or boogeyman.
  b. Death perceived as final and frightening but still not universal. They begin to compromise; i.e., death is final and real but mostly to aged (outside of themselves).
  c. Children can be very curious about death at this age.
Children ages 9 and older.
  a. Death is seen as a process that occurs inevitably according to universal laws based on biological observation.
  b. Usually not seen as punishment or violence; i.e., not outer attack but inner law.
  c. It is viewed as final and universal. A view usually achieved by age 12.

Appendix B

Training Films

1. The Pitch of Grief (30 minutes video cassette, color) by Eric Stange
    The film depicts the emotional process of grieving through intimate interviews with four men and women, young and old, who have lost loved ones and lived through the aftermath.
2. Code Gray: Ethical Dilemmas in Nursing (28 minutes 16 mm and video cassette, color)
    by Ben Achtenberg and Joan Sawyer in collaboration with Christine Mitchell, R.N.
    The film documents four actual situations where nurses confront ethical dilemmas in their work. In the case of a newborn with profound and probably fatal birth defects, nurses must decide what level of care represents *beneficence* or "doing good." The staff in a nursing home must decide between respect for a resident's *autonomy* and the need to restrain her to prevent injury. Nurses in an Intensive Care Unit make daily decisions about the allocation of bed space and nursing resources in accordance with the principle of *justice*. A nurse caring for a terminally ill patient faces a conflict between *fidelity* to her commitment to relieve suffering and the promises made to the patient's family. The film offers no easy answer to the questions. It is designed

to trigger discussion among nurses, physicians, other health workers, and medical, nursing, and social work students.
Available from Fanlight Productions
    47 Halifax Street
    Boston, MA 02130
    Tel: (617) 524-0980
3. Death of a Wished for Child: The Order of the Golden Rule
    by G. W. Davidson
Available from
P.O. Box 3586
Springfield, IL 62708
4. Death and Dying: The Physician's Perspective (29 minutes video
    cassette, color)
    Produced by Elizabeth Bradbury
    Good film for physicians and health personnel who deal with the
dying. Should be required viewing for medical students.
Available from Fanlight Productions
47 Halifax Street
Boston, MA 02130
5. *Suzy's Story* (60 minutes film, color)
    Produced by Carlyon-Gillespie and Pro-Image Productions, dis-
    tributed by 20th Century Fox.
    Excellent film produced by dying patient's husband depicting final
stages of heterosexual AIDS. Filmed in Sidney, Australia, March/April
1987.

APPENDIX C

Purpose: To provide guidelines for handling stillbirths.
Objective: To provide continuity of care to parents experiencing a
           stillbirth.
   I. Support of Parents Prior to Delivery:
     A. Encourage ventilation of feelings.
     B. Encourage support person to stay with mother.
     C. Encourage one-to-one nursing support.
     D. Administer/order pain medications.
     E. Inform mother of her option of being transferred to an-
        other unit after delivery.

    F.   Notify clergy according to parents' wishes.

    G. Note parents' wishes on care plan.

II.   Care of Infant After Delivery:

    A.   Physical care of infant

        1.   Take to soiled utility room to complete care.

        2.   Weigh and measure.

           a.   Save disposable tape measure for parents.

        3.   Cut small piece of hair for parents, tape to infant

III.   A. Memory Sheet

           a.   Save comb for parents

        4.   Apply Hollister cord clamp to cord, remove hemostat.

        5.   Footprint on birth record.

           a.   Obtain mother's thumbprints first.

           b.   Footprint "Infant Memory Sheet."

           c.   Footprints may be deleted if infant is macerated, note this on footprint record.

        6.   Identify with ID band.

           a.   Make two bands so that one can be given to parents.

        7.   Complete two crib cards.

           a.   One for parents

           b.   One to tag outside of blanket prior to taking infant to morgue.

        8.   Baptize infant after obtaining verbal permission from parents.

        9.   Save all above-mentioned baby effects to be given to parents.

           a.   Infant Memory Sheet, hair cutting, tape measure, comb, crib card, ID band.

           b.   Place in manila envelope, place mother's name and date of infant's birth on outside.

           Note: If parents do not claim belongings, save on storage shelf in soiled utility room L/D; retain for five years; if not claimed, they will be discarded.

      10.   Ask parents if they want an instant picture taken of baby; obtain consent form.

      11.   Discuss with parents their options in viewing the baby.

      12.   If infant is very small (*i.e.*, 1 lb.; 16–20 wk.) or very macerated, a properly labeled specimen container is used to transport to morgue.

Common sense will dictate which of the previously listed measures is appropriate and which can be used to support parents.

    B.   Documentation, required forms

        1.   Birth Record (footprint sheet)

           a.   Complete as much as possible prior to delivery to avoid questioning parents later.

           b.   Obtain mother's thumbprints prior to delivery if possible.

           c.   Make parents aware they may name the baby.

           d.   When complete—place in Ward Clerk's file on postpartum unit.

        2.   Stillbirth Certificate (2 certificates with carbon between).

           a.   Required by state law on any stillborn 16 weeks gestation or older; if in doubt of age, follow through with procedure; the pathologist will give final determination of gestational age.

           b.   Physician consulted by coroner.

        1.   Coroner signs certificate on a coroner's case.

        2.   Physician signs certificate otherwise.

           c.   Send original signed certificate to Nursing Office; retain carbon copy on mother's chart.

        3.   Record of Death Sheet

           a.   Send to Nursing Office after infant is taken to the morgue.

        4.   Checklist for Assisting Parents

           a.   Check as items are complete; place on mother's care plan. Remove at time of discharge and file on postpartum unit.

    C.   Infant to morgue

        1.   Be sure parents have had opportunity to hold/view infant.

        2.   Be sure infant is identified.

        3.   Wrap infant in blanket.

        4.   Tag outside of blanket with crib card.

        5.   Notify security to meet you at morgue to open door.

        6.   Take infant to morgue via back stairwell.

        7.   Place in morgue compartment (cooler).

        8.   Complete record of death sheet, forward to Nursing Office.

III. Support of Parents after Delivery:
   A. Allow parents to view/hold baby as desired.
      1. In delivery room
         a. Physician agrees that mother's condition permits.
         b. If physically or emotionally unable, inform parents they may view baby later.
         c. It is preferrable to keep baby in soiled utility room of L/D until all family members have viewed, provided this is a reasonable period of time (*i.e.*, 1–2 hours).
      2. In immediate postpartum period after transfer from delivery room.
         a. As mother's condition permits.
         b. Allow grandparents as couple desires.
      3. After infant has been taken to morgue.
         a. Notify Supervisor and Security of request.
         b. Meet Security at morgue to obtain baby, wrap in a warm blanket.
         c. Use back stairwell to return baby to OB conference room for viewing.
            1a. To meet Infection Control Guidelines, all individuals viewing the baby must wash hands prior to returning to patient's room.
      4. Stay with parents while they view baby.
         a. Silent support sometimes best.
         b. If parent's condition warrants, you may leave them alone for awhile.
         c. *Remember*—some parents may never be able to be left alone.
   B. Make parents aware of necessary decisions
      1. Autopsy
         a. Coroner is notified of all stillborns by the Nursing Supervisor.
         b. Coroner discusses case with attending physician.
         c. If deemed a coroner's case, the need for autopsy is determined by coroner—no autopsy permit needed.
      2. Funerals
         a. Use handout (facing pg.) to parents to guide them in decision making.

Funerals

Upon the death of your baby

You and your family have just experienced the death of a fetus or full-term baby. This is the time when it is difficult to think clearly or make decisions. We know that this is a painful time that you have had no time for which to prepare. This sheet is intended to give you some ideas which you can talk over with your family, clergyperson, friends, and staff. We encourage you to share openly with one another and to make mutual decisions.

Various funeral homes contacted in the area are willing to offer specialized services to families experiencing fetal death or stillbirth. These funeral homes stressed their willingness to help families in the grieving process by providing sensitive, low-cost funeral arrangements. They welcome your questions and will help you in your arrangements at no obligations.

In the next few hours, you will be asked some difficult questions. We, as a hospital, need to know the name of the funeral home you will contact. We will also be approaching you about the possibility of an autopsy. After you have made those decisions, you will have more time to decide what type of funeral arrangements and services you might want.

Funeral Arrangements and Services

A typical funeral might include
- Transportation (moving the body)
- Announcements (for newspapers, memorial folders, etc.)
- Burial container
- Viewing (a chance to see the body before burial or cremation)
- Preservation of body (type of embalming)
- Opening and closing of grave site
- Burial plot
- Religious service (whatever you and your clergyperson have decided upon)

Costs

The services offered by the various funeral homes would vary in terms of cost with regard to each situation, however, most, funeral arrangements totaled less than $100.00. The various funeral homes contacted stressed that cost would be kept at a minimum and that much of the expenses would be at cost or given free of charge.

Various funeral homes offer cremation services at a nominal charge. Cost would range with each individual case but would be made up of transportation and cremation charges.

Planning

Making funeral plans is difficult. It must seem very final and very real. We as a staff will support you in this process. We encourage you to discuss your plans and the feelings they raise. If it becomes necessary for you to be hospitalized for a longer period of time than expected, you might want to think about postponing the actual funeral service until you can participate in it personally.

      b.   Any fetus over 16-weeks gestation is required to have a stillbirth certificate and should be properly disposed of by a funeral director. Notify Nursing Supervisor as soon as parents have decided upon a funeral director so that he can be notified.

      c.   If parents wish to bury their own baby, they should be advised that it would be preferable to arrange for the services of a funeral director who can properly advise on legalities involved in the burial and filing of death certificates. However, if the parents insist, they should sign a release form stating they are aware of their responsibilities in filing a death certificate, obtaining and filing a burial permit, and in observing local and municipal ordinances concerning burial in that area.

      d.   If fetus is determined to be less than 16 weeks gestation, no special forms are needed; fetus is disposed of as any other surgical specimen.

   3.   Picture of baby, personal effects of baby

      a.   Refer to immediate infant care.

      b.   Document Discharge Instruction Sheet that these items have been given to parents.

      c.   If not taken, mother's discharge instructions should include a note that these items are available if the parents should decide to claim them later.

C.   Emotional support of parents

   1.   Allow them to ventilate feelings and ask questions.

      a.   Answer truthfully even if the answer is "I do not know but I will try to find out for you."

      b.   Treat each set of parents individually.

      c.   Do not force your feelings upon the parents.

      d.   If you cannot handle the case, seek out additional help such as the Chaplain or Social Services.

      e.   Develop care plan for continuity of care.

      f.   If mother has been transferred to another unit following delivery, OB nursing staff may be contacted to assist with patient's emotional support.

   2.   Explain grief process

   3.   Administer ordered medications.

4. Notify clergy
   a. Hospital
   b. Their own if parents desire
5. Give information on SHARE
   a. SHARE pamphlet
   b. "When Hello Means Goodbye"
6. Add name of follow-up person to mother's discharge instructions. Follow-up call to be made in 2–3 weeks after discharge. Also include maternity department phone number in case mother wants to call in.

APPENDIX D

Date	Time	Check □ to Indicate Completion:	Signature
		Checklist for Assisting Parent(s) Experiencing Newborn Death, Stillbirth, Neonatal Death, and Miscarriage	
		1. □ Knew of potential difficulties prior to birth _____	
		2. □ Weeks gestation _____ Weight _____ Length _____	
		3. □ Saw baby when born and/or after delivery. Mother ___ Father ___	
		4. □ Touched and/or held baby Mother ___ Father ___ Other family ___	
		5. □ If premature infant is expected to die, are parents given option to stay with infant until dead.	
		6. □ Given option of staying on the maternity floor.	
		7. □ _____ Male _____ Female Was name given _____	
		8. □ Three photos take.° □ Given to parents □ On file □ One picture unclothed. □ Two pictures wrapped in blanket. □ Parents holding baby.	
		9. □ Footprints and complimentary birth certificate made. ___ Yes ___ No □ Given to parents □ On file □ Physician's file	
		10. □ ID bands and/or cribcards, lock of hair or other mementoes. Given to parents □ On file □	
		11. □ Baptism or other religious ceremony offered. Yes □ No □	
		12. □ Social Worker or Nurse Clinician notified. Yes □ No □	
		*13. □ Disposition: Funeral (2 copies) _____ Hospital (2 copies) _____	
		*14. □ Funeral arrangements made by: Mother _____ Father _____	
		*15. □ Informed about postponing funeral until mother able to attend.	
		*16. □ Parents assisted in decisions on: □ Clothes for burial. □ Special psalms or prayers. □ Burial mementoes from family to be placed with baby. □ Baby nursery to be left up or dismantled.	
		*17. □ Signed appropriate Birth/Death certificate (copies of either or both when 20 weeks or beyond).	
		*18. □ Autopsy Yes □ No □ Two permits signed—(take 1 to med. records & 1 to pathology)	
		*19. □ X-rays Yes □ No □	
		*20. □ Reminded to call Dr.'s office for results of autopsy, X-ray other lab tests.	
		*21. □ Description of any infant abnormalities:	
		*22. □ Identify previous losses: □ Adoption □ Elective abortion □ Miscarriage Stillbirth □ Infant death	
		*23. □ Identify other death experiences in immediate family.	
		*24. □ Assistance to family on sibling's special grief reaction.	
		*25. □ Resource information given to parents. □ Informed of H.A.N.D. Phone #'s & Book References □ Would patient like for H.A.N.D. member to call them at home to talk.	

The asterisk* denotes items to be done by the nurse clinician or social worker, when available, in 24 hours.
Houston Organization for Parent Education, Ste. 330, Houston, TX 77098, for use at Women's Hospital of Texas.

1) This knowledge can be gathered from the patient, doctor, or medical report, should be filled out in Labor and Delivery or other place if delivery such as ICU or surgery.
2) It is important to weigh and measure the fetus or infant regardless of gestation whenever possible. The nursery scale can be used; measuring tape is available there also. Exact time and date of birth and death should be noted by the delivering unit or nursery if infant dies in nursery.
3), 4) and 5) It is important to respect the parents' wishes concerning seeing, touching, and staying with the baby. Critically ill infants should be offered for viewing, touching and visiting whenever the opportunity occurs. This is done in delivery, nursery or floor. Chart the date and time of each visit on the check list.
6) Inform the mother that most women prefer the gyn floor due to longer visiting hours, but if she feels the desire she may stay on the ob floor. This is done at the place of delivery.
7) Check appropriate sex if possible: done at delivery, nursery, or floor.
8) Camera available in nursery and labor and delivery. Offer parents picture holding baby if appropriate. This is done in place of delivery, nursery, or floor.
9) Footprints are usually made by labor and delivery nurse. If not, obtain from baby in morgue (or pathology if under 20 weeks). Ink pads are in nursery. Complimentary birth certificates are in Labor and Delivery.
10) This is usually done by labor and delivery nurse. If not obtain from baby. and labor and delivery yourself. One ID band must stay on baby.
11) Let parents know that this is an option and can be arranged at their convenience with their own minister or may be initated by labor and delivery floor nurses.
12) This may be done by the nursing staff at any point in the process.
13) The family is given the option of either hospital disposal or making their own funeral arrangements. The hospital will dispose of the baby by cremation after 2 copies of the "Disposition of fetus" forms are signed. If a private funeral home is preferred, two (2) copies of the "Release to undertaker" form should be signed instead.
14) and 15) Parents are encouraged to take an active part in funeral plans should they choose this option, generally, funerals can be delayed until mother is able to attend. Most obstetricians are willing to give a pass for a few hours if that is helpful.

16) Families should be given option to plan for special mementoes. medals, psalms or prayers that are important for them. Nursery plans need to be discussed. Generally, it is best for the family and friends not to dismantle the nursery, but leave this up to the parents to handle as they see fit.
17) Before discharge it is important that the appropriate vital statistics forms be completed and returned to Medical Records—that is if the pregnancy was 20 weeks or beyond in gestational age. The pink form is to be used if the infant was born dead. The blue and white forms are used if there was a gasp, heartbeat or apgar score before death. (In the case of twins, be sure that 4 copies are filled out for each baby). See sample sheets. One of the copies is filled out and used as a work copy—all are signed by either parent and doctor.
18) An autopsy needs to be discussed with the family. This is usually done on the floor. Two copies of the permit are to be signed and given to the laboratory before it can be done. This is done as a courtesy by the hospital at no charge to the family. The final results are available in writing in about 4–6 weeks.
19) Occasionally, when the cause of death is unclear or a genetic disorder is suspected. X-rays may be helpful. Discussing this with the obstetrician. pediatrician or geneticist will help to decide when films are indicated.
20) Most reports of tests. lab work. etc. are available in 4–6 weeks. Families need to be encouraged to request this.
21) This can be obtained from the patient chart or the physician.
22) and 23) In your assessment, it is helpful to identify other losses the family or person has experienced. This can assist the nurse in better understanding of the current loss and may benefit the family in identifying coping skills.
24) Siblings and their grief deserve special attention. With preparations and parent's agreement, many siblings can benefit from seeing the infant or pictures. Their special grief must be recognized. How to discuss it with them needs to be addressed without giving advice.
25) The parent support group, HAND, can be very helpful to many families. They are available for telephone support and monthly meeting, and newsletters.

Appendix E

Nursing Care Plan for a Patient Hospitalized During a Bereavement Reaction

Behaviors or Problems

> Denial of loss
>
> Guilt feelings
>
> Feelings of anger, hostility, outrage
>
> Inability to express feelings
>
> Depression
>
> Suicidal ideation
>
> Withdrawn behavior

Short-Term Goals

> Encourage expression of feelings
>
> Decrease guilt
>
> Decrease anger
>
> Decrease depression
>
> Decrease suicidal ideation
>
> Help with recuperation from the stress of loss

Long-Term Goals

> Integrate the loss into the griever's life
>
> Help adopt a life-style that incorporates the fact of the loss
>
> Help develop new and healthy coping strategies

Nursing Actions

> Validate the patient's feelings.
>
> Do not put time limits on the stages of grief.
>
> Point out to the patient that these painful feelings of loss will subside in time.

Do not offer explanations for the death such as "He (or she) is better off now" or "It was for the best."

Encourage and accept expressions of angry feelings.

Help patient express anger in constructive ways.

Encourage expressions of feelings of guilt without being judgmental.

Help the patient in daily health needs, exercise, and proper rest and nutrition.

Encourage the patient to talk about what was involved in his or her relationship with the deceased.

Convey to the patient that feelings are painful and uncomfortable, that they are natural and necessary to the grief process, and that there is no way around these feelings but only working through them.

Encourage the patient to accept the fact that a crisis is a time for gathering strength and emotional growth.

Talk with the patient in realistic terms concerning his or her loss and the impact that this has on future plans and life-style.

INDEX

a